Spiritualism in Nineteenth-Century New Orleans

Spiritualism in Nineteenth-Century New Orleans

THE LIFE AND TIMES OF
Henry Louis Rey

MELISSA DAGGETT

University Press of Mississippi / Jackson

www.upress.state.ms.us

Designed by Peter D. Halverson

The University Press of Mississippi is a member of the Association of American University Presses.

Copyright © 2017 by University Press of Mississippi
All rights reserved

First printing 2017
∞

Portions of this work have previously appeared as "Spiritualism among Creoles of Color in Nineteenth-Century New Orleans: The Life and Times of Henry Louis Rey." *Louisiana History* 55 (2014): 409–31.

Library of Congress Cataloging-in-Publication Data

Names: Daggett, Melissa, author.
Title: Spiritualism in nineteenth-century New Orleans : the life and times of Henry Louis Rey / Melissa Daggett.
Description: Jackson : University Press of Mississippi, 2017. | Includes bibliographical references and index. | "Portions of this work have previously appeared as 'Spiritualism among Creoles of Color in Nineteenth-Century New Orleans: The Life and Times of Henry Louis Rey,' Louisiana History, 55 (2014)"—Preliminary pages.
Identifiers: LCCN 2016022490 (print) | LCCN 2016023447 (ebook) | ISBN 9781496810083 (hardcover : alk. paper) | ISBN 9781496810090 (epub single) | ISBN 9781496810106 (epub institutional) | ISBN 9781496810113 (pdf single) | ISBN 9781496810120 (pdf institutional)
Subjects: LCSH: Rey, Henry Louis, 1831–1894. | Free African Americans—Louisiana—New Orleans—Biography. | Creoles—Louisiana—New Orleans—Biography. | Spiritualism—Louisiana—New Orleans—History—19th century. | New Orleans (La.)—History—19th century. | New Orleans (La.)—Race relations.
Classification: LCC BF1283.R425 D34 2017 (print) | LCC BF1283.R425 (ebook) | DDC 133.909763/3509034—dc23
LC record available at https://lccn.loc.gov/2016022490

British Library Cataloging-in-Publication Data available

 IN MEMORY OF

Michael Mizell-Nelson

Ils ne sont pas morts. Parlez-leur, ils vous répondront.
They are not dead. Talk to them, they will answer you.
—*Le Spiritualiste de la Nouvelle-Orléans*, 1857

Contents

Acknowledgments
- xi -

Introduction
- xiii -

Timeline of Henry Louis Rey and Modern American Spiritualism
- xxi -

Prologue: A New Day
- 3 -

1. Father and Son
- 8 -

2. Echoes from Another World
- 19 -

3. Early Forays into Spiritualism
- 39 -

4. Steppingstones
- 61 -

5. Stormy Days in Louisiana
- 78 -

6. Windows of the Soul
- 95 -

7. Le Cercle Harmonique
- 101 -

8. Transitions
- 116 -

9. The Spiritual Rubicon
- 137 -

Epilogue
- 149 -

Notes
- 158 -

Bibliography
- 185 -

Index
- 194 -

Acknowledgments

Behind every story there is another story. The genesis of my debut monograph began as a seminar paper for Arnold Hirsch of the University of New Orleans and later evolved into a manuscript, and after numerous revisions, a published book. Many thanks go to Molly Mitchell, who informed me of valuable resources and made excellent suggestions. I am most grateful for Michael Mizell-Nelson, whose support and unflagging enthusiasm for the subject led me to pursue a rather difficult journey to expand and submit my work for publication.

A special thanks goes to Caryn Cossé Bell, who urged me to research the entire collection of the René Grandjean Séance Registers, calling the collection a "gold mine" of historical information. Her sage advice concerning primary and secondary sources proved to be invaluable. Thanks also go to Jay Edwards, Al Kennedy, Carolyn Morrow Long, Justin Nystrom, Michael Tisserand, and Clare P. Weaver for their historical expertise, encouragement, and advice. I especially want to thank my editor-in-chief Craig Gill and editorial associate Katie Keene for supporting and believing in my book.

Also, thanks go to Fatima Shaik, who answered emails concerning the Economy Society. Another email correspondent, Mary Gehman, was very helpful in researching Creoles and their connections to Mexico. Will Trufant was kind enough to allow me to visit his Spain Street home, which at one time was the site of the First Church of Divine Fellowship of Spiritualism.

Descendants of historical figures mentioned in the book assisted me with family information. Many thanks go to Allaina Wallace, a descendant of Hippolyte Rey; Pat Schexnayder, a descendant of Antoine Dubuclet; and Derrick Pitard, great-great-grandson of Gustave Pitard.

This work would not have been possible without the help of librarians and archivists. Therefore, I would like to express my sincere gratitude to Pamalla Anderson, Lori Birrell, Janet Bloom, James Clifford, Dorenda Dupont, Mary Lou Eichhorn, Florence Jumonville, Tara Laver, Connie Phelps, Sally Reeves, Tracy Timmons, Irene Wainwright, and Mary Wernet.

Not to be forgotten is my family's unfailing support. So thanks to Tim, my husband; Julianne and Christina, my daughters; Michael, my son; and Coco, my cat.

A huge heartfelt thanks goes to Tommy Milliner, my brother, who acted as my copy editor, critic, and main supporter in this academic endeavor. I also would like to thank three friends—Eileen Holt, Chris Kivett, and Adele Mangipano—who gave me words of encouragement and lent a sympathetic ear for my concerns throughout the long and grueling process of research and writing the manuscript.

There is one more person I would like to thank who is no longer alive but whose spirit lives on. He is René Grandjean, whom I would like to thank for reading, researching, and adding insightful historical information into the Séance Registers. And most importantly, thank you René Grandjean for preserving and donating the René Grandjean Séance Registers, your notes, photographs, and ephemera to the Earl K. Long Library, Special Collections Department of the University of New Orleans. You have added immensely to the historiography of the Creoles of color in nineteenth-century New Orleans.

Introduction

The free people of color in antebellum New Orleans lived during an era of conflicts and dilemmas as Louisiana moved away from a fluid three-tiered racial system inherited from the French and the Spanish to a rigid, binary American racial system that denied them a special legal, social, and economic status. The free black community managed to survive and flourish in spite of social ostracism and the draconian legislation in Louisiana of the mid-nineteenth century that severely curtailed their civil rights. Their remarkable story of survival speaks well of their solidarity in the face of adversity during the antebellum years, the Civil War, and Reconstruction.

During the colonial days of Louisiana, a multiracial social structure developed similar to existing ones in the Caribbean. Between the privileged whites and the enslaved blacks was inserted a middle stratum, *les gens de couleur libre* (free people of color), a class of marginal status. Though they lacked political rights such as the right to vote, free people of color could own property, make contracts, and testify in court against whites. The free community of color in New Orleans constituted the most literate and prosperous free black population in the United States. Approximately 70 percent of free people of color in 1860 were of mixed blood, and their skin color varied from near white to dark complexion.[1]

Among the elite of this middle tier in the unique, tripartite society of New Orleans were outstanding community leaders in the fields of business, education, literature, the arts, religion, and medicine. One such leader was Henry Louis Rey. Born in 1831 to a wealthy and prominent black Creole family with Saint-Domingue roots, Rey's leadership qualities blossomed during the Civil War and Reconstruction. Henry Rey's father and grandparents had been part of the massive diaspora known as the Second Wave of Emigration (1809–1810). Many free people of color originally immigrated to Cuba from war-torn Saint-Domingue during the Haitian Revolution in the 1790s and early 1800s. Still later, more free people of color were forced to move after the Cuban government determined the francophone population to be a security threat during the ongoing Napoleonic Wars. Many of these émigrés fled to New Orleans. During the first half the nineteenth century, the Saint-Domingue émigrés and their descendants formed a vibrant, flourishing, and cohesive community in the Faubourgs Tremé and Marigny. Forced diaspora transformed New Orleans into a permanent home for those who escaped the catastrophic Haitian Revolution.

Henry Rey became actively involved with the Modern American Spiritualism movement that swept the nation starting in the early 1850s. At first, Rey was a participant and observer, but soon he became recognized for his talents as a medium. He formed his own séance circles after Valmour, a charismatic black Creole medium, ceased private and public séances at his home in the New Orleans suburb of Tremé.

Rey and his séance participants kept registers in which they recorded communications received from the spiritual world. According to a contemporary account, the French Creoles "kept a careful record of all its sittings, and of spirit writings received, until their records number many volumes." The Creole séance circles considered the communications to be sacred texts, and the séance circle members meticulously recorded these messages and carefully preserved the journals in which they were written. However, over time none of these journals survived into the twentieth-first century with the exception of the René Grandjean Séance Registers, housed in the Special Collections Department of the Earl K. Long Library at the University of New Orleans.[2]

The René Grandjean Séance Registers consist of thirty-five volumes containing thousands of pages of séance transcriptions conducted by Henry Louis Rey and his fellow Afro-Creole mediums, beginning in 1858 and terminating in 1877. The first register contains an autobiographical essay in which Rey described his early encounters with Spiritualism and his strong anticlerical feelings. Rey himself transcribed most of the séances, and almost all of the communications are in French. The French language has been a daunting barrier to historians who have attempted to research and write about this important primary source, and these manuscripts have remained basically untapped primary documents. I have translated all of the French spiritual communications quoted in this book as well as other French-language primary documents. If the original spiritual message was in English, that is stated in an endnote.

François "Petit" Dubuclet became Henry Rey's friend, faithful member of his Cercle Harmonique, fellow medium, and self-appointed curator of the registers for half a century. Dubuclet moved to Jamaica in 1913 for health reasons and in 1918, at the age of eighty-two, returned to New Orleans to spend his sunset years with his daughter, Assitha, and her French-born husband, René Grandjean.

As a young man, René Grandjean had traveled from France to Haiti, where he lived for two years. In 1911, he moved to New Orleans and became acquainted with members of the once vibrant community of the Creoles of color, including the Dubuclets and Rodolphe Desdunes, author of *Our People and Our History: Fifty Creole Portraits* ([1911] 1973). Desdunes's book was an ode to the extraordinary legacy of the Creoles of color and consisted of fifty vignettes of famous black Creoles in the nineteenth century. Grandjean, a Caucasian, married François Dubuclet's daughter, Assitha, in St. Andrew, Jamaica, on October 29, 1913, and remained in Jamaica for seven years. The foreign location was necessary because at that time interracial marriages were outlawed in the southern states.[3]

After the family returned to New Orleans in 1920, René Grandjean began meticulously reading the registers and made copious margin notes in the registers with information obtained from his father-in-law, the last surviving member of the Henry Rey séance circles. Grandjean took an active interest in both Spiritualism and the history and legacy of the black Creoles. As he listened to Dubuclet's fascinating stories from a forgotten era, René Grandjean scribbled historically significant notes on whatever was available—postcards, old receipts from a Kingston bakery, used envelopes, scraps of paper, and notices of bank holiday closings in New Orleans. François Dubuclet's oral history provides invaluable information of a contemporary who lived during the turbulent years of Reconstruction. François Dubuclet personally knew many of the important historical figures of antebellum Louisiana and those of Reconstruction. His father, Antoine Dubuclet, had been the Louisiana state secretary of the treasury for ten years. François Dubuclet's keen intellect and astute observations add immeasurably to the historiography of the black Creoles and Spiritualism during the nineteenth century. Using Grandjean's margin notes and a careful reading of the spiritual communications open a window into the hearts and minds of the black Creoles in nineteenth-century New Orleans. Their lost world lies within the covers of these séance registers. (René Grandjean's notes in the registers are identified in the endnotes as "Grandjean Séance Margin Notes." A separate collection of notes is identified as "Grandjean Notes.")

François Dubuclet died in 1924, and the registers passed down to René Grandjean. Fifty-two years later, in 1976—as the result of a friendship with Dr. Joseph Logsdon, a professor of history at the University of New

Orleans—Grandjean donated his priceless collection of séance registers, notes, books, photographs, and ephemera to the Special Collections Department of the Earl K. Long Library at the University of New Orleans.[4]

Spiritualism in Nineteenth-Century New Orleans: The Life and Times of Henry Louis Rey weaves together the closely intertwined histories of the black Creoles, Louisiana history, Reconstruction, Modern American Spiritualism, and the personal and political histories of the Cercle Harmonique's charismatic leader, Henry Louis Rey. Not intended to be a traditional history of Modern American Spiritualism, this book seeks to look past the messages of the departed to more fully understand the black Creoles and the difficult social and political dilemmas they faced during the postbellum years. The voices of the dead were reflections of the contemporary political situation in Louisiana. Denied access to the traditional outlets of free speech and free press, Afro-Creoles articulated their hopes and dreams at séances safely ensconced in their homes and businesses.

The late antebellum and postbellum years in New Orleans were troubled times set against a grand panorama of war, destruction, oppression, and unfulfilled dreams. Other than the short-lived black Creole newspapers, *L'Union* and the *New Orleans Tribune/La Tribune de la Nouvelle-Orléans*, the Grandjean Registers are the only existing historical records of the black Creoles' political philosophy during those pivotal years. There were other French and Anglo séance circles in New Orleans during the late antebellum years and the postbellum years, but the historical record is sketchy about their composition, philosophy, numbers of devotees, and influence in Louisiana. Therefore, my primary focus is on Henry Louis Rey's séance circles, which span these turbulent years.

I have included information in chapter 2, "Echoes from Another World," about northern Spiritualism and itinerant mediums who made their way down the Mississippi River to shore up the faithful and expand their base of Spiritualists in New Orleans prior to the Civil War. Among these peripatetic mediums were Thomas Lake Harris, an early convert to Spiritualism; two newspaper editors—Thomas Gales Forster and J. Rollin M. Squire—of the premier spiritualist Boston newspaper, the *Banner of Light*; Emma Hardinge, a trance medium and prolific chronicler of Spiritualism; James V. Mansfield, the Spiritual Postmaster; and James M. Peebles, sometimes called the Spiritual Pilgrim because of his journeys abroad and across the continental United States.

Not to be forgotten was a well-known medium of the 1850s, Cora L. V. Hatch Daniels, who escaped the local spotlight when she lived briefly in New

Orleans in 1867 with her husband and infant daughter, Henrietta. Her only public appearance was as an invited guest speaker at the first-year memorial of the famous Mechanics' Institute Massacre, sometimes called the New Orleans Riots or the New Orleans Massacre. After the tragic deaths of both her husband and daughter within two weeks in October 1867, Cora Daniels returned to the North to resume her Spiritualist activities.

Culling information from contemporary newspapers and other primary sources, I have reconstructed what transpired in a nineteenth-century New Orleans séance in the chapter titled "Windows of the Soul." During the 1870s, two competing New Orleans newspapers—the *New Orleans Times* and the *Daily Picayune*—published a series of articles that investigated private séances and described the sometimes horrific details of nightly paranormal encounters with the dead.

Henry Rey, despite the voluminous transcriptions found in the Grandjean Collection, offered little information about the exact nature of his spiritual encounters. A few details emerge about the protocol of a séance, the membership of the circles, and situations and questions to avoid when the spirits arrived. However, the transcriptions and Grandjean's margin notes provide few details about what the spirits actually looked like, how they entered the room, reactions of the séance members, and the spiritual method of communication.[5]

The advent of Modern American Spiritualism took place in the 1850s and continued as a viable faith into the 1860s and the 1870s. The Crescent City provided fertile ground to nurture the new movement. Because of the city's diversity and openness to new cultures and religions, New Orleans developed into an outpost of Spiritualism within the confines of a very conservative antebellum South. At certain junctures during its ascendancy, northern Spiritualism intersected with the French Creoles' branch of Spiritualism and its unique hallmarks, which included Francophile spiritual messengers; meticulously transcribed and preserved communications from the spiritual world; private venues in Faubourgs Tremé and Marigny; politically connected mediums; abhorrence of the Catholic Church; and the preservation of the extraordinary nineteenth-century legacy of Afro-Creoles in New Orleans.[6]

Spiritualism in Nineteenth-Century New Orleans sheds new light on Henry Louis Rey's pivotal role as a key civil rights activist, author, medium, and Civil War and Reconstruction leader whose lifetime achievements have largely remained in the shadows owing, in part, to a language barrier. Now that this barrier has been broken, a more complete understanding is rendered of New

René Grandjean (ca. 1920), Grandjean Collection. *Photo courtesy of Special Collections, Earl K. Long Library, University of New Orleans.*

Orleans and Louisiana's rich and complex history, filling a historiographical gap.

Historians have written about Henry Rey and Spiritualism in nineteenth-century New Orleans, but none have done a full monograph treatment of these important and overlooked historical subjects. Presently, there exist three brief studies. In *Revolution, Romanticism, and the Afro-Creole Protest Tradition in Louisiana 1718–1868* (1997), historian Caryn Cossé Bell dedicated a chapter to New Orleans Spiritualism in which she briefly sketched the movement's presence in the city and pointed to its transatlantic links. Far from being isolated in New Orleans, the elite Creoles of color were part of a vast global network, connected horizontally to France and by a vertical axis to the French Caribbean colonies. This elite group transformed its French intellectual heritage to demand *liberté, égalité, fraternité* in their new American postbellum order. Bell's use of the Grandjean Séance Registers as primary sources marks the first time that a historian has used the Registers as a window into the lives of Creoles of color. Quoting spiritual communications,

Francois Dubuclet (1918), Grandjean Collection. *Photo courtesy of Special Collections, Earl K. Long Library, University of New Orleans.*

Bell helped to break down the traditional view of black Creoles as an elitist group jealously defending a dated, self-serving agenda to shore up their fading Gallic culture and to prevent the newly freed Anglo blacks from political and economic ascendancy in postbellum Louisiana.[7]

Robert S. Cox, a historian of Spiritualism, has also chronicled Rey's Cercle Harmonique in *Body and Soul: A Sympathetic History of American Spiritualism* (2003). Using the framework of the changing social climate and the volatile politics of the era, Cox expanded the historical and religious conversation about Rey's circle during the 1860s and the 1870s.[8]

The literary merits of Rey's spiritual communications have since 2004 received attention from French scholars in Louisiana, most notably Chris Michaelides in *Paroles d'honneur: Écrits de Créoles de couleur néo-orléanais 1837–1872* (2004). This French-language anthology of writings of the black Creole intelligentsia included a final chapter devoted to selected communications from eight of the Grandjean Registers. Michaelides considered Henry Louis Rey to be a *poète visionnaire* and likened him to such French Romantic writers as Lamennais, Lamartine, and Béranger—and closer to home, Charles Testut, a white French émigré and early convert to Spiritualism. Spiritual messages were sometimes communicated by the French Romantic writers, and Rey himself was a gifted writer who contributed poems and editorial letters to the two black Creole newspapers—*L'Union* and the *New Orleans Tribune*.[9]

This book uses as a framework the life and times of Henry Louis Rey. His lifetime and that of his father, Barthélemy Louis Rey, spanned most of the nineteenth century and mirror the rise and fall of the black Creoles of New Orleans as a community. Although Henry Rey was a minor historical figure, there is much to be learned by studying his life and times. Thus, *Spiritualism in Nineteenth-Century New Orleans: The Life and Times of Henry Louis Rey* is partially a microhistory, which is the use of the experiences and mentalities of a hitherto obscure historical person to better understand the social and political forces during that person's lifetime. As historian Jill Lepore explains, "However singular a person's life may be, the value of examining it lies not in its uniqueness, but in its exemplariness, in how that individual's life serves as an allegory for broader issues affecting the culture as a whole."[10]

By examining Henry Rey Louis's life and the spiritual communications, we can use previously untapped archival material to better understand Spiritualism in nineteenth-century New Orleans and as an allegory for broader issues affecting the culture as a whole. A meticulous and systematic reading of the René Grandjean Registers provides unparalleled insights into Afro-Creole thought and the Afro-Creoles' society and visions during the turbulent postbellum years. Henry Louis Rey has much to teach us about the Afro-Creoles of New Orleans, not just as intellectuals or political leaders or Spiritualists, but also as social reformers.

It is a story that has been waiting for over 150 years to be told.

Timeline of Henry Louis Rey and Modern American Spiritualism

1791 Saint-Domingue (Haitian) Revolution.
1802 Flux of refugees from Saint-Domingue to Cuba.
1803 December 20: Louisiana becomes an American territory.
1804 Birth of Barthélemy Louis Rey in Cuba.
1809 Second emigration from Cuba of Saint-Domingue refugees to New Orleans.
1810 Claude Tremé's plantation is subdivided for development. Many black Creoles, especially those from Saint-Domingue, populate Faubourg Tremé.
1812 April 30: Louisiana enters the Union as the eighteenth state.
1815 January 8: Battle of New Orleans.
1829 January 19–23: Père Antoine (Antonio de Sedella) dies, lies in state, and is buried. July 2: Barthélemy Louis Rey marries Rose Agnès Sacriste.
1830 Linguistic turning point: French loses importance as English becomes the dominant language in Louisiana.
1831 February 20: Henry Louis Rey is born. August 21: Nat Turner Rebellion.
1833 March 22: Henry Hippolyte Rey is born.
1834 Parish Prison in Tremé is built.
1836 New Orleans is divided into three separate cities; the Third Municipality is mostly Creole. March 1: La Société d'Economie et d'Assistance Mutuelle (Economy Society) is founded.
1837 June 26: Birth of Felix Octave Rey. Panic of 1837. Adèle Crocker is born.
1839 Tremé Market is built.
1842 St. Augustine Church is dedicated in Tremé.
1843 Andrew Jackson Davis, the Poughkeepsie Seer, gains spiritual prominence as a subject of mesmeric trances.
1845 April 9: Joseph Barthet, a French émigré, founds La Société du Magnétisme de la Nouvelle-Orléans.

1847 A. J. Davis begins publication of a weekly newspaper in New York City that promotes his Harmonial Spiritualism, based on the philosophy of the Swedish mystic Swedenborg.

1848 March 31: The Fox sisters report mysterious raps in Hydesville, New York. L'institution Catholique pour l'instruction des orphelins dans l'indigence (Catholic Institution or Couvent School) opens.

1850s Many Creoles of color move to Mexico or to France as a result of draconian laws to limit their freedom. *Le Propagateur Catholique* attacks mesmerism and Spiritualism. Henry Louis Rey works as a bookbinder in the early 1850s.

1852 May 29: Barthélemy Rey dies. June 8: Memorial service officiated by Father Morisot at Annunciation Church. The division of the city into three municipalities is abandoned. December: The earliest documented report of northern mediumship in New Orleans, as the Reverend Thomas Lake Harris of New York City conducts private séances. Joseph Barthet begins his séance circle.

1853 The city experiences its worst yellow fever epidemic.

1855 February 11: Henry Louis Rey travels from New Orleans to Tampico, Mexico.

1856 January 17: Rose Agnès Sacriste Rey, Henry's mother, dies. April 18: Henry Louis Rey returns to New Orleans on the schooner *Red Fox*.

1857 January: *Le Spiritualist de la Nouvelle-Orléans* of Joseph Barthet begins publication. March 6: Dred Scott decision. April 11: The *Banner of Light* begins publication in Boston. July 9: Pierre Crocker dies. September 3: Henry Louis Rey marries Adèle Crocker in St. Augustine Church. The Louisiana legislature prohibits all manumissions (freeings of slaves).

1858 Rivalry between Abbé Perché and Joseph Barthet heats up over Spiritualism. City ordinances prohibit freedom of speech and assembly to free people of color. Henry Louis Rey works as a clerk at Eugène Hacker's hardware store. January–April: J. Rollin M. Squire and Thomas Gales Forster, editors of the *Banner of Light*, visit New Orleans. June 19: Henry Louis Rey begins his first séance register.

1859 February 7: Lucia Rose Rey is born. March: Henry Louis Rey moves from St. Philip Street to 95 Columbus Street. September 1: Free people of color are ordered by the Louisiana state legislature to enslave themselves. December: Emma Hardinge, northern medium and author of *Modern American Spiritualism* (1869), arrives in New Orleans and gives lectures.

1860 January: Emma Hardinge leaves New Orleans. April 14: Henry Joseph Rey is born. April 25: Last entry recorded at Joanni Questy's house in Henry Louis Rey's first séance register before the Civil War begins. November 6: Abraham Lincoln is elected president. December 21: Death of Rose Adèle Gignac Crocker, wife of Pierre Crocker. December: James V. Mansfield, the Spiritual Postmaster, visits New Orleans

1861 January 26: Louisiana secedes from the Union. Late January: James Mansfield leaves New Orleans. March 4: Lincoln becomes the sixteenth president. April 12: The Civil War begins. May 2: The Confederate Native Guards is formed. July: Henry Louis Rey adopts Myrtille Raphaël Crocker, the minor child of Rose Crocker.

1862 May 1: General Benjamin Butler occupies New Orleans. Henry Louis Rey, Edgar Davis, Eugène Rapp, and Octave Rey surrender weapons to Butler. September 27: First issue of *L'Union* appears, and the First Regiment of the Union Native Guards is mustered in.

1863 April 6: Henry Louis Rey resigns from the Union army. May 27: Port Hudson battle. July 4: Union gains control of the Upper Mississippi River. November 5: A meeting is held at Economy Hall to discuss securing the rights of franchise.

1864 May 10: Séance register is resumed. November 28: Albert Louis Rey is born. December 27: National Equal Rights League holds a mass meeting.

1865 April 9: The Civil War ends. April 14: Lincoln is assassinated. July 5: Henry Louis Rey begins second séance register. Séances resume at Valmour's house. September 13: Henry Louis Rey resigns as secretary to the Friends of Universal Suffrage. November: Séance entries are recorded in the register after several months of absence.

1866 July 30: The Mechanics' Institute Massacre occurs. September 3: Placide Augustin Rey is born.

1867 Cholera and yellow fever claim thousands of lives. March 2: Henry Louis Rey begins his Cercle Harmonique. May 16: Masonic Temples are opened to African Americans. Henry Louis Rey joins Fraternité #20. May 29: Cora L. V. Hatch Daniels travels to New Orleans with her husband, Colonel Nathaniel Daniels. July 30: Cora Daniels recites her poem at the memorial service commemorating the one-year anniversary of the Mechanics' Institute Massacre.

1868 March 7: Placide Rey dies. April: A liberal Louisiana constitution is enacted. Henry Louis Rey is elected a member of the Louisiana House of Representatives; Henry Clay Warmoth becomes governor; Oscar J.

Dunn becomes lieutenant governor; and Antoine Dubuclet is chosen state treasurer.

1869 February 6: Valmour dies. March 4: Ulysses S. Grant becomes president.

1870s Minerva Hall becomes the center for Spiritualist societies and Spiritualist lecturers.

1870 January: Henry Louis Rey is appointed director of the Couvent School. April 4: Governor Henry Clay Warmoth appoints Benjamin Flanders mayor of New Orleans. April 13: Henry Louis Rey becomes the New Orleans Third District tax assessor. July 6: The second séance register ends. Séances are held at Joseph Lavigne's cigar shop on the corner of Esplanade Avenue and St. Claude Avenue (now Henriette Delille Street).

1871 August 7: Henry Louis Rey as a Republican Party official holds an election for party delegates to a state convention that is declared by the Warmoth faction to be fraudulent. November 22: Oscar Dunn dies under mysterious circumstances. P. B. S. Pinchback replaces him as lieutenant governor. December: The Reverend James Peebles, the so-called Spiritual Pilgrim, visits New Orleans.

1872 March 5: Henry Louis Rey's appointment as tax assessor expires. November 3: Grant is reelected president. William Kellogg is elected Louisiana governor in a disputed election.

1873 Henry Louis Rey is appointed director of the Orleans Parish School Board. May 20: Henry Louis Rey and his wife deposit money in the Freedman Bank.

1874 The Freedman's Bank fails. September 14: The Battle of Liberty Place occurs. December: White males eject African American pupils from integrated New Orleans public schools.

1875 Henry Louis Rey's Cercle Harmonique terminates. He continues his séance registers alone. December 3: Henry Louis Rey's house at 341 Villere Street burns down, and he moves back to 95 Columbus Street.

1877 Gustave Pitard employs Henry Louis Rey as first clerk. March 1: Henry Louis Rey is elected secretary of the Economy Society. March 4: Rutherford B. Hayes becomes president, and Reconstruction ends. April: Henry Louis Rey is replaced on the New Orleans Parish School Board. April 25: Federal troops are withdrawn. June 11: Joseph Vignaud Lavigne dies. November 24: The séance registers stop.

1879 Louisiana Redeemer constitution is adopted.

1882 The New Orleans Spiritualist Association is organized.

1889 April 21: Georges Henri René Grandjean is born in Vouziers, France.

1890 April: A reunion séance is held with Soeur Louise and Valmour. July 10: The Louisiana Separate Car Act is adopted. July 22: Adèle Rey dies.
1891 September 1: Le Comité des Citoyens (Citizens Committee) is founded.
1892 June 7: Homer Plessy challenges the Separate Car Act. July 2: Catherine (Kate) Fox Jencken dies. August 27: Henry Louis Rey applies for a Union Invalid Veteran pension.
1893 The National Spiritualist Association is founded. March 8: Margaretta (Maggie) Fox Kane dies.
1894 April 19: Henry Louis Rey dies.
1896 May 18: US Supreme Court decides *Plessy v. Ferguson*. June 7: Cora L. V. Richmond becomes pastor of the Church of the Soul in Chicago.
1907 The *Banner of Light* ceases publication.
1911 René Grandjean moves to New Orleans from France via Haiti.
1913 October 29: Grandjean marries Assitha Dubuclet, the daughter of François Dubuclet, in St. Andrew, Jamaica.
1920 The First Church of Divine Fellowship of Spiritualism, Grandjean's Spiritualist Church, is founded. July 16: François Dubuclet and the Grandjeans return to New Orleans from Jamaica.
1921 April 17: Mother Leafy Anderson establishes a Spiritual church, the Eternal Life Christian Church.
1922 February 16: James M. Peebles, the Spiritual Pilgrim, dies in Los Angeles at the age of ninety-nine.
1923 January 2: Cora L. V. Scott Hatch Daniels Tappan Richmond, matriarch and last of the nineteenth-century Spiritualist leaders, dies in Chicago.
1924 March 2: François "Petit" Dubuclet dies, the last Rey séance member and longtime curator of the séance registers.
1976 As the result of a friendship with Dr. Joseph Logsdon—a professor of history at the University of New Orleans—René Grandjean donates his collection of séance registers, notes, books, photographs, and ephemera to the Special Collections Department, Earl K. Long Library, University of New Orleans.

Spiritualism in Nineteenth-Century New Orleans

PROLOGUE

A New Day

The first sign was a frigate bird, the swallow of the ocean, which soared across the twilight sky; spread its large, dark, powerful wings; and then plunged into the choppy blue waters seeking the bounty of the sea. The frigate bird was, as all sailors knew, the harbinger of land and safe passage. The next sign came the following day when branches floated on the gentle swells and occasionally brushed against the ship's hull. Next came flocks of brown pelicans and more branches, trees, and vegetation, which assured the crew and passengers of the proximity of the Father of Waters. Still, there was no sight of land.

A heavy fog descended at nightfall, and the passengers could hear the muffled, mournful sounds of foghorns from invisible ships. The anticipation and excitement mounted. At daybreak the fog dissipated and clearly visible were the yellow murky waters of the mighty Mississippi mixing with the blue salty waters of the Gulf of Mexico. On the horizon was La Balize, the first port of call for all who entered the river. La Balize was the desolate home of pilots who made their living navigating the last treacherous ninety miles upriver to New Orleans, the capital of the Territory of Orleans. The wretched village consisted of a cluster of low, ramshackle, wooden buildings huddled around a lighthouse. The new arrivals now waited for favorable winds to guide their small ship up the Mississippi River against the strong current. Contrary winds could mean a delay of weeks to complete the final leg of their voyage. Added to the uncertainty of climatic conditions was the uncertainty of what their reception would be once they docked in New Orleans, their final destination.[1]

The year was 1809, and the passengers were refugees from Saint-Domingue (present-day Haiti) who originally fled to Santiago de Cuba in the early years of the nineteenth century to escape the chaos and catastrophic destruction of the Saint-Domingue or Haitian Revolution. The vessel was the schooner *Louise*, the first of many ships to make the treacherous voyage across the Gulf of Mexico from Cuba, a virtual flotilla of émigrés seeking permanent homes in Louisiana.[2]

Saint-Domingue had been the crown jewel of the French Caribbean colonial empire. The colony brought fabulous wealth to the plantation owners and traders whose income rested largely on the backs of African slaves toiling incessantly under unbelievably harsh conditions. The agricultural linchpins of the economy were sugar and coffee, two crops not grown in Europe but in huge demand during the eighteenth century. Three-quarters of the sugar and coffee produced in the Caribbean and exported to France were later sold to other European countries. Metropolitan merchants in the French port towns amassed enormous fortunes, and it was to their economic advantage to continue the transatlantic slave trade despite all of its human suffering. Huge profits generated incessant demands for slaves, who were needed to cultivate, harvest, and process these labor-intensive crops.[3]

The plantation owners and the French colonial government should have seen it coming, but they failed to see the obvious until it was too late. By the time of the French Revolution (1789), 90 percent of the population were slaves living in despair and horrendous living conditions while the privileged few lived in sumptuous mansions. Many plantation owners were basically absentee landlords who left the control and daily management of their lands to cruel and corrupt managers. It was just a matter of time before the downtrodden many rose up to eliminate the privileged few. And that time began in 1791, under the leadership of Toussaint Louverture, a charismatic free black man who commanded the adoration and support of the enslaved blacks. The slave revolt resulted in the defeat of the white French aristocracy that had controlled and ruled the slaves from birth until death.

The Haitian Revolution took place in phases from 1791 to 1804, and with each phase there was a corresponding migratory movement of displaced colonials, sometimes accompanied by slaves. The primary destinations included the East Coast of the United States in 1793, Jamaica in 1798, and Cuba in 1803.[4] The refugees thought of their diaspora as temporary. They believed that political conditions would revert back to those of pre-revolutionary Saint-Domingue and that the slaves would be defeated by the superior military might and intelligence of France. And so, they waited and watched events unfold in Saint-Domingue, safely ensconced in their temporary locations in the Caribbean; on the East Coast of the United States; and in Louisiana, now part of the Spanish colonial empire.

The anticipated counterrevolution never occurred. In 1801, Emperor Napoleon Bonaparte ordered an army of forty-three thousand men under the leadership of his brother-in-law, General Charles Leclerc, to regain control of the French colony. Leclerc landed at Cap Français (frequently called Le Cap) in February 1802, and a few months later deported the insurgents' leader, Toussaint Louverture, to France, where he died the following year on April 8, 1803, in a prison located in the remote Jura Mountains. However, Leclerc and his army were unable to regain France's most valuable colony, Saint-Domingue. Almost half of the French army died, including General Leclerc, mostly as victims of tropical diseases. Yellow fever decimated the French forces, and by October 1803 Louverture's lieutenant, Jean-Jacques Dessalines, regained control of the lost colony. The French army evacuated, and Dessalines ordered all plantations, the cornerstone of economic stability, burnt to the ground. Many whites, unfortunate enough to have stayed, were massacred. On New Year's Day 1804, Dessalines proclaimed a new republic, the nation of Haiti. After the apocalyptic year of 1803, the expatriates knew that returning to their homeland was no longer an option.[5]

The Haitian Revolution was not just a simple story of enslaved blacks fighting rich whites. It was much more complex. For the previous century, a third racial group had evolved in Saint-Domingue: *les gens de couleur libre*, free people of color. Generally, the free people of color were racially mixed, the product of the union of white males and African women in a colony with few available white women. Many free people of color had been emancipated by their white fathers, and some even became plantation owners and slave owners themselves. Frequently, the white father would leave part or all of his inheritance to his African partner and children of the union. The children of the first union would later, as adults, have their children with either someone from within their own mixed-race ethnic group or with whites.[6]

Thus, a middle tier in the Saint-Domingue society evolved. They were freed people, but restricted to a type of quasi-citizenship. Many members of this middle tier in the Caribbean society identified with whites during the Haitian Revolution, thus incurring the wrath of the black insurgents. As the Haitian Revolution progressed, the free people of color fled the war-torn country because they too became the targets of racial and class animosity.[7]

For many of the refugees, Santiago de Cuba on the southeastern coast of Cuba was a natural primary destination because of its geographical proximity to the northern coast of Haiti. It was here, at this outpost, that the émigrés waited for political and social changes that never materialized. As they waited, they put down roots and attempted to duplicate the society of the motherland by establishing coffee plantations and building libraries, billiard rooms, and bars.[8]

In March 1809, the Cuban government issued a proclamation commanding the French refugees to leave Cuba because of Napoleon's invasion of Spain and his subsequent failed attempt to place his brother, Joseph, on the Spanish throne. Most of the émigrés left in 1809 and early 1810, and the preferred secondary destination was Louisiana. There were many reasons for so many Cuban exiles to move to Louisiana. Perhaps the most important one was the similarity in cultures. Both Saint-Domingue and Louisiana were French-speaking with a strong Gallic culture.

The largest and most important secondary migratory wave began in late April 1809, and the first ship reached New Orleans on May 19, 1809, much to the consternation and chagrin of the US territorial governor, William C. C. Claiborne. The governor was firmly against increasing the number of free people of color in Louisiana. In a letter to Robert Smith, the secretary of state, Claiborne railed against allowing additional free people of color to enter the Territory of Orleans (present-day Louisiana) because it already had "a much greater proportion of that kind of population than comports with our interest." The large population of free people of color was a problem for the new American leaders accustomed to the Anglo-American dualistic society of blacks and whites in most of the southern states.[9]

Claiborne proposed excluding males over fifteen, but this proved to be impractical for families that had already disembarked and were being quickly assimilated into the existing free people of color community. The existence of a strong vibrant community of free people of color was another reason why exiles from Cuba chose Louisiana as their next exile destination. The addition of 3,102 free people of color in 1809–1810 more than doubled the population of that caste in New Orleans. The percentage of the total population formed by the free people of color mushroomed from 19 percent in 1805 to 28.7 percent in 1810, forever changing the cultural and political landscapes of New Orleans.[10]

Among the free men of color Claiborne fought to exclude was Joseph Rey, who had made the voyage with his wife, Elizabeth Mickline, and their five-year-old son, Barthélemy.[11] New Orleans was a feast for their eyes and ears.

The first day off the crowded ship was a day to explore and see the sights of this new, exciting, exotic city before returning to mundane daily chores. Upon landing at the levee, which fronted the Public Square (now Jackson Square), the family disembarked, climbed a few feet up the riverside of the levee, walked across the top, which was 50 feet wide, and made an easy descent on a gently sloping levee to the banquette (sidewalk), a distance of about 150 feet from the edge of the levee. Along the levee, as far as the eye could see, were two rows of market people, some having stalls or tables with a tilt or awning of canvass, but most displaying their wares on the ground either on a piece of canvas or a spread of palmetto leaves. Their wares consisted of wild ducks, oysters, poultry, fish, bananas, oranges, sugarcane, Irish potatoes, tinware, dry goods, and books in English and French. It was like a Tower of Babel, with so many languages being heard: English, French, Spanish, Italian, American Indian dialects, and German.[12]

For little Barthélemy, it was a new day, the perfect ending for a perilous journey. But in some ways, the journey had just begun.

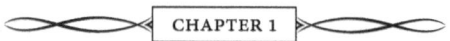

Father and Son

Twenty years later, the boy who landed in New Orleans after being exiled from Cuba was now a young man preparing for his upcoming nuptials less than a mile away from where he had disembarked on that life-changing day in 1809. On July 1, 1829, Barthélemy Rey and his future wife appeared before the New Orleans notary, Carlile Pollock, to legally affirm their intentions to share future property as man and wife and, perhaps more importantly, to legalize their three-month-old daughter, Elizabeth.

The bride was Rose Agnès Sacriste, natural daughter of Jean Marie Sacriste and Rositte Frère; the groom was the son of Joseph Rey and Elizabeth Mickline.[1] The notary duly inscribed the letters H.C.L. (*homme de couleur libre*—free man of color) for Barthélemy and F.C.L. (*femme de couleur libre*—free woman of color) for Rose, thereby conforming to the Louisiana law that required all legal documents to identify free people of color.

Upon completing the document, Carlile Pollack read it to the young couple and the witnesses. The notary then asked them to sign the marriage contract. Rose, unable to read or write, took the quill and scratched a shaky black "X" in the two-inch space dividing the names "Rose Agnès" and "Sacriste," which the notary had already written on the document. Barthélemy signed his first and last names underneath and added a flourish of several decorative loops as if to emphasize his firm agreement to the legal document.

The union of the Sacriste and Rey families represented in one small way the cohesiveness and solidarity of émigrés with Saint-Domingue roots. Barthélemy and Rose were both first generation immigrants from Cuba and Saint-Domingue. In the marriage contract, Barthélemy listed his birthplace as

Santiago de Cuba, which had been the initial destination for many refugees fleeing the chaos of the Saint-Domingue (Haitian) Revolution, and Rose was originally from Saint-Domingue.[2]

Legal documents, like the marriage contract between Barthélemy Rey and Rose Sacriste, attest to the significance and legacy of Saint-Domingue ancestry. The connection was important literally from cradle to grave. Baptismal records often mentioned a parent's place of birth if the parent had been born in Saint-Domingue or in a primary immigration location like Cuba. Death certificates and succession papers frequently mentioned the connection of the deceased to Saint-Domingue. This enduring link to the lost French Caribbean colony was important for both whites and free people of color.[3]

Once the marriage contract was completed with its requisite signatures, Rose and Barthélemy left the notary's office on the corner of Chartres and Conti Streets behind Exchange Alley.[4] Less than a block away was an auction house, Hewlett's Exchange, a two-story building with arched openings, a tile roof, and a stucco exterior. The daily slave auctions took place from 10:00 a.m. until 3:00 p.m., with a huge attendance of local businessmen, visitors, and buyers from Louisiana and Mississippi. New Orleans was the premier city for the domestic slave trade in the United States, and Hewlett's was the premier auction house and something of a tourist attraction. Visitors to the city often documented what they had witnessed at Hewlett's Exchange—some appalled with the selling of human flesh, but others ambivalent about the auctions. Many of the notaries' offices were located near Hewlett's to make it convenient for the slave owners to record their new purchases.[5]

Chartres Street was the most prominent shopping street in New Orleans during the early part of the nineteenth century and earned the sobriquet of "The Broadway of New Orleans," alluding to the bustling, fashionable shopping and the place to be seen while promenading on the banquettes.[6] From Canal Street to St. Louis Cathedral, the shoppers purchased the latest Parisian fashions. The fashionable Creole and Anglo-American ladies could select such luxurious fabrics as silks, organdies, and French calicoes and then order custom-made dresses. The fabrics were tastefully displayed on shelves and counters, and generally there were no show windows, which were considered too gauche for the refined upper crust.[7]

In 1829, Chartres Street ran parallel to the Public Square, and on the other side of the St. Louis Cathedral the name of the street was later changed to Condé, named for Louis Henri, the powerful Prince of Condé who was father of the Duke of Bourbon in the ancien régime. It was here on rue de

Condé that the Reys first lived as man and wife with their infant daughter, Elizabeth.[8]

To support his new family, Barthélemy Rey worked a few blocks away on rue Bourbon, famous today for its bars and lively nightlife. City directories in the early 1830s identify Rey as a tailor at 261 Bourbon Street (old numbering). At this time, Bourbon Street was in a filthy condition with deplorable sidewalks and huge potholes dotting the earthen streets, with the holes collecting water that later stagnated and produced mosquitoes, algae, slime, and stench. Geographer Richard Campanella characterizes Bourbon Street in this era as "middle class, generally residential, and mostly francophone, Catholic, and Creole." Because tailoring was a profession that many Afro-Creole men successfully undertook, they were considered to be superior to white tailors and were the preferred choice for any tailoring needs of the white upper class.[9]

The Reys welcomed their first son and second child, Henry Louis Rey, on Sunday, February 20, 1831. Eight months later, on October 30, 1831, the Reverend Felipe Asensio baptized the baby boy at St. Louis Cathedral. Joseph Rey, his grandfather, stood as his godfather, and his godmother is listed as Marie Antoinette Godin, but it is unclear who she was or what her relationship was with the younger Rey.[10]

After Henry Rey's birth, his parents welcomed five more children to a total of seven: four girls and three boys. All seven children lived to adulthood, which was extremely unusual in the nineteenth century, particularly in New Orleans with its frequent outbreaks of yellow fever and cholera epidemics.[11]

Barthélemy Rey's days as a modest tailor on Bourbon Street ended in the mid-1830s when he embarked upon a new career as a real estate broker in the booming markets of New Orleans, the suburbs, and even across Lake Pontchartrain in St. Tammany Parish. His business partners were typically free people of color with Saint-Domingue roots. Two frequent partners were Nelson Fouché and Chazal Thomas, who both later were teachers at the Couvent School. Often sellers and buyers were white Creoles and the foreign French at the pinnacle of their success. The foreign French were people who were born in France and entered the city from 1820 to 1860, shoring up the existing Gallic community, which had been declining in numbers and importance since the Louisiana Purchase in 1803.[12]

The New Orleans Notarial Archives contain numerous records of Barthélemy Rey's real estate dealings beginning in the early 1830s and continuing until his death in 1852. Louis Bouligny and Pierre Soulé occasionally appear in the notarial records as sellers or buyers involved in Rey's real estate transactions, especially in the mid-1830s. Historian Joseph Tregle characterized

Pierre Soulé and Louis Bouligny's father, Pierre, as "mainstays of the foreign French faction."[13]

Pierre Soulé, an idealistic and handsome lawyer, was expelled from France for attacking the restored Bourbons in a series of newspaper articles. After moving to England, Haiti, and Baltimore, the young revolutionary eventually settled in New Orleans. He later served as a US senator, ambassador to Spain, and Confederate official. In *My Travels in America* (1963), Henry Herz described Pierre Soulé as "the most eloquent lawyer in New Orleans" and his home as "the meeting place of the distinguished people in the region." Contemporaries remarked on his amazing resemblance to Napoleon, which he apparently relished and cultivated by styling his long raven black hair like the emperor's.[14]

The career path chosen by Barthélemy Rey proved to be a lucrative one, rewarding his family with wealth and the prestige accorded to the upper echelon of the black Creoles. The Rey family had many close friends in the black Creole elite: Bazile Crocker, Drausin Macarty, Pierre Casanave, François Boisdoré, and François Lacroix.[15] Interestingly, Barthélemy Rey was a slave owner. According to the 1850 Schedule of Slaves, Barthélemy Rey owned eight slaves ranging in age from two months to fifty years old.[16] The notarial acts of Paul E. Laresche from 1847 to 1852 document six transactions in which Barthélemy Rey either bought or sold slaves. The question arises whether the elder Rey was a benevolent slave owner who was protecting people of his race against harsh white owners or an exploitive owner, no different from white owners who treated slaves as property and as vastly inferior to them, socially and legally.[17]

The perplexing issue of slave ownership among the elite free people of color is a subject that has long hidden in the shadows of historiography but is currently a subject of an ongoing debate among historians of the era. The traditional view is that free people of color who owned slaves were related to the slaves and had simply bought them to protect them from exploitive whites who might mistreat them or possibly resell them to plantation owners who lived far away from New Orleans. There is some evidence to support this benevolence theory. Legal scholar Judith Schafer documents numerous manumissions of slaves owned by free people of color during the 1850s. Schafer proposes the theory that the manumitted slaves were actually family members. First, despite the free people of color's relatively small numbers in the city's total population, this enclave of slave owners made up nearly half of all who freed their slaves in the 1850s. Second, demographics support Schafer's theory because the now-freed slaves were overwhelmingly women and described as "mulattoes," a phenotype that generally meant of half white and half African descent. This would correlate with the demographics of the free community in New Orleans. And third, court cases stipulated that the freed people must be allowed to remain in Louisiana. This legal condition was deemed necessary because of the Louisiana Act of 1852, which stipulated that manumitted slaves depart for Liberia after manumission. Putting all of the court evidence together, Judith Schafer maintains that the slave-owning free people of color were basically benevolent owners protecting relatives and friends from a harsher and crueler form of slavery.[18]

More recent scholarship of 2006 depicts a more nuanced view of slave ownership among the free black community, one that reveals a darker and more exploitive picture. Using the records of the Orleans Parish Notarial Archives Research Center, which document the purchase, sale, transfer, or manumission of a slave, Ben Hobratsch found numerous transactions that recorded the sale of English-speaking slaves from Virginia who were obviously not relatives of their new black owners. The notarial records also document that the *gens de couleur libre* sold slaves at a greater frequency than they purchased them and that many of these transactions were to white buyers. And finally, the Hobratsch study found that manumission records were mostly for biracial slaves with French heritage, leaving the black anglophone slaves still in bondage. This more recent study contradicts the Schafer study, and the trend now is to view many free black slaveholders as exploitive of their slaves' labor rather than being benevolent and protective of their racial brothers and sisters.[19]

So where did Barthélemy Rey fall in these divergent categories of slave owners? Looking at the number of transactions recorded in the Notarial Archives of New Orleans and considering that he owned more than a few slaves, the elder Rey fell into the category of the more exploitive type of owner who viewed slaves as property to sell or buy according to his individual economic and domestic interests. Perhaps some slaves were related, but that is unlikely in the case of the transaction of March 9, 1852, in which Barthélemy Rey sold Fanny—who was noted in the records as a "negress about 42 years old"—and fetched the price of $260 from a white buyer, Louis Mestier. Rey distanced himself from the city's black and enslaved population and was more akin socially to the white slave owners.[20]

The next question to consider is why his son later emerged as a prominent leader of a civil rights movement on behalf of all men of color and how this change came about. It is difficult to determine the answer, but perhaps it was a combination of a generational shift to move away from an antiquated form of social structure, slavery, and a recognition that during the postbellum years, the three-tiered racial system conflated to a binary one in which all people of African descent were amalgamated into just one class. Whatever the reasons, Henry Louis Rey became a leading civil rights advocate for all people of African descent in his séance circles, the Louisiana legislature, and on the Orleans Parish School Board.

Despite the negatives of his slave ownership, Barthélemy Rey provided leadership for the free black community in education and in the exploding real estate market. Barthélemy Rey and other Afro-Creoles helped to build the two Creole suburbs: Faubourg Marigny and Faubourg Tremé. The Faubourg Marigny developed when Bernard de Marigny inherited his father's downriver plantation in 1800. Five years later, the land was subdivided, and Marigny began to sell 30-by-120-foot lots to the French and Creoles. Americans tended to congregate on the other side of Canal Street in the Faubourg St. Mary (Ste. Marie), sometimes called the American Sector, marking a physical, cultural, and political division between the Creoles and the Anglo-Americans in New Orleans.

Bernard Marigny became a very successful real estate broker and sold lots for $300 to $400. Temporary Creole cabins of two rooms were often built on the lots and were later replaced with larger and more substantial houses. After the 1809 migration of the Saint-Domingue refugees, Marigny's sales experienced a major upswing because of the greater need for housing.

Joseph Rey, Barthélemy's father, bought a lot on Craps Street from Bernard Marigny on April 5, 1820, for $400. Joseph Rey is listed in the 1822 City Directory as a grocer, so he probably had his place of business in or near his residence. Marigny named Craps Street for the dice game that contributed to his financial ruin. Barthélemy Rey later moved to another house on Craps Street from his French Quarter residence on Condé Street.[21]

The second Creole suburb, Faubourg Tremé, was originally owned by the Frenchman Claude Tremé and his Creole wife, Julia Moreau (sometimes written as Moró). Tremé had acquired the land in 1794 through his wife's inheritance of the Morand-Latil-Prévost-Moreau holdings. After his marriage and the clearing of the title, Claude Tremé began to sell lots between 1798 and 1810, mostly to free people of color. He then sold the remaining tract to the City Corporation in 1810, and the Tremés moved downriver. Like the Faubourg Marigny, the influx of émigrés from Saint-Domingue in 1809 and 1810 ensured the economic viability of Faubourg Tremé.[22] The Faubourg Tremé was located north of the French Quarter in what was then dubbed "the back of the city." Tremé was bordered by Rampart Street on the south,

Broad Street on the north, St. Louis Street on the west, and Esplanade Avenue on the east (see map on page 47).

Leading into Tremé from the north was the Carondelet Canal (sometimes called the Old Basin Canal), which made it possible for boats to sail from Lake Pontchartrain into Bayou St. John and continue on the canal into Faubourg Tremé, where the boat would unload its cargo on or near the turning basin. Once unloaded, the boat would turn around in the rectangular-shaped turning basin, float up the Carondelet Canal, and return to the lake. From that point the boat could sail either to the north shore of Lake Pontchartrain or out to the Gulf of Mexico. Boats that used the Carondelet Canal avoided extra miles and the tricky navigation of sailing against the strong current of the Mississippi River, especially before the invention of the steamboat. Thus, New Orleans consistently received produce, lumber, and many other products, which contributed to an economic boom in an area already experiencing rapid growth.

Just east of the Carondelet Canal was the heart of Tremé, the famed Tremé Market, which was built in 1839. The original plans in the Notarial Archives Research Center show buildings to be erected on Orleans Street for $27,000, a considerable sum of money in those days. The architectural plans were based on the existing Poydras Market and included cast iron fluted columns with wood coffered butchers' tables, fifteen market stalls under arcades, and cast iron arch fan inserts with exquisite cornucopia details.[23] Crowning the archway over Villere Street was a cupola, which dominated the neighborhood and served as a beacon of community cohesion.[24]

Adjacent to the Tremé Market was the Orleans Parish Prison, erected between 1832 and 1836 on the site of an old soap factory that over the years had become a nuisance to the neighborhood and a blighted piece of property. The prison's twin, three-storied buildings complemented the architecture of the marketplace with its two belvederes for surveillance and alarm bells. The rat-infested prison was notorious for its horrid conditions, even by nineteenth-century standards. A contemporary account described the prison cells as a hell on earth—filthy, overcrowded, smelly, unventilated, and overall appalling.[25]

If Tremé Market was the heart of Tremé, then Congo Square was the heartbeat of Tremé with its thunderous din of pounding African instruments: drums, gourds, and banjo-like instruments. Free people of color and slaves rendezvoused for a relaxing and entertaining Sunday afternoon of music and dancing witnessed by an occasional curious white visitor. A few vendors milled around and peddled gingerbread, rice cakes, and pralines. Over the last two centuries, the square has been known by various monikers: Place des Nègres, Public Square, Circus Square, Beauregard Square, and Congo Square.[26] Together, the Tremé Market and Congo Square formed an unofficial town center for the Creole community.

The Tremé neighborhoods experienced a building boom as a result of the city's robust commercial economy. The most popular housing style was the Creole cottage set flush on the wooden banquette with gardens on the side and behind the house. This style of architecture featured full-length casement openings with transoms or overlights and dormers. Yellow ochre paint with Paris green shutters and off-white woodwork was a popular color combination.[27]

As more families moved into the burgeoning Faubourgs Tremé and Marigny, the need for a new church became more apparent. Up until this time, the spiritual needs of the Creole community had been met by attendance and membership in St. Louis Cathedral in the French Quarter. But over the years, there had been a spiritual and personal schism between Catholic Church leaders and the Afro-Creoles. There was also a need for a church physically closer to the new neighborhoods. Saint Augustine Church was completed in 1842 with donations from the white and black Creoles and French émigrés. The Reys were active members of the congregation and purchased a pew to use for Sunday mass.[28]

The lucrative real estate market exploded, and the fortunes of the real estate brokers mounted, fueling more investments and more brokers vying for financial success. Except for a temporary economic downturn related to the national Panic of 1837, New Orleans was a booming southern city and one of America's largest cities until the Civil War, which decimated its economy. Anglo-Americans flooded the city during the first half of the nineteenth century, seeking their fortunes and recrafting the ethnic, linguistic, and political landscapes.

There is no specific information about Henry Rey's education, but judging by the excellent quality of his writings, the fact that he was bilingual, and his career choices, the younger Rey must have received a superb foundation. The question then arises: who taught Henry Rey and his siblings? More than likely, the older Rey children were educated privately. During the 1830s and 1840s, there were no public schools, even for white children. However, there were small private schools taught by local Creole men or Frenchmen in their homes.[29]

The lack of schools for black Creole children led Barthélemy Rey to play a prominent role in the founding of the L'Institution Catholique pour l'instruction des orphelins dans l'indigence (Catholic Institution for the Instruction of Poor Orphans), better known today as the Catholic Institution or the Couvent School. The Afro-Creole school was first incorporated by Louisiana in 1847, more than a decade after the death of Madame Marie Justine Cirnaire Couvent, whose generous bequest stipulated the foundation of a school. In her 1832 will, Madame Couvent, the widow of Bernard Couvent, named Henry Fletcher, a free man of color, to be executor of her will. Her lot on the corner of Grands-hommes and Union (now Touro and Dauphine Streets) was to be the home for a free school for orphans of color (*orphelins de couleur*), and money after the payment of her debts was to be dedicated to support the school.[30]

Henry Fletcher failed to fulfill the conditions of Madame Couvent's will upon her death in 1836. He kept the legacy a secret and misappropriated some of the funds. According to Rodolphe Desdunes, "Mr. Fletcher had been engaged in his crooked work for some time before the discovery of the abuse. Instead of beginning work to carry out the last intention, he disposed of some of the [property] and applied the fruits of these disposition to his own use." Father Constantine Manehault of St. Louis Church (now St. Louis Cathedral), who had been named in Madame Couvent's will as the director of the future school, informed François Lacroix belatedly of the fraud, who then alerted the community to legally direct the remaining funds and the land to the establishment of the school. As evidence of Lacroix's pivotal role, Desdunes noted that Lacroix was named the first president of the school.[31]

There is some evidence in the René Grandjean collection that says otherwise. An interview between René Grandjean and Eugène Rapp on July 17, 1921, at Rapp's home on St. Anthony Street, gives the place of honor to Barthélemy Rey as being the first to realize that there was something amiss and to reveal the existence of Madame Bernard Couvent's generous bequest to the community.[32]

At the time of the Grandjean interview, the ailing Rapp was eighty-five years old, and one month later he died. Rapp was an old family friend of the Reys and very involved with the Couvent School. He served with Henry Rey in the Native Guards (Confederate and Union regiments) and married Rey's youngest sister, Henriette. Marie Collins,[33] Eugène Rapp's daughter who was also Barthélemy Rey's granddaughter, substantiated her father's version of the discovery during the July 1921 interview. In the Rapp version, Father Manehault played no part in the discovery, and it is certainly curious that a priest would have waited over a decade to alert the black Creole community of improprieties involving the founding of a Catholic school.[34]

In any case, Barthélemy Rey played a prominent role in the history of the Couvent School, staffed by a highly politicized teaching corps that instructed their students in the democratic advances of the American, French, and Haitian Revolutions. Historians today recognize the Couvent School as the "nursery school for revolution in Louisiana." The elder Rey was named the first secretary of the overseeing organization, la Société Catholique pour l'instruction des orphelins dans l'indigence.[35] In 1852, the school moved from a temporary location to the corner of Greatman and Union in the Faubourg Marigny, now 1941 Dauphine Street. Historian Molly Mitchell credits the school's directors and teachers as being some of the leading French-speaking free black intellectuals and writers in Louisiana. "The Catholic Institution was the cornerstone of the Afro-Creoles' political work," she has written.[36]

In February 1851, Barthélemy Rey's name appeared as "President" in a notarized copy of amendments to the incorporation.[37] Two months later, the first entry in the Séance Register for the Couvent School named Barthélemy Rey as the president and François Lacroix as a director.[38] By 1852, 165 students had been enrolled, the number of boys and girls being nearly equal. The school was ostensibly under the guidance of the Catholic Church, but in reality it was a secular institution. Orphans and the destitute attended free of charge, and other children paid a small monthly tuition. The school was a source of pride for black Creoles as well as a community of writers and political activists. The list of directors and teachers included such black Creole notables as Paul Trévigne, Armand Lanusse, Rodolphe Desdunes, Joanni Questy, and Henry Louis Rey.[39]

However, Barthélemy Rey's days as president were numbered. On May 29, 1852, he died. The cause of death is unknown. No death certificate was filed, and Henry Rey did not mention in his séance registers the cause of death. If the elder Rey died from natural causes, it was not an extended illness because there were numerous notarial acts documenting property transfers filed during the first part of the year.

A week later, the Board of Directors of the Couvent School at a school assembly read a letter from Henry Rey inviting them to attend a memorial mass on June 8, 1852. The Board urged all directors and students to attend the mass for their president, which was to be celebrated by Father Joseph Morisot at Annunciation Church.[40]

The torch was passed from the father, Barthélemy Rey, to his eldest son, Henry Louis Rey. It was now up to Henry to continue his father's work as a pioneering educator, an active community leader, and a successful businessman. The first generation of Saint-Domingue émigrés began to pass away, and members of the second generation assumed leadership roles within their communities. As the second generation descended into the political maelstrom of the 1850s, their Saint-Domingue and French legacies invigorated the struggle for liberty, equality, and brotherhood.

A thousand miles away in western New York, Modern American Spiritualism awakened the hearts and minds of Americans who searched for ways to communicate with departed loved ones. The rise of Spiritualism in the North would later be molded into a unique expression of Afro-Creoles' hopes and aspirations during the late 1850s and continuing through the Civil War and the postbellum years.

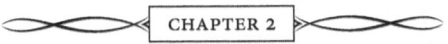

Echoes from Another World

The year 1848 was a pivotal one in American history. In Washington, James K. Polk was completing his final year as president and ensuring his lasting legacy as the main architect of Manifest Destiny—the expansion of the United States into a continental nation from the Atlantic to the Pacific, from sea to shining sea. At the conclusion of the Mexican War, the Treaty of Guadalupe Hidalgo added a vast amount of land to the United States, including the new western territory of California. Rumors of a major gold strike at Sutter's Mill in California circulated soon after the treaty was signed, and the rumors had been confirmed by March 1848. And on Friday night, March 31, 1848, in the hamlet of Hydesville, New York, the adolescent Fox sisters—Kate and Maggie—reported mysterious rappings emanating from their small rustic farmhouse.

The strange events at the Fox household attracted the attention of excited and curious neighbors and relatives. The sisters soon discovered that they could communicate with the spirit by commanding one knock for an affirmative answer and two for a negative response. Repeating the alphabet and the spirit responding with a knock for the correct letter expanded the spiritual conversation. Using this telegraphic code, the girls determined that the spirit was a traveling peddler who years earlier had lodged at their house and was killed by the previous residents for money. Efforts to find a body in the earthen basement proved futile, as the springtime digging consistently hit a persistent, gushing stream of underground water.

The eerie tale of the murdered peddler might have ended at this point had not the older, divorced sister, Leah Fish, intervened and brought the frightened family to her home in Rochester, about twenty miles east of rural Hydesville in western New York. For Leah—a struggling thirty-year-old single mother—the nocturnal rappings were an opportunity knocking. The younger sisters acquiesced to Leah's tutelage and agreed to perform private séances among Rochester's elite families, the first of whom was a radical activist Quaker couple, Amy and Isaac Post. The Posts were dedicated and intrepid reformers who championed the radical causes of abolitionism and women's suffrage in Rochester, a city nationally known as a storm center for political and social reforms. Their home served as a hub of discussion and support for famous reform lecturers and abolitionists such as Frederick Douglass and William Lloyd Garrison.[1]

Although the Posts were initially skeptical of the young Fox sisters' canny ability to communicate with the dead, they became fervent lifelong believers in Spiritualism after their first séance, in which Kate and Maggie received messages from the couple's deceased children. For the Posts, Spiritualism conformed to their Quaker religious belief of the individual possessing an inner light or spark of the divine. As historian Catherine Albanese notes in *A Republic of Mind and Spirit* (2007), the Quakers believed in an unbroken chain of communication between all beings and spirits. The theological Quaker compass was set "in a direction that could point comfortably toward spirit communication." The young Fox sisters, acting as mediums, were able to use their inner lights to hear and translate echoes from another world. No ministers or priests were required for a connection to the spiritual realm, and common people were able to commune with the dead.[2]

After a round of successful and lucrative private séances in Rochester, Leah Fish—ever the opportunist—brought the nascent séance Spiritualism to the next level: public forums. On November 14, 1849, the older sister arranged for Kate and Maggie to perform at the Corinthian Hall in Rochester, charging twenty-five cents a person to hear mysterious rappings, which were translated by the girls. The raucous audience had its share of disbelievers who later demanded that a committee investigate the true source of the rappings. The Rochester investigators were unsuccessful in their attempts to expose the girls' suspected chicanery, and the committee's lack of success fueled more public interest and support for Kate and Maggie's public performances.

Newspaper reports added to the girls' newfound celebrity as they toured major cities in New York, with Leah Fox acting as a type of stage manager. Their arrival in New York City in early June 1850 attracted the eye of Horace Greeley, the influential and decidedly liberal editor of the *New York Tribune*. Greeley and his wife, Molly, attended one of the private séances the Fox sisters were holding at Barnum's Hotel and, like the Posts, became strong devotees of the now flourishing Spiritualist movement. Kate and Maggie convinced the Greeleys that they were able to cross the spiritual divide and contact the Greeleys' five-year-old son, Pickie, who had died of cholera in 1849. The skilled mediumship of the attractive and charming Fox sisters was deemed by Greeley to be genuine and not legerdemain.[3]

Horace Greeley's positive coverage of the girls' uncanny abilities in the prestigious *New York Tribune* ensured the viability and national growth of Modern American Spiritualism. Following the lead of the *New York Tribune*, newspapers throughout the country reported on the supernatural events, which had originated in western New York. By the mid-nineteenth century, western New York had developed into a venue for numerous religious activities and radical social movements that arose quickly, spread quickly, and then quietly disappeared from the American scene. Revivalism, new sects, and social reforms occurred so frequently that western New York became known as the Burned-over District, an epithet alluding to fires of the forest and fires of the human spirit.[4] The Fox sisters' spiritual encounters were the latest spark in a scorched area and engendered a renewed interest in contacting the departed in the early 1850s. What later became known as Modern American Spiritualism spread like a contagion throughout New York State to the Northeast and the Midwest.

Historians of Spiritualism credit the seismic changes that American society was undergoing during the 1850s as one reason for the movement's popularity. According to Robert S. Cox, the "spiritual hothouse in which Spiritualism developed was in some sense a product of an unusual conjunction of social stresses, ranging from the increasing pace of geographic and social mobility and the fallout of industrialization, urbanization, immigration, 'modernization,' and democratization to the extension of market relations, religious diversity and the sinuous careers of religion and science and of class, race, and gender relations."[5]

The nature of contact with the spiritual world evolved as séance Spiritualism gained popularity. The original communication method relied on rappings and translations of the raps, similar to the tapping on a telegraph key and the decoding of the message using Morse code, which had been recently developed during the 1840s by Samuel Morse. The term *spiritual telegraph* was frequently used in the early 1850s and even applied as a name for one of the earliest Spiritualist periodicals, founded by Samuel Byron Brittan and Charles Partridge in 1852.[6] Later, mediums used automatic writing, trances, moving of furniture, and playing of musical instruments to make communication faster, more efficient, and perhaps more entertaining and phenomenal. No longer did the Fox sisters enjoy a monopoly over spiritual communication. The popularity of Modern American Spiritualism spawned a proliferation of adept mediums who deftly used these new, innovative methods to their advantage. No training was required; anybody had the capability to receive spiritual communications. In the words of a contemporary, "Every man his own prophet."[7]

Many mediums were young women and girls who were considered to be excellent conduits of messages from the spiritual world because of their innocence and increased sensitivity to spiritual matters. Women who had previously been barred from speaking in the public sphere were now allowed to speak openly because they were simply relaying messages from the departed and not speaking in their own voice. Historian Ann Braude contends in *Radical Spirits: Spiritualism and Women's Rights in Nineteenth-Century America* (1989) that women were able to break out of their male-imposed private spheres and find success as leaders in the patriarchal religious world. Women also benefited financially from traveling on lecture circuits and conducting private séances. Braude links Spiritualism to radical social reforms such as women's rights and abolition during the 1850s. "Spiritualism," she says, "became a magnet for social and political radicals throughout the nineteenth century."[8]

At the dawn of Modern American Spiritualism in the early 1850s, women were indeed the most important mediums. The Fox sisters and other early women mediums attracted a huge sectional following, so it is natural that some historians regard Spiritualism as a vehicle for upward social and economic mobility for women in a male-dominated world. As Spiritualism spread and became more popular, favorite male mediums and lecturers such as James Peebles, James V. Mansfield, and the *Banner of Light* editors became more visible to the American public. Within private séance circles, men were equally used as the circle's mediums. Men were drawn to Spiritualism and were counted among its celebrity trance lecturers, private séance mediums, and participants at the table during Spiritualism's heyday and beyond.

News of the Fox sisters and Spiritualism eventually crossed the Mason-Dixon Line and spread to the South, where literary editors, reporters, and religious leaders generally dismissed the movement with a mixture of derision and skepticism, often referring to the Fox sisters as the "Rochester knocking girls." The influential and prestigious *Southern Literary Messenger*, published in Richmond, denounced "the buffooneries of the Foxes and the Fishes" and labeled their followers as "ardent zealots, weak-minded enthusiasts and gullible dreamers" who were easily seduced by superstition and charlatans.⁹ The editorial staff issued a scathing condemnation in 1854, stating that

> *the history of the last twenty years is a series of chapters on Phrenology, Mesmerism, Clairvoyance, Animal Electricity, and the last though not the least humbug of all, Spiritual Rappings. And here we have the edifying spectacle of a multitude of the old and the young, the grave and the gay, the rich and the poor, gray-headed judges, illustrious senators, staid matrons and even ministers of religion alternately excited to enthusiasm or standing aghast with wonder and astonishment at the stupid tricks of one of the grossest species of [fraud] that was ever practiced upon poor, gullible man.*[10]

But there was more to the southern opposition to Spiritualism. It was an "ism" that had originated in the North, and Spiritualism was closely associated with other dangerous northern "isms," such as abolitionism, feminism, and radicalism. Therefore, Spiritualism arrived belatedly and had far fewer followers in the South.[11] The early sponsorship of Quaker activists Amy and Isaac Post, together with the support of the influential and liberal northern editor, Horace Greeley, were reasons enough to resist the national obsession with spiritual rappings. Antebellum southerners were a conservative group that viewed with suspicion and aversion new movements, which they considered to be part of northern "depravity."

Nevertheless, despite the strident opposition of newspapers, influential periodicals, and some leaders, Spiritualism did find adherents in the South. Within four years after its inception in New York, Spiritualism had invaded the Queen City of the South, New Orleans.[12]

The earliest written reports of local mediums relate to the séance circles and to the leadership of Joseph Barthet, a French émigré. Barthet was one of the "foreign French" in New Orleans who immigrated to Louisiana because of political upheavals in France. The foreign French "provided not only crucial skilled, literate, and experienced reinforcement of the local Creole elite, but also shored up French and Franco-African society in New Orleans from top to bottom." French-speaking immigrants like Barthet were instrumental in the persistence of an active and politically powerful Gallic community for decades after the Louisiana Purchase.[13]

On April 9, 1845, Joseph Barthet founded his mesmerist society, La Société du Magnétisme de la Nouvelle-Orléans, which counted seventy-one members from the Gallic community and was patterned after mesmerist societies organized in France. The group met every Monday to discuss a healing science called mesmerism that involved submerging patients in a large oak tub filled with water and magnetic substances. This eighteenth-century pseudoscience was based on the premise that everything in the universe, including the human body, was composed of an electromagnetic fluid, and that illness developed when the fluid was out of balance. The patient would sit in the tub, and the magnetized water would allegedly modify or cure disease.[14]

In the 1770s, the Viennese founder of this medical therapy, Franz Anton Mesmer, observed that patients sometimes went into trances called magnetic sleep and descended into dark spheres inhabited by spiritual beings. Today we would call the trances a hypnotic state. While undergoing the healing process of magnetism, patients would sometimes speak in languages they had never studied, or would play musical instruments of which they had no previous knowledge, or communicate with the dead. Later, the magnetic-charged tub was discarded, and all that remained of mesmerism was the doctrine of spiritual communication through subjects operating in blissful, trance-induced states. According to historian Cathy Gutierrez, modern Spiritualists later took "the trance state as a necessary injunction for mediums who would enter an alternate consciousness and communicate with the dead from this intermediary state." New Orleans's French connection was further strengthened by direct correspondence with mesmeric societies in Paris.[15] In the early 1850s, mesmerism dovetailed on a national level into Modern American Spiritualism, with Joseph Barthet as its leading ardent advocate in New Orleans. The transition in New Orleans from mesmerism into séance Spiritualism mirrored the same transition observed in the northern states.

Historian Caryn Bell describes the naissance of Spiritualism in the Crescent City as beginning with a Creole séance circle founded by Joseph Barthet. As with his Société du Magnétisme de la Nouvelle-Orléans, Barthet provided leadership in a new metaphysical religion as well as in controversy, particularly with the conservative Catholic Church leadership in New Orleans. Barthet enthusiastically embraced Spiritualism and welcomed the conversion of new members, including a medical doctor, Charles Testut, a white French émigré like Barthet and a literary colleague of the literary elite within the free people of color community. Testut, an acerbic French gadfly, attended his first séance in December 1852 that he later recalled as having a large number of participants seated around a large oblong table with their open hands resting on the table's surface. Questions were posed by the participants, and the spirits responded by raising the table and striking the ground once for "no" and twice for an affirmative answer.[16]

Testut's first encounter with the spirits may have been a séance lead by the Reverend Thomas Lake Harris of New York City, who in December 1852 lodged for several months at the Veranda Hotel on St. Charles Avenue, across from the St. Charles Hotel and the First Congregational Church of New Orleans, ministered by the Reverend Theodore Clapp. Harris's winter sojourn was spent receiving visitors in his hotel room and holding private séances, similar to what Kate and Maggie Fox had done at Barnum's Hotel in 1850. The Reverend was a former Universalist minister who, together with Reverend James L. Scott, had established a utopian community called Mountain Cove in early 1852. Scott, a Baptist minister, declared that the community would be for true believers in Spiritualism awaiting the second coming of Christ and under the direction of the spirits. Mountain Cove was a ten-thousand-acre tract located in Fayette County, Virginia (now West Virginia). According to Rev. Clapp, the land was composed of fertile and beautiful valleys, springs, and brooks and was complete with a school, church, and printing press.[17]

The *New Orleans Daily Crescent* announced that "one of the apostles of the tribe of Spiritual Rappers [Thomas Harris] has recently arrived in our city" seeking "an army of converts to the faith." The reporter observed that

> *some of our most respectable citizens are either partial or entire converts to the faith of the Spiritual Rappers. They believe that these invisible nomads can tell them truly of the past and the present, of the dead and the living; control the present and predict the future; amuse themselves in the spiritual recreation of titling tables, making them revolve or stand on one leg, compel furniture to dance, answer a thousand meaningless knocks, etc.*[18]

After his winter sojourn in the Crescent City, Rev. Harris returned to his fledgling utopian community, which failed in 1853. Catherine Albanese credits the misguided co-leadership of Scott and Harris as the reason for its failure. Scott and Harris had assumed apostolic authority and governed Mountain Cove with "divine insight." The community fell apart as its inhabitants chafed under threats of blood authority, sexual allegations regarding Scott's adultery, the self-imposed, semi-divine status for the founders, and questionable financial dealings. Rev. Harris traveled one more time to the Crescent City in 1854, where he lectured on Spiritualism at the Mechanics' Institute in public forums, beginning in January and concluding in February.[19]

Although séance Spiritualism failed to make the same connection to the populace of New Orleans in the early 1850s that it had in the North and Midwest, there is evidence of at least a few devotees to the new religion. Advertisements in the *Daily Picayune* announced the meeting of the Spiritualists of the Harmonical Philosophy School at Temperance Hall in the Fourth District, and J. C. Morgan's bookstore on Exchange Place in the French Quarter alerted potential buyers of books about Spiritualism. A prominent northern trance medium, Mrs. G. B. Bushnell Marks, traveled by land to reach New Orleans, where in January 1854 she observed in a letter written to Amy Post that the spirits "don't visit the South much, where slavery is so poisonous to the atmosphere. Mr. Marks and I have private circles sometimes, and they talk well to us." However, Mrs. Bushnell Marks was optimistic about the future of Spiritualism in New Orleans when she announced in her letter that "the napping spirits are just coming to this town."[20]

Apparently the spirits had already arrived in January 1854 for some clergy of the Catholic Church. *Le Propagateur Catholique*, the official weekly Catholic newspaper of New Orleans, reported in the January 28, 1854, issue that the tipping table mania "had invaded some poor empty heads that are empty because their brains have been pulled out." A front-page article in the diocesan paper was vague about spiritual incidents occurring in New Orleans and was more concerned about the rapid growth of what it characterized as a new sect spreading rapidly in France like a fever from America. The author documented the arrival of Modern American Spiritualism in France, comparing it to a fever that targeted the cities where families passed the evenings at the séance table unaware of the dangers of conversing with spirits. Pastoral letters were directed to combat Spiritualism by alerting the congregations of the dangers of *"tables tournantes et parlantes."* The resistance to what was characterized as the new contagious mania was troubling for the Catholic Church leadership and proved to be more popular and more persistent than the short-lived mesmerism.[21]

Some local Catholic Church leaders had taken a lenient view toward mesmerism during its heyday and tread lightly on its founder, Joseph Barthet, and his organization, although most conservative Catholic officials were adamantly opposed to new pseudoscience. That was not the case with Spiritualism, which was viewed by the entire leadership as a threat to Catholicism; a no tolerance policy was issued through editorials and front page articles in Le Propagateur Catholique, condemning the *tables tournantes*, a term originated in France meaning spirit manifestations of all types.[22]

Modern American Spiritualism had taken France and other European countries by storm in the early 1850s, with French Catholic critics issuing polemics against the *tables*, comparing Spiritualism to a diabolical plague. Proponents of the *tables tournantes* were primarily members of the bourgeois class, including educated professionals, doctors, and French bureaucrats. According to John Monroe, the middle class tended to be disillusioned with Catholicism while nevertheless maintaining a respect for Christian morality. Rather than seeing the *tables tournantes* as an amusement or devilry, they wished to make them the basis of a new religion, and some even considered the *tables* to be harbingers of a new era. Devout Catholics hotly contested this benign view of spiritual manifestations. For the devout, spirit phenomena were a diabolical ploy to lead astray those who had lost their Catholic roots and now were engaged in an evil allegiance with the devil who exploited their naïveté.[23]

Spiritualism in the United States actually antedated the famous Fox sisters and the more phenomenal aspects of public and private séances. Andrew Jackson Davis provided the impetus and the leadership for the spiritual transformation to séance Spiritualism during the mid-1840s. A. J. Davis—often referred to as the Poughkeepsie Seer by contemporaries—first gained national prominence in 1843, when as a shoemaker's apprentice he was introduced to mesmerism by J. Stanley Grimes, who used him as a willing subject easily put in a trance. The young apprentice from western New York proved to be a talented medical clairvoyant in his own right and in 1845 began to lecture in an entranced state. One hundred and fifty-seven of Davis's trance lectures were recorded and later published in 1847 in *The Principles of Nature, Her Divine Revelations, and a Voice to Mankind*. The lectures were anticlerical, foreshadowing Davis's later acrimonious relationship with orthodox Christianity. Davis considered organized religion to be an obstacle to humanity's progressive development. During the same year, Davis and his friends began the publication of *The Univercoelum and Spiritual Philosopher*, a weekly newspaper that appeared in New York City to advance Davis's views. Samuel B. Brittan and Thomas Lake Harris—both former Universalist ministers and later proponents of Modern American Spiritualism—served as editors and writers. A. J. Davis borrowed heavily from Franz Anton Mesmer's healing science and developed his Harmonial philosophy, "a master plan for the radical transformation of existing social, economic and religious institutions."[24]

Another important influence on A. J. Davis's visions of an earthly utopia and the spiritual realm was Emanuel Swedenborg, the eighteenth-century

Swedish scientist and mystic. According to Robert S. Cox, "Swedenborgian thought cast a long shadow over the idiosyncratic writings of A.J. Davis, and through him and others, Swedenborg's spiritual geography and epistemology exerted an enormous influence over early Spiritualism." The Swedish seer's cosmos geography consisted of seven concentric spheres inhabited by beings of increasing spiritual advancement. These sympathetic and helpful inhabitants pointed the way to the higher spheres. Swedenborg's philosophy resonated with Spiritualists and the burgeoning social reformist population in the mid-nineteenth century America.[25]

Emanuel Swedenborg's philosophy of one great common brotherhood and his cosmology meshed well with Davis's Harmonial philosophy, whose hallmarks included questioning of authority, belief in the advancement of human society, a universal brotherhood, and the doctrine of progression. The visionary Davis and his followers believed in a series of concentric spheres of increasing harmony, beauty, and wisdom through which the soul advances after death, similar to Swedenborg's cosmos cartography. Davis explained that the more spiritually advanced individual would later be rewarded with a more advanced sphere after death. The mortal world represented the lowest of these spheres, so there was a spiritual continuum between the living and the dead. The earthly world was but a counterpart of the spiritual world. The philosophy of Harmonialism was based on an active and ever-changing afterlife in which more highly developed spirits would impart their knowledge and spiritual comforting to those in the lower spheres.[26]

The philosophical transition from revised Swedenborgian thought to mesmerism and A. J. Davis's Harmonial philosophy paved the way for séance Spiritualism where the living communed with the dead in darkened Victorian parlors, spirit rooms, and lecture halls. The visionary lineage beginning in the eighteenth century in Sweden and progressing to the first raps heard in the Fox sisters' home in Hydesville, New York, provided the theoretical framework for nineteenth-century Modern American Spiritualism. Spiritualism of the 1850s reflects the conjunction of a set of practices partially developed from the Fox sisters with ideas derived from A. J. Davis, Emanuel Swedenborg, Franz Mesmer, phrenologists, and to varying degrees from a number of popular and folk theories and practices.

Spiritualism, then, did not begin in 1848 with the famous Hydesville raps of the Fox sisters. It was a complex phenomenon whose philosophical roots reached back to Europe in the eighteenth century. Modern American Spiritualism captured the interest of Americans by its emphasis on phenomenal aspects at the expense of the philosophical aspects of other Spiritualists. The

American connection began when Andrew Jackson Davis took the first steps in the 1840s with his Harmonial philosophy in which men and women were placed into harmonious relations with each other, resulting in a bonding brotherhood. Davis's philosophy ran counter to mainstream Christianity. A. J. Davis's ideas of harmony and brotherhood would later find firm philosophical ground in Henry Louis Rey's Cercle Harmonique in the 1860s and 1870s.[27]

The 1850s witnessed the emergence of a bevy of newly minted mediums, some of whom gained national celebrity status as mainstream newspapers, and a burgeoning number of Spiritualist newspapers, chronicled their expertise in communing with the departed in both private and public venues. But what was this new form of Spiritualism? Was it a new religion that spoke to the spiritual needs of Americans weary of conventional congregations, a passing dalliance with black magic that harkened back to the days of Salem witchcraft, an entertaining way to while away the evening hours in parlor séances, chicanery perpetuated on a naïve public for ill-gotten financial gain, or more than one of these?

A look at some of the era's Spiritualist writings reveals that Spiritualism was a popular religious movement that had enormous resonance for a significant part of the population. Emma Hardinge, the indefatigable and prolific chronicler of Spiritualism, considered Spiritualism to be a serious religion and declared enthusiastically in *Modern American Spiritualism* ([1869] 1970), "Spiritualism, with a large majority of its American adherents, is *a religion*, separate in all respects from any existing sect, because it bases its affirmations purely upon the demonstrations of fact, science, and natural law, and admits of no creed or denominational boundary."[28]

Another prolific Spiritualist writer, James Martin Peebles, delivered high praise for Spiritualism, calling it "a grand, moral, science, and a wisdom religion," which was the cornerstone for all of the ancient faiths. Peebles, a long-lived Spiritualist, announced the dawning of a new religion not governed by a Roman pope and freed from a cast-iron creed and traditional clergy closely regulating its congregations. The traditional Protestant clergy and priests were supplanted by mediums who officiated at séance circles, which evolved into the most well-known hallmark of nineteenth-century Spiritualism.[29]

Although Hardinge and Peebles emphasized the religious aspects of Spiritualism, a more balanced, nuanced view is that Spiritualism was not strictly a religious movement but also a secular philosophy. Modern American Spiritualism was a broad-based series of ideas and practices that ranged from purely secular and scientific to highly Christianized and faith-based. It meant many different things to divergent segments of the American population. For some it was part of a liberal reform movement championing the causes of abolitionism and feminism; others considered it a philosophy; and still others like Emma Hardinge declared Spiritualism to be a religion, albeit not a traditional mainstream nineteenth-century religion. It was a new and distinctly democratic American religion that emphasized the importance of the individual and deemphasized the importance of the clergy and the authority of the Bible.

There were certain organizational characteristics that support the Hardinge religious viewpoint. Séance circles met on a regular basis and were similar to very small churches, each with its own set of regular members who developed over time specific spiritual protocols. These protocols sometimes included seating arrangements, hymn singing, prayer, and calls for meditative quiet to entice the hesitant spirits to enter the room and to impart their spiritual knowledge of the afterworld. Some séance circles even had their own names.[30]

Trance lectures were another way to convey the message of Spiritualism to the American public. Often the lecturers were women who attracted admiring male patronage to their paid audiences, thus providing the lecturer with opportunities to reap financial rewards. According to Catherine Albanese, "Platform trance speakers pronounced inspirational messages, bland and sentimental in the platitudinous style of popularized Romanticism or Transcendentalism." The lifestyle of some of the traveling women lecturers garnered them an overstated reputation of sexual looseness and immorality.[31]

The pace of Spiritualism in New Orleans quickened in 1857, when Joseph Barthet launched a Spiritualist newspaper, *Le Spiritualiste de la Nouvelle-Orléans*—the only French-language newspaper in North America devoted exclusively to Spiritualism. Barthet used his monthly journal as a forum to explain the Spiritualist philosophy; report on séances in other states; and publish reviews of recently published Spiritualist books and articles from sister Spiritualist publications in the United States, such as the *Spiritual Telegraph*, the *Spiritual Age*, and the *Banner of Light*. In addition, the newspaper passed on information about coming attractions to the Crescent City such as conventions, speakers, itinerant mediums, and public séances. Articles from French publications such as *Mystères de Paris* and *Journal du Magnétism* were also summarized.[32]

Spirit communications formed the major portion of *Le Spiritualiste*, and these communications had a distinctive Francophile flavor to them. Many spirit guides were deceased French writers and philosophers such as Honoré de Balzac, Jean-Jacques Rousseau, and Pierre-Jean de Béranger. Especially active at the séance table were deceased Catholic figures like Père Ambroise and St. Vincent de Paule. All of these French spirit guides would later find their way to Henry Rey's Cercle Harmonique in the 1870s.[33]

Joseph Barthet also criticized the increasingly conservative Catholic Church. His acerbic criticism targeted *Le Propagateur Catholique* and its powerful French editor, Abbé Napoléon Joseph Perché. The acrimonious debate raged on for two years. Abbé Perché countered Barthet's criticism by publishing his own scathing editorials and blasting the zealous French émigré and his followers. The Abbé had already used his vitriolic pen to lance Barthet and his mesmeric society in a series of articles during the early 1850s, calling mesmerists "charlatans" seduced by Satan. Those who crossed the spiritual divide and contacted the dead were godless creatures, the Abbé wrote.[34]

The mounting radical challenge to the Church and the persistent lampooning of Abbé Perché doomed *Le Spiritualiste*, especially when the periodical reported on public séances of a charismatic healing medium. All of New Orleans and the surrounding areas knew the medium by one name: Valmour.[35] In 1858, Barthet reported that Valmour, a free man of color, had generously given his time and energy to holding public séances and to healing the sick at his blacksmith shop and home. Ailing Spiritualists seeking instant cures at the hands of the skilled healing medium besieged his shop nightly, making it difficult for Valmour to earn a living. Abbé Perché, jealous of Valmour's popularity, used his ecclesiastical prominence to pressure the police to descend upon his home on the Carondelet Canal and force Valmour to discontinue the popular nightly public séances. Exasperated, Barthet angrily wrote that the police and Abbé Perché had no right to disperse the assemblies and went on to emphatically state, "as if these little despots have the right!"[36]

Joseph Barthet's séance circle was the best-known in antebellum New Orleans because of his journal and his connections to northern Spiritualists. Barthet commented on the state of Spiritualism in his adopted city when he wrote that the northern states were much more involved in Spiritualism than was Louisiana and that consequently there were more mediums and stranger phenomena in the North; however, in the local séance circles, what he called the invisibles cured the sick and corrected old dogmatic errors (*vielles erreurs dogmatiques*), which were presumably errors committed by Barthet's nemesis, Abbé Perché, and other clergy members.[37]

Joseph Barthet's circle crossed racial, gender, linguistic, and sectional barriers. Besides references to the revered free man of color, Valmour, Barthet mentioned Tampico several times in *Le Spiritualiste*. In the 1850s, Tampico became the destination for free people of color who had become disenchanted with the increasingly oppressive political situation in Louisiana and had moved out of the United States to Eureka, a community in Mexico outside of Tampico, Mexico, composed of like-minded Afro-Creoles.[38] In 1857, Louis-Nelson Fouché established a colony of one hundred families in Eureka. The village burned in 1861, and the colonists moved to Tampico. Originally from Jamaica, Fouché had been a business partner of Barthélemy Rey and a mathematics teacher at the Couvent School. Henry Rey sailed to Tampico on February 11, 1855, with two Frenchmen, Edmund Valmont and Tomas Vidal, and returned to New Orleans on April 18, 1856, on the schooner *Red Fox*. His younger brother Octave also visited Tampico in 1856. There are occasional references in the Grandjean Registers to "our brothers in Tampico," indicating an ongoing correspondence between the two black Creole communities. The Reys and other black Creoles traveled to Tampico but did not stay permanently in Mexico. They may have been in Tampico for business or pleasure or to establish a permanent residence only to change their minds and return to the Crescent City.[39]

Women played important roles as participants and mediums at the Barthet séances. As in the North, it was recommended, but not always followed, to have an equal number of males and females at the séance table. Sometimes Barthet's circles were much larger when a celebrity medium from the North appeared—so numerous that two séances would have to be conducted to accommodate the larger crowd.[40]

In a tradition established in the North, many of the Barthet's séance circle mediums were women. In his journal, he mentioned a preferred medium, "Mlle Eugénie D___." Typically, Joseph Barthet did not list the names of the participants or of the mediums. When he did list the names, there was roughly an even number of men and women. Judging from the last names, most of the participants were of French origin, although there were a number of Anglo last names such as Harris, Gray, and Taylor, indicating interaction between these two diverse ethnic groups in nineteenth-century New Orleans.[41]

For Joseph Barthet and other Spiritualists in New Orleans, the year 1858 was a particularly eventful and exciting one. Two editors of the *Banner of*

The *Banner of Light*, the premier Spiritualist newspaper, began publication in 1857 and terminated in 1907. *Courtesy of the DeGolyer Library, Southern Methodist University.*

Light, Thomas Gales Forster and J. Rollin M. Squire, made the long and arduous journey from Boston to Buffalo, across the Ohio Valley, and down the Mississippi River to lecture on Spiritualism and to hold private circles in New Orleans. The weekly *Banner of Light* was the premier Spiritualist newspaper in the nation. According to its staff, subscribers existed in every state and territory, and the periodical received correspondence from across the nation. This may have been a bit of hyperbole, but there was no doubt that the national newspaper was very popular, especially in Massachusetts, New York, Ohio, and Illinois. The *Banner of Light*'s readership formed an impressive national network of Spiritualists united by their common belief in communication with the dead. During the 1850s, a sales agent in New Orleans was listed in every weekly issue along with the names of the editorial staff. The New Orleanian agent was one of about eight listed in the journal whose job was to solicit new subscriptions and to distribute issues to existing subscribers. New Orleans was the only southern city that had a sales agent.[42]

Prior to the publication of the *Banner of Light* starting in 1857, there existed other Spiritualist newspapers such as the *New England Spiritualist*, the *Spiritual Age*, and the *Spiritual Telegraph*. Barthet corresponded with the *Spiritual Telegraph*, which published some of his letters. In a letter dated March 8, 1855, a rather long-winded Joseph Barthet recounted some spiritual episodes involving a young orphan girl. The letter concluded with his firm opposition to the local Catholic clergy, which according to Barthet was "the most hostile to the new faith." He rhetorically asked, "Will the clergy of the Roman Church persist in declaring that we are in commerce with his satanic majesty?"[43]

The advent of the Spiritualist newspapers throughout the country was a cultural and literary phenomenon. In the absence of a formal organization and clergy, the plethora of periodicals helped to connect Spiritualists around the country to the new religion and solidified the movement. This was especially important for Spiritualists who lived in an isolated area with few converts and virulent opposition from the local population.

The *Banner of Light* defined itself as A Weekly Journal of Romance Literature and Central Intelligence. This motto appeared on its massive, ornate masthead. Founded in 1857 by Luther Colby and distributed every Saturday, about half of the oversized paper was devoted to sentimental serialized stories, mediocre poetry, and predictable novelettes. The rest of the Bostonian periodical was dedicated to Spiritualism and, to a lesser extent, national politics, entertainment, and reform movements.

Much of the Spiritualist portion concerned printed communications from the dead channeled through Jennie H. Conant, correspondence from readers, summaries of sister spiritual publications, and reprints of lectures delivered by celebrity mediums like Cora L. V. Hatch and Thomas Gales Forster. The *Banner of Light* also ran a weekly column called Movements of Mediums, which detailed the lecture circuits of the peripatetic mediums who traveled from one major American city to another giving lectures and holding private séances. The *Banner of Light* carried numerous advertisements for mediums, bookstores that specialized in spiritual tomes, and specialty spiritual services. In summary, the *Banner of Light* was depicted by its editorial staff as "a popular Family Paper, and at the same time the harbinger of a glorious Scientific Religion."[44]

J. Rollin M. Squire's first foray in print was in the issue of July 23, 1857, when the Boston periodical published a letter in which Squire railed against Harvard professors who publicly denounced Spiritualism and, in particular, his ability to commune with the dead. A few months later, the *Banner of Light* published an article that mentioned Squire as an assistant to the older and more experienced medium, Thomas Gales Forster. The article reported that the handsome law student opened a prayer at services by channeling a spirit and gushed that "J. Rollin M. Squire gives promise of arriving at a high station of mediumship." Both Squire and Forster became editors in November 1857, and one month later they traveled separately to the Crescent City, presumably to expand the reach of Spiritualism into the Deep South as well as the readership of the *Banner of Light*. Squire arrived in January 1858, and Forster arrived a few weeks later, having made making a detour to St. Louis.[45]

The young and charming Rollin Squire impressed Joseph Barthet and his spiritual circles. *Le Spiritualiste* described the twenty-year-old celebrity medium as intelligent with very good manners, two essential characteristics for young men in the nineteenth century. Squire was originally from

Springfield, Vermont, and had moved to Boston with his family as a teenager. Squire attracted numerous Barthet circle participants to private séances and rewarded them with a display of his impressive supernatural powers such as raising a round table weighing about fifty pounds during the séance. Squire further dazzled the participants by placing a sheet of paper and a pencil under the séance table. The distinctive crackling of the pencil over the paper was heard, and the message was read: *Good evening all. Bonsoir Madame et Monsieur.* Even Barthet noted the obvious French error that *Madame* and *Monsieur* were in the singular instead of in the plural. Other paranormal activities included the traditional table tipping.[46]

Two additional séances with Rollin Squire had less than prodigious results. The first took place at a private home with just a few attendees and the other transpired in what Barthet described as a quasi-public room where a large crowd, including many vocal disbelievers, gathered. Squire was subjected to a rowdy group who insisted on the public séance being conducted without darkness, which according to Barthet prevented the production of the earlier paranormal results.[47]

Thomas Gales Forster received less praise and attention from Barthet. Forster lectured in February and March at Armory Hall on Camp Street and Odd Fellow's Hall. Forster was tall with a full beard and was a fast talker. As part of his presentation, he showed portraits that according to Forster had been executed under the power of a spirit by a trance-induced medium who knew nothing of the art of painting. At the conclusion of the lecture, a hat was passed around to collect donations to cover the cost of the hall and "for the benefit of the speaker." Local newspapers reported that his lectures had created a furor among not only believers, but also among nonbelievers.[48]

Both Squire and Forster corresponded with the *Banner of Light* during their sojourn, giving readers lively updates and making commentaries on the state of Spiritualism in New Orleans. The youthful Rollin Squire joyfully penned upon his arrival, "I am in the city of gayeties."[49] What greeted him upon disembarking from the steamer must have been an amazing sight. A contemporary correspondent for the *Illustrated London News* wrote this description of the levee in 1858: "The fine open space, the clear atmosphere, the countless throngs of people, the forests of funnels and masts, the plethora of cotton and corn, the roar of arriving and departing steam-boats, the deeper and more constant roar of the multitude, all combine to impress the imagination with visions of wealth, power, and dominion."[50]

Squire noted that there were many Spiritualists in the city, but that they were not in the public's eye. He described the French Spiritualists of Barthet's circle as "a quiet, calm and respectful people." Joseph Barthet's Spiritualist journal, *Le Spiritualist de la Nouvelle-Orléans,* had been mentioned in the July 23, 1857, issue of the *Banner of Light,* so apparently there had been some prior contact between Barthet and the editorial staff. While waiting for his mentor's arrival, Rollin Squire made inquiries about conducting services at established Protestant churches but to no avail.[51]

During the Squire/Forster sojourn, an anonymous correspondent from New Orleans wrote the *Banner of Light* about the grand progress of Spiritualism in that city. The writer described his early experience with northern Spiritualism, saying that he had met Forster four years earlier, in 1854, in New Orleans during Spiritualism's infancy. At this time, according to the correspondent, Spiritualism was a "by-word and a mockery to all who dared to believe.... There were probably not over 100 believers." The current state of Spiritualism had much improved with "the number of believers increasing from year to year" and the city receiving more lectures from itinerant mediums. The large audiences attending Mr. Forster's lectures and the increased number of readers of the *Banner of Light* were all indications of progress in the spread of Spiritualism.[52]

J. Rollin M. Squire informed the *Banner of Light* readers in his letter of March 12, 1858, that the audiences were growing despite opposition from the New Orleans churches. Squire and Forster continued their efforts to hold services at a Protestant church, this time applying at the First Congregation Church with Dr. Boles as minister, but they were again unsuccessful. The use of churches as a Spiritualist lecture venue was probably an attempt to circumvent the expensive meeting halls.[53]

John R. Grymes's letter of April 9, 1858, described the Forster lectures at Armory Hall as a success and praised their erudition and eloquence. The letter was a reprint of a letter published in the New Orleans *Sunday Delta.* Grymes reasoned that New Orleans was logically the premier city for Spiritualism because "if there is one city in our universe that the spirits of the departed are in abundance hovering over, anxious for its conversion, it is [New Orleans]." Echoing the criticisms of Barthet and the anonymous letter writer, Grymes lamented the interference of priests, clergy, and professors in the grand progress of Spiritualism.[54]

The correspondence and references in *Le Spiritualiste de la Nouvelle-Orléans* and the *Banner of Light* all attest to Spiritualist connections in the mid-1850s between New Orleans and Boston, the capital city of Spiritualism. Spiritualist newspapers were a method of networking and coalescing the isolated, far-flung séance circles around the country without the confining theology and conventional clergy of an established church. Joseph Barthet and his séance circle members knew and admired Thomas Gales Forster through the pages of the prestigious *Banner of Light* and other Spiritual newspapers, even before Forster and Squire arrived in the Crescent City. According to Emma Hardinge, their visit awakened an irrepressible interest in Spiritualism, which paved the way for other Spiritualist speakers to be warmly received and for more local mediums to be developed among the French and American portions of the population. New Orleans became the premier destination city in the South for the peripatetic mediums of the North.[55]

The city's cosmopolitan nature, the more relaxed Creole culture, and its Gallic connections are partly responsible for New Orleans being the most important southern center for Spiritualism in the 1850s and, earlier, of mesmerism in the 1840s. New Orleans developed into an island of Spiritualist activity in a sea of southern conservatism. The steady stream of itinerant mediums to New Orleans beginning in 1852 and continuing throughout the decade was small but significant. These traveling emissaries of the Spiritualist philosophy converted new adherents and helped to reinforce the convictions of an already-established community of believers.

Historically, many New Orleanians believed in spiritual manifestations. Joseph Barthet's mesmerist group of the 1840s was founded on the belief of trance-induced communications from the spiritual world. Voodoo (sometimes called Voudou) had for generations been a vibrant and popular African-based religion, finding its devotees among both whites and African Americans. Many residents believed in haunted houses, most notably the infamous French Quarter mansion of Madame Lalaurie, which was said to have been haunted by her mistreated slaves. For all of these reasons, New Orleans proved to be rich fertile ground for planting the seeds of nineteenth-century Spiritualism by traveling northern mediums.

In December 1858, six months after Squire and Forster departed, Joseph Barthet terminated his short-lived publication. In his last issue, Barthet attributed the demise of *Le Spiritualiste de La Nouvelle-Orléans* to a reduced readership. But perhaps the combined presence of the fiery Abbé Perché and the vigilant police might have been too much for the French émigré. Joseph Barthet's final words in his short-lived publication were, "I have done what I could; another must take my place: there are still many things to accomplish on the road [of Spiritualism]."[56]

At this point, Spiritualist activity in the francophone community shifted away from the foreign French to the local black Creole elite. The Francophile flavor of Barthet's séance circle and its clandestine nature, now that the Abbé Perché had vilified its basic tenets, appealed to the elite black Creoles. The syncretism of its belief system with an emphasis on the spiritual world, the disenchantment with the Catholic Church, and the promise of social and political reforms all conspired to attract Creoles of color to this new religion from the North.

On the national level, African Americans were a small fraction of the Spiritualist movement, which is perplexing considering the talk of universal brotherhood and West African worship of ancestors. African Americans showed relatively little interest in the spirits. In the northern region of the country, African Americans never adopted Spiritualism to any great extent. Ironically, it was in the South—the region with little interest in Spiritualism—that a strong and culturally significant black Spiritualist movement flourished.[57]

The spark of enthusiasm generated by J. Rollin M. Squire and Thomas Gales Forster that Emma Hardinge mentioned in her spiritual tome energized the black Creoles to form their own circles. It was surely no accident that Henry Louis Rey began his first séance register on June 19, 1858, just one month after the zealous editors of the *Banner of Light* returned to Boston.[58]

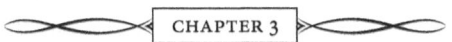

Early Forays into Spiritualism

As a teenager in the early 1850s, Henry Rey was employed as a bookbinder.[1] Sometime during the mid-1850s, he entered into an apprenticeship as a clerk under Eugène Hacker, a white Saint-Domingue émigré who owned a hardware store directly across from the Tremé Market. It was at Hacker's store on June 19, 1858, that Henry Rey began his first of many spiritual registers in which he recorded communications received in séances.

From his vantage point in the hardware store, Rey could see the famed Tremé Market with its constant flow of shoppers, merchants, and delivery carts. To the right of the store was Parish Prison, with its Black Maries (police vans) arriving periodically to discharge loads of new prisoners. To the left of the hardware store was A. Massel's, the corner liquor store on St. Peter and Marais Streets with the traditional Parisian green shutters and grey stucco exterior. Jutting out from the peaked roof was an extended protective overhang with words painted underneath that advertised wines, champagne, cognac, and whiskies.[2]

When Rey was not working on his account books, he could view through the windows an ever-changing panorama of humanity. Strolling African American women proudly wore elaborate tignons, which identified them as free women of color. The tignons were headscarves similar to turbans, which were supposed to hide their beauty and make them less attractive to white men. The women circumvented the Spanish restrictive decree of 1786 and often wore tignons with brilliant, flamboyant colors complimenting the hue of their skins and making them more alluring and stylish. A more common choice of headdress was the traditional madras elaborately arranged so as to allow locks of hair to peek out along with the glimmer of gold earrings.[3]

The Tremé location of Hacker's store had one more advantage. It was just a few blocks away from the house of a young lady who had captured Henry's heart—Adèle Crocker, the teenage daughter of Pierre Crocker and Rose Gignac. She was described by François Dubuclet as "*très intelligente, trop intelligente*," meaning she was very intelligent, too intelligent.[4] What did Dubuclet mean by "too intelligent"? He probably meant that Adèle was so intelligent that she was bored and had none of the intellectual outlets that were available to the elite black Creole males.

The only suitable trades for black Creole women who out of dire financial necessity were forced to work outside the home were the lowly positions of house servant or washerwoman. Daunting cultural and economic barriers erected by both whites and Creole men prevented Creole women from obtaining independence in the highly circumscribed nineteenth-century work world. John Blassingame notes that both white and black women in the mid-nineteenth century did not typically venture outside their homes to work, and that wives in general depended upon their husbands for financial support and their social status. The black Creole patriarchal society ensured that women were economically dependent on their men. Career aspirations for free women of color in the antebellum years were almost nonexistent, and the situation did not substantially change in the postbellum years.[5]

By 1850, free men of color had carved out a niche in New Orleans society of relatively high occupational status. According to historian Robert Reinders, only 10 percent of males were unskilled workers, with the other 90 percent working in valued professions as clerks, coopers, draymen, tailors, and even doctors and architects. The figures were reversed for women. Reinders states "women were more likely to be unskilled than men ... [and were] largely employed in domestic service or at home as washerwomen."[6] Mary Gehman identifies the few occupations open to free women of color, noting that occupations such as washerwoman, street vendor, or domestic servant were not considered to be important enough to enumerate in the US Census of 1850. Gehman lists three occupations of free women of color and their numbers: seamstress (189), dressmaker (21), and hairdresser (10). City directories document some free women of color who owned grocery stores and market stands. All in all, the 1850 US Census and the city directories paint a dismal picture of the economic status for free women of color who did not have the luxury of well-heeled husbands.[7]

Decades later, Rodolphe Lucien Desdunes celebrated the legacy of the black Creoles in a book titled *Our People and Our History: Fifty Creole Portraits*. He profiled Afro-Creoles from the nineteenth century who had been doctors, lawyers, teachers, musicians, artists, writers, actors, craftsmen, politicians, and philanthropists. Of these Afro-Creoles, only three were women: Louisa Lamotte, Virginie Girodeau, and Madame Bernard Couvent. Lamotte was an educator, Girodeau was an actress, and Couvent was the generous philanthropist whose inheritance started the Couvent School. Only one of these three was noted for her intellectual talent, Louisa Lamotte. Madame Couvent was instrumental in founding a school, but she herself was illiterate. The idealized role of women within the black Creole elite was that of being mothers and wives. A good Creole woman, as described by Desdunes, was "generous, helpful, and pious. Her virtue, her charity and her devotedness could never be doubted."[8]

Afro-Creole women were basically excluded from the vibrant literary scene in nineteenth-century New Orleans. *Les Cenelles*, the seminal anthology of black Creole poets and writers published in 1845, was totally male dominated. During the 1920s, Edward Larocque Tinker inventoried important francophone writers in Louisiana during the nineteenth century in *Les Écrits de langue française en Louisiane au XIXe siècle* (1923). Without an exception, all writers from the free people of color group were men. Among the white Creoles and French émigré writers, there was a sizable minority of women writers, yet within the elite black Creole community, literary pursuits were the exclusive providence of male authors.[9]

There are no existing photographs or paintings of Adèle. She was likely a very light-skinned black Creole, being a quadroon, a phenotype term applied to people whose genetic makeup was imagined to have been one-fourth African. Adele's mother, Rose Adèle Gignac, is listed in the US Census of 1850 as a mulatto (one-half white, one-half black) born in Louisiana around 1805.[10] Adèle's father, Pierre Crocker, was born on March 3, 1803, in New Orleans. In the baptismal records of St. Louis Cathedral, Father Antonio de Sedella recorded Pierre as a free quadroon. Pierre's father was Rafael Croker, a soldier originally from Guatemala, and his mother was Celeste Camasac, a mixed-race free woman of color.[11]

Pierre Crocker and Barthélemy Rey shared many similarities. Pierre was just one year older than Barthélemy; they were both free men of color involved in the booming real estate markets of the faubourgs and city during the 1830s, 1840s, and early 1850s; they both married women named Rose only two years apart (1827 for Pierre and 1829 for Barthélemy); both were active in the Couvent School; they both had large families—Pierre with eight legitimate children and Barthélemy with seven; and the two men were both active parishioners of St. Augustine Church. Pierre Crocker was a founding member of La Société d'Economie et d'Assistance Mutuelle, the Economy Society, which was a benevolent organization for free men of color established in 1836 with a membership of fifteen free men of color. Pierre was also known for being the brother of Bazile Crocker—fencing master, superb craftsman, math teacher at the Couvent School, and frequently mentioned by contemporaries as one of the most handsome men of New Orleans.[12]

There was one significant difference between Barthélemy Rey and Pierre Crocker. This involved the sixteen-year-old daughter of Christophe Glapion, a white businessman, and Marie Laveau, the reigning Voodoo Princess of New Orleans. The daughter's full legal name was Marie Heloïse Euchariste Glapion, but as she became more deeply involved in Voodoo, she adopted the name of her famous mother. Many contemporaries confused the two Marie Laveaus, thinking that the high priestess of Voodoo had discovered a supernatural way to stay eternally young. In reality, it was the younger Marie Laveau who had assumed her mother's exalted position among the devotees as the elder Marie Laveau retired from Voodoo activities. Some modern biographers, like Martha Ward in *Voodoo Queen: The Spirited Lives of Marie Laveau* (2004), refer to her as Marie the Second to differentiate the daughter from the mother.[13]

The younger Marie Laveau met Pierre Crocker, a married man twenty-four years older than her, and began a long relationship that would last until his death on July 9, 1857. The relationship had begun by June 1843 at the latest because the first illegitimate child was born on February 28, 1844. The unlikely pair probably met through Marie's father, Christophe Glapion, who was a close friend and business associate of Pierre Crocker. Two years prior to the birth of Pierre's first illegitimate child, Glapion orchestrated bankruptcy proceedings for Crocker, who owed thousands of dollars to many Creoles, including Glapion, who was owed $507. The largest debt was $4,000, which Crocker owed to his mother-in-law, Manon Montreuil. It is not clear why Crocker was so heavily in debt after a long, successful career as a real estate broker. Pierre Crocker was forced to liquidate most of his properties, which included eight slaves. His assets included property in Mandeville and Pass Christian as well as lots in Faubourg Marigny and the French Quarter. By law, Crocker was able to retain his family's clothing and furniture and his home on St. Philip Street, valued at $12,500.[14]

Five children were born to this union, but only two lived to adulthood: Adelai Aldina Crocker (also called Malvina and Alzina) and Victor Pierre Crocker. Pierre Crocker had a total of thirteen children with his legal wife, Rose Gignac, and Marie Heloïse Euchariste Glapion. Out of thirteen children, only five lived to adulthood, and two of them—Pierre Jr. and Malvina—died in their early twenties. This is quite a commentary on the high rate of child mortality and low life expectancy in nineteenth-century New Orleans.[15]

Pierre Crocker passed away on the morning of July 9, 1857. There was no death certificate to verify the cause of death, and Ludger Boguille, the secretary of the Economy Society, announced Crocker's death and funeral arrangements in the newspapers. Crocker lived a short distance away from Economy Hall, located on the 1400 block of Ursulines Street. Henry Louis Rey never mentioned Pierre Crocker's second illegitimate family or the younger Marie Laveau in his séance registers. Occasionally "superstition" is mentioned in a spirit message, which René Grandjean explained in his margin notes as meaning "Voudou," which today is often spelled "Voodoo."[16]

Henry Rey and Adèle Crocker may have known each other since childhood as their fathers' paths crossed so frequently over the years. Barthélemy Rey was the president of the Couvent School during its early years of existence, and Pierre Crocker was on the Board of Directors and the Examination Committee. Crocker's attendance record was spotty at best, and the Board of Directors removed him from his position as director.[17]

Less than two months after the death of the elder Pierre Crocker, Adèle Crocker and Henry Rey were joined in holy matrimony at St. Augustine Church on September 3, 1857. Witnesses included Adèle's older brother, Pierre Jr.[18] Soon afterward, Henry Rey moved to the Crocker family home on St. Philip Street to live with his bride, his mother-in-law, and Adèle's minor brother, Myrtille Raphaël.

The Reys welcomed their first child, Lucia Rose Rey, on February 7, 1859. The following month, the Reys, Rose Crocker, and Myrtille Raphaël moved into a new home on Columbus Street. Adèle purchased the property for $700 from Jacques Monière and Catherine Thiebaud. The house was located on a typical lot in that area: only 30 feet wide, but extending back for 120 feet, perfect for the traditional narrow New Orleans shotgun house.[19]

Rose Crocker lived three more years after the death of her husband. She died on December 21, 1860. Her estate was divided into thirds between Rose's two living children, Adèle and Raphaël, and the children of Pierre Jr., who had died sometime between September 1857 and October 1859. A family meeting in 1861 decided who would be the tutor (guardian) of Rose's minor

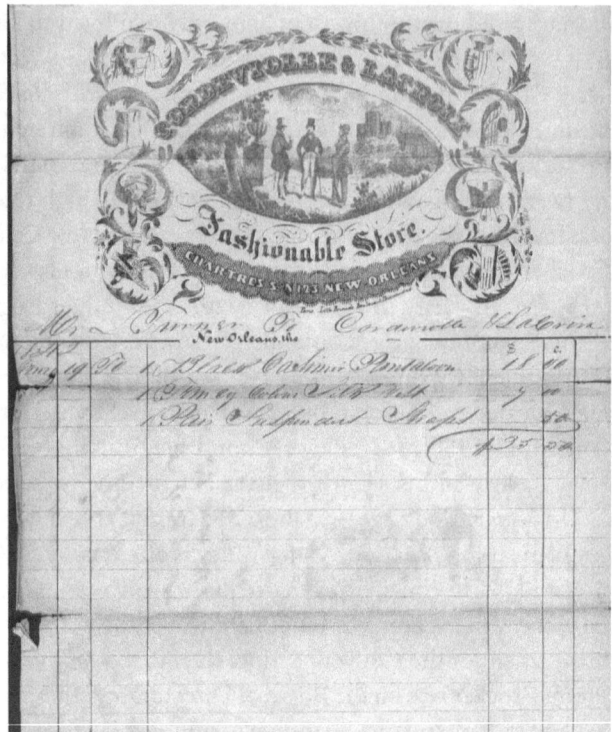

François Lacroix, a fellow émigré of Saint-Domingue ancestry and close friend of Barthélemy Rey, was a successful tailor and dressed the upper elite in New Orleans high society. This receipt, dated August 19, 1842, shows the buyer bought black cashmere pants, a silk vest, and a pair of suspenders. *Courtesy of the Louisiana Division, City Archives of the New Orleans Public Library.*

child, Myrtille Raphaël. Family friends appointed Henry Rey as guardian of the orphan, who was eleven at the time of his mother's death. The friends at this meeting were all members of the upper echelon of black Creole society: François Lacroix, Pierre Casanave, Bazile Crocker, Drausin Macarty, and François Boisdoré.[20]

There were many roads that led to Spiritualism, and the road taken by Henry Louis Rey involved encounters with the spiritual world when his father passed away. On October 26, 1858, Henry Louis Rey composed an autobiographical essay in his first séance register in which he recounted his first encounter with the spiritual world as a bereaved young man of twenty-one. On May 29, 1852, just one hour after his father's death, Henry Rey was home alone at 126 rue de Craps,[21] when he saw his father's spirit appear. The younger Rey attempted to embrace him, but the fleeting apparition vanished as quickly as it had appeared. Years later, in an 1858 séance, the spirit of Barthélemy Rey admonished his wife and related how Father Joseph Morisot had cajoled Rose out of his entire fortune. "The next day, there wasn't a *sou* [a penny] to feed the large family ... you gave him everything."[22]

Catholic Church archival records hint at a less than an exemplary priest. In 1843, Father Morisot was appointed to a rural parish across Lake Pontchartrain near Mandeville, Louisiana, on the banks of Bayou Lacombe, much to Morisot's chagrin. The country lifestyle was apparently not to his liking, and letters addressed to Father Rousselon and Bishop Anthony Blanc pleaded his case to return to New Orleans while acknowledging a sin that he has paid for by suffering in a rural environment. A few years later, Father Morisot was appointed to a post at Annunciation Church in New Orleans, but complaints from parishioners decried the father as "a rascal, who collects revenue that does not belong to him."[23]

Nevertheless, church leaders retained the embattled priest at the prestigious Annunciation Church despite complaints until 1859, when he retired and moved to Fleury-sur-Ouche, France, living the rest of his days there in poverty. Years later, Morisot's greed still resonated with Henry Rey. According to an 1872 spiritual communication, the now-deceased Father Morisot regretted his past transgressions and explained to the circle, "I wore a black robe that hid in part my weaknesses. Here I exist in dishonor and I must lower my head in front of those who move forward on the glorious Route. Excuse my despicable actions." The humble and apologetic Father Morisot followed a similar spiritual path as that of other departed Creoles and French nationals who visited the séance table to repent and beg forgiveness for past sins.[24]

The loss of Henry Rey's father's substantial inheritance had a profound and lasting effect on Henry Rey. He abandoned the Catholic Church, and the séance registers, especially the early ones, often served as a forum for diatribes and polemics against what was perceived as the Catholic Church's avarice and excessive monetary demands.[25]

According to Henry Rey, he heard about Spiritualism four or five months after seeing the spirit of his father in 1852, roughly corresponding with the time that the northern Spiritualist, Thomas Lake Harris, visited the Crescent City. Rey out of curiosity tried to communicate with the spirits while alone in his home. His initial efforts proved successful, and he levitated a heavy table that three strong men would have had difficulty in raising. Rey began attending séances with the black Creole Spiritualist Charles Veque and his uncle, Captain Jean François Chatry, who was his aunt's common-law husband.

Chatry, a wealthy white with Saint-Domingue roots, and Marie Josephine Rey were never legally married because interracial marriages were banned in Louisiana and throughout the South; however, they lived together for decades in a stable relationship and had eight children.

One Sunday evening in the 1850s, Henry Rey attended a séance at the home of Soeur (Sister) Louise, a neighbor and a popular black Creole Spiritualist.[26] In the flickering glow of gaslight, Rey levitated a heavy wooden table, and then Soeur Louise presented him with a pencil and some paper. The fatigued Rey reluctantly took the pencil, and at this point an invisible hand seized his hand. His deceased father commanded, "Write our dictation, and then you will not be tired." Thus began Rey's vocation as a medium—a vocation that he excelled at and was proud of throughout his adult life.[27]

News of a young, gifted medium spread quickly among the elite. As part of his early forays in Spiritualism, Rey conducted séances in the late 1850s at the homes of Soeur Louise and other neighborhood devotees. Included in these séance circles were members of the elite black Creole intelligentsia, among them Samuel Snaër, Adolphe Duhart, Nelson Desbrosses, and Joanni Questy. The participants were interracial, but predominantly members of the free people of color community and connected to the Couvent School. Joanni Questy was the assistant principal and upon the death of Armand Lanusse in 1867, he became principal. Questy was also a very popular and flamboyant Spanish and French teacher, affectionately addressed as "Monsieur Joanni" by his students. In 1843, Questy founded a short-lived interracial literary journal, *L'album litteraire*, and later he collaborated with Paul Trévigne as a staff writer on the *New Orleans Tribune*.[28]

But not all of the black Creoles believed in his amazing mediumistic abilities, including his own younger brother, Octave, who flatly dismissed the possibility of supernatural powers, saying, "I don't believe it." As evidence of his ability to communicate with the dead, Henry instructed Octave to go to Chartres Street where he would find some money. Octave returned half an hour later and excitedly reported that he had found "five piastres (dollars) on Chartres near St. Louis Street." A vindicated Rey rhetorically asked his younger brother, "Was this by accident or not? I tell you the truth."[29]

Henry Rey's wife Adèle also doubted the new faith, but the newly minted medium was determined to make her a believer as well. One day at midnight, according to Henry Rey, his bedroom was lit up as if by a "thousand candles." He turned to his wife and calmly demanded, "Now do you believe in Spiritualism?" Another time Rey asked a spirit to knock in his bedroom at midnight to prove to his wife the presence of spirits. Exactly at midnight

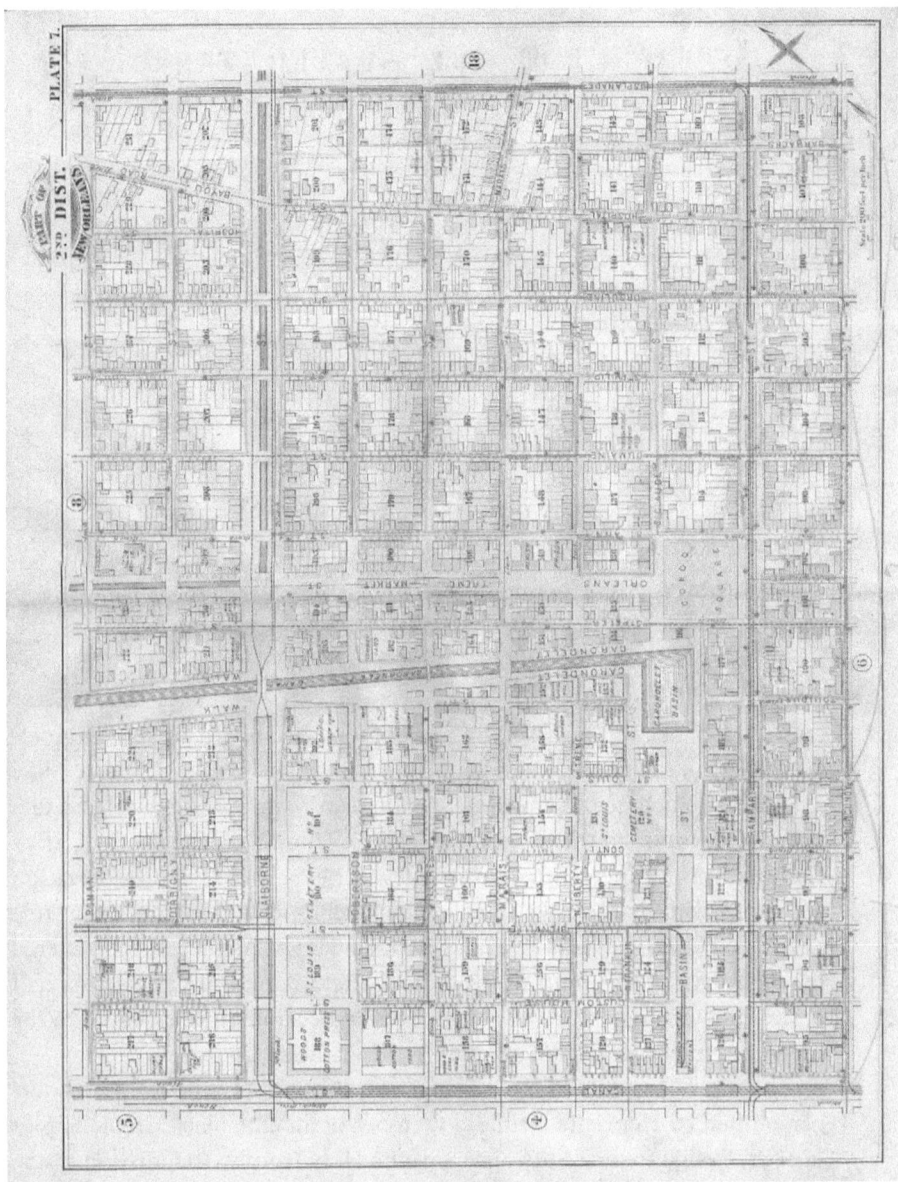

Faubourg Tremé refers to the area bordered by Esplanade Avenue to the east, St. Louis Street to the west, North Rampart to the south, and North Broad to the north. The Carondelet (Old Basin) Canal bisected the community with the turning basin on Basin Street. The town center was composed of the Tremé Market, Parish Prison, and Congo Square. *Plate 7, Robinson's Atlas of the City of New Orleans, 1883.*

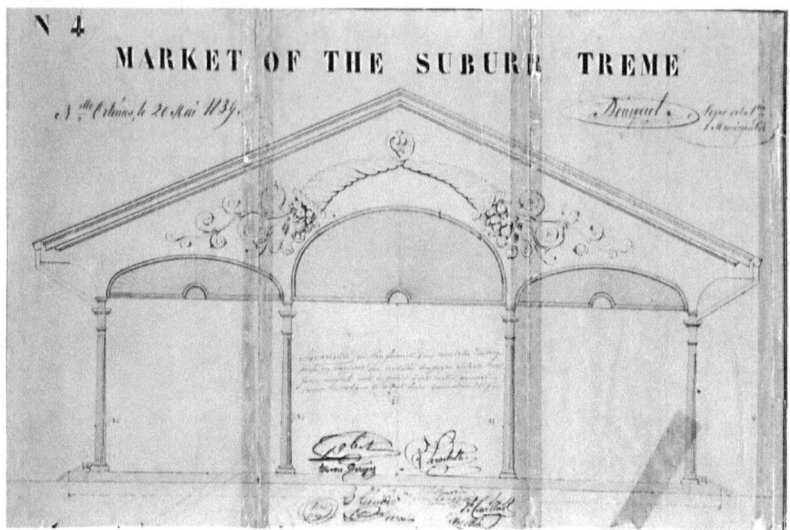

The Tremé Market was designed and completed in 1839. The architectural plans were based on the existing Poydras Market and included cast iron fluted columns with wood coffered butchers' tables, fifteen market stalls under arcades, and cast iron arch fan inserts with exquisite cornucopia details. The above drawing is part of the original plans. Tremé Market Sheet 4, Joseph Cuvillier, November 28, 1839. *Courtesy of Dale N. Atkins, Clerk of Civil District Court, Parish of Orleans.*

one heavy knock was heard on the back of their bed board, waking up Adèle and others in the house.[30]

Adèle's reluctance to embrace Spiritualism may have been related to a stronger devotion to the traditional Catholic Church. Key features of Afro-Catholicism in nineteenth-century New Orleans were the appropriation of Catholicism by the city's free women of color and their important role as the dedicated partners of the white male clergy. As the church suffered the onslaught of the influx of Protestant Anglo-Americans in the first half of the nineteenth century, the women's role became more essential to the preservation of black influence within the Catholic Church.[31]

The prominent role of free women of color in the Catholic Church was personified by Henriette Delille, a member of an elite black Creole family. In 1842, Delille founded the Sisters of the Holy Family. The mission of the order was to provide a hospice for the indigent and religious instruction and medical care for free blacks and slaves. Ten years later, Henriette Delille and the Sisters of the Holy Family took their formal vows in St. Augustine Church.[32]

Even more detrimental to the Church's viability than the ongoing flux of Anglo whites was the increasingly conservative clergy, which now stalwartly adhered to the ever-expanding and harsh racial order of America. As the Catholic Church's influence faltered and the new power elite within the Church became more Americanized, Afro-Catholic women held firm and continued to resist popular religious alternatives such as Spiritualism and Protestant sects. Despite the prominent presence of free women of color in the Catholic Church, many male black Creoles, more than women black Creoles, joined Anglo whites and became firm believers in the new American faith, Modern American Spiritualism.

In the last month of the turbulent 1850s, another celebrated northern medium appeared in New Orleans following the lecture circuit footsteps of Thomas L. Harris and the *Banner of Light* editorial duo, J. Rollin M. Squire and Thomas Gales Forster. From December 1859 into January 1860, Emma Hardinge (Britten) visited the Crescent City and noted that Spiritualism was thriving in both the American and French communities.[33] However, a few weeks prior to Hardinge's arrival, a letter from New Orleans published in the *Banner of Light* described the dismal state of Spiritualism in New Orleans. The anonymous correspondent blamed the lack of a formal organization for the decline in Spiritualists. "Chercheur" (Searcher) named two organizations that had recently disbanded: the Conference Meeting of the Harmonialists and the Brothers of the Swedenborgian and New Jerusalem Church.[34] The letter writer asked, "How are we to know our strength, unless there is a general organization?" The lack of a formal organization was an ongoing dilemma for Spiritualism, which rested on the tenet of individual mediumship yet struggled to connect to the public in a nation that now stretched across the continent.

During her stay in New Orleans, Hardinge lectured without charge for five Sundays and two weeknights per week. According to Emma Hardinge and local newspaper reports, the lectures were always well attended. The venue had to be changed to a larger venue, Odd Fellow's Hall, to accommodate the overflow crowds.[35] The enthusiastic crowds forsook their usual evening attractions to listen attentively to the petite brunette from the North lecture about Spiritualism. The interracial attendees included "the finest minds and clearest heads in this city," as Emma Hardinge later admiringly penned. After the lecture, the audience was asked to contribute money to help defray the high costs of the hall and advertising. Hats were passed around the hall and were filled with "many shining gold pieces."[36]

Hardinge astutely commented on the unusual number of people who possessed medium power despite the humidity, which is "so unfavorable to the production of these electro-spiritual manifestations." Ever the optimist,

Emma Hardinge speculated that there were enough mediums of the phenomena "in New Orleans to spiritualize the entire South." She also noted the large number of séance circles being held in New Orleans among both the French and Anglo populations.[37]

One evening Emma Hardinge interrupted her prepared lecture when a "French Creole named Dr. Valmour" entered the hall. Valmour, the charismatic medium who two years earlier had terminated his public séances under duress from the Catholic Church, started to walk pass Odd Fellow's Hall, an impressive four-storied building in the American sector, when he was seized by a supernatural force forcing him to stop and enter the hall. As he crossed the threshold in the lecture room, Hardinge loudly commanded, "Let that Brother come up here to me, to give me strength to speak! He is filled with electricity!" Valmour complied with her urgent summons and sat on the dais for the rest of the lecture as the medium continued for two more hours to hold the audience spellbound. Hardinge terminated her lecture tour in New Orleans during early January with mixed feelings. She was content to return to Boston yet sad to leave New Orleans, "the land of the shining orange grove and fair magnolia—strange and beautiful city of life and death." Years later, Hardinge raved about Valmour in her seminal history *Modern American Spiritualism*, describing him as a celebrity because of his legendary healing ability. Valmour "performed the most astonishing feats of healing . . . under the influence of his father's spirit, who was a physician before him." In her postwar addendum to *Modern American Spiritualism*, Hardinge went on to say that she remained optimistic even in the war's aftermath, noting that "Spiritualism still lives, and is still fondly cherished there: In fact it has been maintained as the 'magic staff' on which alone many a breaking heart and bereaved spirit could lean, and find assured strength and consolation. . . . Spiritualism is a fixed fact in Louisiana."[38]

One year after Hardinge's successful lecture tour on the eve of the Civil War, another well-known northern emissary of Spiritualism appeared in New Orleans. James V. Mansfield, like other northern mediums, visited the Crescent City during the winter. While in Massachusetts, Mansfield offered an interesting service through the Boston-based *Banner of Light* that involved answering questions in sealed letters destined for a departed loved one for a one dollar fee and three postage stamps. According to Emma Hardinge, the Spiritual Postmaster's modus operandi consisted of clairvoyantly reading the sealed letters, which were carefully marked and secured so that it would have been virtually impossible to open them without detection. The celebrated writing medium communicated with denizens of the spiritual realm and then transmitted their responses to living relatives and friends, sometimes in a foreign language that he had never studied.[39]

James Mansfield meticulously recorded the names of the living and the departed loved ones, the place of residence of the living, and the date that the clairvoyant reading took place in alphabetized account books, similar to what Henry Rey and François Dubuclet accomplished with their spiritual communications. Mansfield did not record the contents of the actual letters or his responses relayed from the spiritual realm. Unfortunately, only the first register, containing last names beginning with the letters A or B, has survived. Nevertheless, this register reveals some invaluable insights into the extent and scope of Spiritualism during the nineteenth century. Among the names of the living letter writers were the Reverend Thomas K. Beecher, a Congregational minister of Elmira, New York, and Edwin Booth. Beecher came from the famous Beecher family, which included his sister Harriet Beecher Stowe, author of *Uncle Tom's Cabin* and an ardent abolitionist. The Spiritual Postmaster noted that Edwin Booth's letters of January 22, 1871, were addressed to his first wife, Mary Devlin Booth; his father, Junius Brutus Booth; and his brother, John Wilkes Booth, the assassin of Abraham Lincoln. Spiritual correspondence to the infamous brother indicates Edwin's steadfast fraternal loyalty despite John Wilkes Booth's horrific and treasonous deed. A few years earlier, in 1857, Edwin Booth had asked the *Banner of Life* medium, Jennie H. Conant, to reach across the spiritual divide to communicate with his father. The elder Booth responded in her weekly column by saying, "But my time has expired on earth, and another is on the stage, which I wish to raise to the highest pinnacle of fame." It is intriguing that both a Booth family member and Mary Todd Lincoln reached out to Spiritualism to communicate with their departed loved ones, indicating the importance and extent of this popular and democratic religious movement in American society.[40]

James V. Mansfield attempted to widen his unique spiritual niche by traveling to cities receptive to Spiritualism. For financial reasons, Mansfield—throughout his long spiritual career—left his home in Chelsea, Massachusetts, seeking work. He earned money as a medium on the road but returned later to his Massachusetts home. While he stayed in New Orleans during December 1860 and January 1861, the Spiritual Postmaster advertised his exceptional mediumistic ability in the local newspaper. The "world-renowned Writing Test Medium" received visitors in his parlor on Canal Street daily from 9:00 a.m. until 3:00 p.m., except for Sundays.[41]

Mansfield recorded twelve séances/readings during this time in the A/B account book. Most of the names are Anglo-American, but some Creole

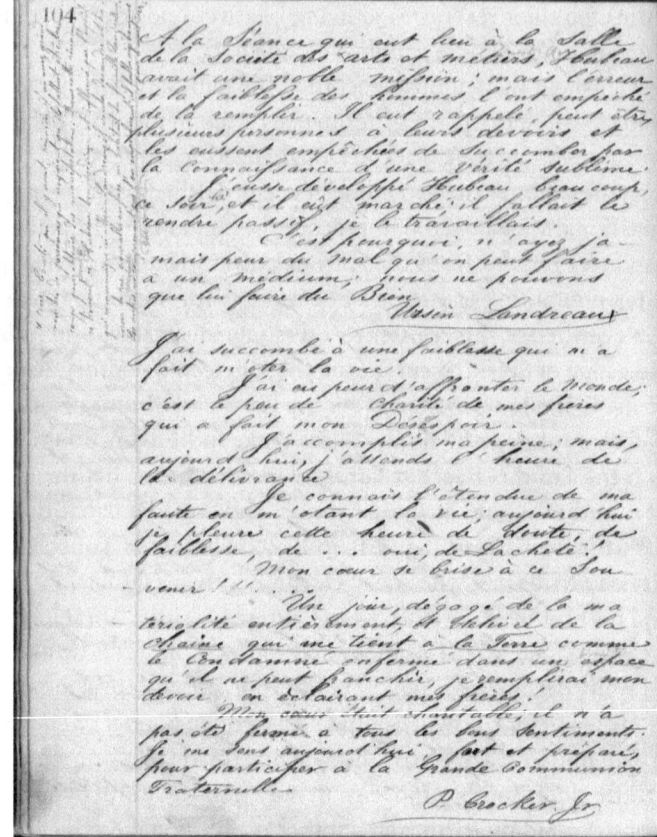

In the first paragraph of this spiritual communication, Pierre Crocker, Henry Rey's brother-in-law, related how he succumbed to a weakness that made him commit suicide. In the third paragraph, Crocker declares that he knows the extent of his mistake in taking his life. René Grandjean wrote the margin notes on the upper left in the 1920s from information obtained from François Dubuclet. Grandjean Register 85-34, November 30, 1871, 104. René Grandjean Collection. *Courtesy of Special Collections, Earl K. Long Library, University of New Orleans.*

names appear as well. Mr. J. W. Allen's name appears on page one of the account book. Later, Allen was a founding member of the New Orleans Spiritualist Association and an officer for several decades. None of the A/B last names can be connected to Henry Rey and his black Creole circles.[42]

In early February 1861, the Spiritual Postmaster departed from New Orleans just a few days after Louisiana had seceded from the Union on January 26, 1861. Perhaps he would have stayed longer in the Crescent City, but by early 1861 the volatile national political situation had pulled apart the city and state governments in Louisiana and an impending apocalyptic civil war loomed on the horizon. Local and state elected officials ignored basic freedoms guaranteed in the US Constitution when people publicly supported abolition and Lincoln's election. In New Orleans, citizens and visitors suspected of advocating radical northern causes were routinely arrested and brought before Mayor John T. Monroe for "further inquiry."[43]

When the Civil War began in April 1861, the liberal *Banner of Light* defended the Union side. The editors railed against the leaders and demagogues of the South, saying that neither harm had been done to them nor had rights been withheld. Secession, they claimed, was simply an attempt to preserve slavery and an antiquated antebellum culture for a privileged few. The Spiritualist newspaper continued its vociferous opposition to the war throughout the next four years.[44]

Henry Rey's early forays into Spiritualism were abruptly curtailed when the Civil War broke out. In April 1861, several meetings were held at the Couvent School at which time it was decided that the free men of color would offer their allegiance to the Confederacy. Louisiana Governor Thomas Overton Moore accepted their offer of military service, and on May 2, 1861, the Confederate Native Guards was authorized.[45] Rey, along with one thousand other free men of color, answered the Confederate call for volunteers. He formed the Economy Unit, which was named after La Société d'Economie et d'Assistance Mutuelle (Economy Society), with himself as captain.[46]

Historians have advanced various explanations as to why the free men of color volunteered for military service to fight for the Confederacy. Some of the former Native Guards later explained to Union officers that they were coerced to join; some probably joined with the notion of improving and protecting their insecure civil and political status; some may have identified more with southern whites than black slaves; and still others may have wanted to reinstitute a bygone tradition of black military participation in Louisiana that dated back to the Spanish period, but especially the Battle of New Orleans (1814–1815). The Battle of New Orleans was not only a huge victory for the Anglo-Americans in Louisiana but also a victory for the free men of color who fought on an equal footing with their white comrades-in-arms. Captain Henry Rey recalled the bygone tradition when he demanded that his regiment "be worthy sons of the heroes of the plains of Chalmette of 1814 and 1815."[47]

In any case, the Confederate Native Guards was activated with capable men like Captain Henry Louis Rey providing the leadership. The Economy Unit remained in New Orleans and did not actively participate in any Confederate battle. Interest in military engagements waned and was replaced with a growing enthusiasm for the northern cause. On December 26, 1861,

Captain Rey lifted his glass and offered a Christmas toast to the staff and officers of the Economy Regiment, exclaiming poetically,

> *Beautiful starry banner, the majestic folds finally extend over us! The chains of our brothers are breaking. The whips of the planters, reeking with blood are going to dry! Immense happiness!*[48]

The Confederates had a small force stationed in New Orleans because the high command in Richmond was confident that Forts St. Philip and Jackson on the Mississippi River would prevent the Union navy from reaching New Orleans. Navigating against the strong, tricky current would also deter the most determined Union naval officers. This misguided military mindset led Secretary of War Judah P. Benjamin to unwisely move troops from Louisiana eastward to battlefields in Tennessee. The remaining troops, under the command of Confederate Major General Mansfield Lovell, were left to defend the largest city in the South. Thus, there were few Confederate troops to control and monitor the Native Guards. The Native Guards' tenuous allegiance to the rebel cause later transformed into open, enthusiastic support for the victorious Union army a few months later. After encountering some resistance on the Mississippi River, Union admiral David G. Farragut's fleet moved past Forts St. Philip and Jackson and paved the way for the fall of the largest and most important city in the South in April 1862. New Orleans fell to the Union forces like a house of cards. Moreover, because the mouth of the river was now controlled by the Union, river commerce and transportation from all points outside lower Louisiana were regulated by Union forces. Later, the Union army would split the Confederacy in two with the fall of Vicksburg in July 4, 1863.[49]

Now that the Union navy had cleared the way for the Union army, Major General Benjamin Franklin Butler, the commander of the Department of the Gulf, entered the city on May 1 and quickly set up offices and barracks in the US Custom House and his personal living quarters at the St. Charles Hotel. Soon after his triumphal entry, General Butler met with five of the Confederate Native Guard officers: Captain Edgar Davis; Captain Henry Rey; Lieutenant Octave Rey; Lieutenant Charles Sauvenet; and Lieutenant Eugène Rapp, Rey's brother-in-law. Lieutenant Charles Sauvenet, who was now working as a translator in the Provost Court, arranged the meeting to decide how to demobilize the Confederate Native Guards and for General Butler to determine their true allegiance. Where and exactly when this meeting took place is unclear. More than likely, it took place in General Butler's headquarters on the second floor on the northeast corner at the federal Custom House sometime in late May. The massive, uncompleted Custom House on Canal Street by the river now housed the post office, the courts, and the military center of operations for the Department of the Gulf.[50]

The five officers made a positive impression on General Butler and his officers. Four of the five were bilingual, and Lieutenant Sauvenet spoke German, Spanish, French, and English. It was obvious to Butler that the Confederate Native Guard officers were well-educated, intelligent men who exuded the confidence of accomplished officers. Octave Rey was particularly remarkable in his physical appearance. He was very tall for the era—six foot four—and of Herculean proportions. According to Rodolphe Desdunes, Octave Rey was "energetic, powerful and dynamic in his thinking. Everyone respected him for his tremendous courage and his strong determination."[51]

While visiting the First Louisiana Regiment Native Guard, a *New York Times* reporter described Henry Rey "as possessing a fine personal appearance and soldierly bearing." Pension records noted that Rey was a "bright mulatto," meaning that he was a very light-skinned African American. Unfortunately, there are no surviving photographs or paintings of Rey, so these descriptions are the closest we have to a visual image of Henry Rey.[52]

On the other hand, General Butler, now in his mid-forties, lacked impressive physical attributes. He was short, overweight, and balding. Already he had lost much of hair, leaving a bald crown ringed by stringy, slightly wavy brown hair. His face was deeply lined, and he had a disturbingly droopy eyelid and bags under his eyes, which resembled those of an old English bulldog. But it was the general's eyes that were the most alarming of his misshapen features. Because Butler had since childhood suffered from a severe case of strabismus (cross-eyes), speakers addressing the general had difficulty determining exactly what Butler was looking at. His appearance and strict enforcement of martial law in New Orleans soon earned him the lasting nickname of Beast Butler.

At the meeting, the five black Creole officers offered to surrender their arms and to enlist in the Union army. General Butler initially declined their offer. In the spring of 1862, African Americans could not enlist in the US army, and Butler could not officially muster in the former Confederate Native Guards. Moreover, in the early days of occupation, Butler was more concerned with establishing federal control over the city and the outlying areas.[53]

New Orleans was in chaos. Its once robust economy had been decimated by the federal blockade, and the citizens were on the verge of starvation. Foreign nationals and the remaining white citizens were for the most part still loyal to the Confederacy. Women in particular were vicious and vocal in their attacks on the federal occupying forces, sometimes taunting the soldiers as they patrolled the streets, and even more offensively, dumping the chamber pots' foul contents over the balcony onto the passing soldiers. The white citizens were particularly incensed by Benjamin Butler's infamous General Order No. 28, which decreed "when any female shall, by word, gesture, or movement, insult, or show contempt for any officer or soldier of the United States she shall be . . . treated as a woman of the town plying her avocation."

Butler firmly enforced martial law and respect for the US Army and the Union flag. Men and women who were guilty of even minor violations were sentenced to prisons outside New Orleans, most notably Ship Island off the coast of Mississippi, which had earlier been General Butler's staging area for the capture of New Orleans.[54]

Another major problem that Butler encountered in New Orleans was the presence of the criminal element. In the absence of the regular city police during the Civil War, a gang of what François Dubuclet called "vagabonds and bandits" terrorized the city.[55] In an article published in the *New York Times*, Rey described how the New Orleans criminals were creating mayhem in the lawless city, calling them "rowdies and assassins."[56] Among these criminals were Arthur Guerin, Benjamin Leggett, and Oscar Blasco—all career criminals who would return after the Civil War to wreak havoc in the Crescent City. When Benjamin Butler arrived in New Orleans, he made "short work" of the rampant criminal activity. The expression Dubuclet admiringly used was a *"bon coup de balai de ces petits bandits"*—a good sweep of the broom to these little bandits.[57]

Despite Benjamin "Beast" Butler's unpopularity and the universal hatred directed against him by Confederate supporters, he continued to ride the streets unprotected, seemingly oblivious to the endless vitriol that swirled around him. One British visitor observed that the general "could be seen any day riding up and down the street, sometimes with, but often without escort; and in fact acting as though [he] was the most pure and popular ruler the city ever knew." Although the white population detested Butler, he obtained rock-star popularity amongst the black Creoles, who later closely followed his military career after his removal from his post in New Orleans.[58]

By August 1862, the Union army had exhausted its recruiting efforts to bolster troops of the Department of the Gulf with men from New Orleans. The military situation was becoming more serious with each passing day. On August 15, Captain Henry Rey and three of his fellow officers from the now-defunct Confederate Native Guards took the initiative and met once again with General Butler. The men assured him of their loyalty to the Union and pressed the general to allow free blacks to enlist in the Union army. On September 27, Rey was officially mustered into the army as captain in the First Louisiana Native Guard (Union), the first officially authorized regiment of African American soldiers in the US Army. Later his brother, Octave, would enlist in the Second Regiment of the Louisiana Native Guard, and still later his other brother, Hippolyte, would volunteer for the Third Regiment. Black men were now empowered as the military equals of white males, at least in theory.[59]

A few days prior to being mustered into the Union army, an effusive Rey displayed his intellectual support for the Union cause when he penned:

It [ignorance] is the evil of Humanity,
It is the ever-gnawing canker, which consumes it,
That which always controls It,
And suppresses Liberty ...

Yes, in the political,
Social or religious world,
As in the artistic world,
Ignorance is enthroned everywhere ... [60]

Henry Rey reported to Camp Strong for training on October 1, 1862. While based there, at the Louisiana racetrack in the suburb of Gentilly, Captain Rey complained bitterly about white prejudice in an editorial letter to *L'Union*, a new biweekly French language newspaper published by the black Creole intelligentsia and founded by Dr. Louis Charles Roudanez. In his letter, Rey vented his anger against streetcar drivers who prevented black soldiers from boarding their cars, and he asserted that the Native Guard soldiers "have no prejudice; that we receive anyone at our camp, except the sellers of human flesh." Captain Rey sang the praises of a diverse army coalescing to form a united front with the aim of racial equality. He pointed out the newly formed panracial alliance when he wrote, "You can ... see the enthusiasm of the negro soldiers, and at the parade, you see a thousand white bayonets gleaming in the sun, held up by black, yellow or white hands."[61] The mustering and parading in military regalia, along with the display of the accouterments of war, placed black Creoles on the same level of manhood as the white males in the South. No longer was the military the uncontested, exclusive enclave for white men to demonstrate their valor and physical prowess.

On October 24, 1862, the newly formed First Regiment of the Native Guards marched the whole length of Canal Street on a cool, crisp Saturday afternoon with the Stars and Stripes flying in the breeze, shiny bayonets fixed and glinting in the sun, drums beating, and the band sprightly playing "Yankee Doodle." The parade route was lined with Confederate sympathizers who glared at the Union Native Guards with sullen faces and, according to one observer, the soldiers seemed to be afraid of the crowd. The regiment was dispatched to Algiers on the west side of the Mississippi River, across from New Orleans, for their first official military mission under the command of Colonel Spencer H. Stafford. General Godfrey Weitzel, despite his vehement protests against commanding an all-black unit, issued the official orders for the First Regiment Native Guards to move through western Louisiana for the dual purposes of repairing a railroad line damaged by the Confederates and dispersing the forces under Confederate General Richard Taylor. According to Captain James Ingraham, the men were delighted to finally be fighting under the American flag and declared that "we can and will be a wall of fire and death to the enemies of this country, our birthplace."[62]

It was soon after the march commenced in late October that Rey, according to pension records, fell while marching between Bayou Des Allemands and Lafourche Crossing. Although in obvious pain, Captain Rey insisted on continuing the march and reached Bayou Lafourche Crossing, at the march's end, on November 2, 1862.[63]

Now out of their native city and thrust into a mind-numbing routine of garrison and fatigue duty in the mosquito-infested swamps of southern Louisiana, the Union Native Guards began to realize that martial glory was elusive at best. The men made slow but steady progress repairing the railroad, which involved dealing with overgrown grass and missing rails that had been removed by the Confederates and with additional obstructions placed on the remaining tracks. After several weeks, the Native Guards had cleared fifty-two miles of track, having acquitted themselves well. In his letter to the commander-in-chief of the US Army, Major General H. W. Halleck, Butler commended the Eighth Vermont who were "assisted by the first Native Guard (colored), under the command of Colonel Stafford." Treasury agent George S. Denison also commended the First Regiment Native Guard when he informed Secretary of the Treasury Salmon P. Chase that "they have done well and accomplished all that has been given them to do. The company officers of the 1st Reg't are educated men, and each speaks at least two languages. General Butler will soon give his colored troops a chance to show themselves."[64]

In March 1863, the First Regiment of the Native Guards was ordered to meet the Third Regiment in Baton Rouge to prepare for an assault on Port Hudson, a Confederate stronghold on the Mississippi River. After six months of active duty without any significant military action, the drudgery of garrison duty and tedious repair work was beginning to tax even the most ardent Union supporter. Morale within the regiment continued to plummet because of the disparity between the white and the black soldiers' pay and equipment. Henry Rey's regiment had been issued obsolete muskets, second-hand uniforms, and damaged knapsacks. The soldiers had not been paid, and they had not received the bonus promised for enlisting in the Union army. The hardest pill to swallow was the prejudice and strident racism that the black soldiers had endured for six long months.[65]

Years later Aristide Desdunes, a private in the First Regiment Native Guards and older brother of Rodolphe Desdunes, penned a poem titled "Imitation—Les Voeux d'un jeune soldat" ("The Wishes of a Young Soldier") in which he recalled his comrades' boredom. Each soldier dealt with the monotony in his own unique way.

> Weariness: one stretched out on a simple mat,
> Another chatted softly;
> The commander, at last, amused himself among these men of war
> Each in his own fashion
> Attempting to cheat the oppressive and obscene boredom
> Born of the garrison.
> For me, alone, following the smoke of my pipe with the black stem,
> Cured the misery![66]

Despairing of the lost opportunity for martial glory and suffering from unrelenting racial harassment by white Union soldiers, Captain Henry Louis Rey and other black officers tendered their resignations in early spring 1863. Rey received an honorable discharge on April 6, 1863, for medical reasons while deployed in Baton Rouge. The physician, Dr. J. T. Paine, diagnosed him with "syphilitic rheumatism and sore throat."[67]

Despite the many negatives of his abbreviated military career, Captain Henry Rey did reap some economic, social, and future political rewards. Because of his high rank as captain, and more importantly because of the lucrative bonuses received from recruiting efforts, Captain Henry Louis Rey was deployed with the princely sum of three hundred dollars. Because of this, during the Union occupation, Rey was one of the few Creoles of color in New

Orleans who was not in dire financial straits resulting from the decimated economy.[68]

The six months in the Union army brought contacts with a wide spectrum of Union officers and enlisted men from across the country—from Major General Benjamin Butler of Massachusetts, the commander of the Department of the Gulf, to privates in the Eighth Vermont. The men of African descent that Rey recruited were mostly men of his social and economic milieu in New Orleans, but now numerous fugitive slaves joined the Native Guards as they moved through the hinterlands of South Louisiana. As captain of the well-respected First Regiment Native Guards, Henry Rey received their respect and admiration, and conversely, Rey recognized their valor and allegiance to the Union cause. Captain Rey would later parlay the leadership skills that he had honed while deployed with the federals into state and local political positions as well as into becoming the leader and medium of the Cercle Harmonique. Other black Union Native Guard officers like James Ingraham, Arnold Bertonneau, and P. B. S. Pinchback would play important roles in the nascent Louisiana Republican Party and the franchise movement for African Americans during the 1860s and 1870s.

On his return trip to New Orleans, Captain Rey traveled down the flood-swollen Mississippi River past a flotilla of federal gunboats preparing for an assault on Port Hudson. What Rey thought about is a matter of conjuncture, but surely he must have been disappointed with his brief, uneventful military career. Less than a year after his enlistment, Rey was mustered out of the army without any of the anticipated martial glory. The soldiers in the Union army, for the most part, were just as prejudiced as the rebels. Henry Rey's two brothers had also been mustered out of the army for reasons of prejudice. His wife and two young children awaited his arrival in New Orleans. Lucia Rose was now four, and her brother, Henry Jr., was about to celebrate his third birthday.[69]

The return voyage down the Mississippi River was a time of peaceful reflection, relaxation, and anticipation of a new egalitarian racial order in Louisiana. As he traveled past the abandoned plantation homes and the deserted sugarcane fields, Rey must have thought of what this new racial order in Louisiana would mean. For the planters, the halcyon days of the antebellum plantation system had ended; for the free people of color and the newly liberated blacks, the halcyon days of a new birth of freedom had just begun.

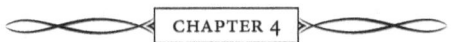

CHAPTER 4

Steppingstones

In April 1863, Henry Louis Rey returned to his beloved native city, which was hardly recognizable from the one he had known in antebellum days. New Orleans, still under martial law, had the appearance of a deserted city now that men had departed for the Civil War, most fighting for the Confederates, but some recently recruited for the Union army. The stringent curfew of 9:00 p.m. closed clubs, coffeehouses, and the ubiquitous barrooms that dotted the urban landscape.[1]

The despised and widely vilified Major General Benjamin Butler had also departed from the Crescent City. Alarms had sounded in Washington that the general and his brother, Andrew Butler, had been involved in illegal activities and extensive corruption, which enriched the Butler brothers at the expense of the citizens and foreign residents. Major General Nathaniel Prentiss Banks replaced Butler on December 16, 1862, and was initially greeted by the white populace as the lesser of two evils. Rancorous relations between the conquered and the conqueror were replaced with token civility. And for least a few months that seemed to be the case, especially since General Banks immediately began releasing Butler's political prisoners from Ship Island.[2]

The massive, granite US Custom House at the end of Canal Street, near the Mississippi River, was used as barracks and offices for the Union army. The unfinished Custom House ranked among the largest and most impressive American government buildings in the United States and represented the financial power generated by the port of New Orleans in antebellum days. Canal Street was one of the few paved streets in New Orleans.

Beginning in 1859, large square-cut stones were installed as well as flagstone sidewalks and granite-lined gutters.³

After the fall of New Orleans to Union forces, sanitary measures taken by General Butler substantially improved the state of the city's streets and, consequently, New Orleans enjoyed a lower mortality rate. Yellow fever was almost totally wiped out. Pickets patrolled the nearby streets, earning themselves insults and the disparaging stares of the disgruntled Confederate women. From all accounts, the young Union soldiers exhibited excellent behavior and only occasionally irritated the women with a spontaneous chorus of "Yankee Doodle Dandy." The steady, measured tread of the patrol guard rang out from the sun-heated wooden sidewalks, called banquettes by the locals. The constant traffic of artillery and weapons of war being dragged to various barracks in or around the city made a distinctive rumbling sound on the cobbled streets, unsettling to both the natives and Yankees.⁴

On the riverfront, the once familiar, omnipresent sound of steamboat whistles was replaced with frequent communication signals from the US Custom House with the Union gunboats that lined the docks. River travel was opened on the Lower Mississippi River, now reaching its annual flood stage, but the Confederates still controlled the Upper Mississippi in April 1863. A steady trickle of river commerce from the South down to New Orleans began to revive the moribund city economy, bringing much needed supplies and food to its beleaguered citizens.⁵

The following month brought the distressing news that Captain André Cailloux, Henry Rey's close friend and former comrade-in-arms, had been killed at the pitched Battle of Port Hudson in an effort to gain control of the Upper Mississippi and divide the Confederacy. Soldiers in Rey's former regiment were among the fifteen thousand Union soldiers who besieged the Confederate stronghold in May 1863. As the First Regiment of the Native Guards inched up the steep embankment along the Mississippi, Captain Cailloux led the ill-fated charge, "steadying the men with words of encouragement in both French and English." Cailloux, a Creole of color who proudly proclaimed himself as the blackest man in New Orleans, was wounded in the left arm, which left the limb paralyzed and useless; but he heroically led the charge to within two hundred yards of the main line, when he was slain in a barrage of shots. The Confederates blocked efforts of the Union army to retrieve Captain Cailloux's body, which deteriorated under the hot, oppressive summer sun. The Union army finally retrieved the badly decomposed body after Port Hudson surrendered on July 9, 1863.⁶

On July 29, a memorial mass was officiated by Father Claude Maistre and followed by an elaborate funeral procession on Esplanade Avenue complete with marching units of Mutual Aid Clubs and a hearse drawn by two jet black horses, guided by a coachman wearing a long black frock coat and a top silk hat. Among the more than thirty organizations participating was the Economy Society. The body was interred at St. Louis Cemetery No. 2.[7]

The Battle of Port Hudson in May 1863 was a defeat for the Union army but a victory for the black Creoles in New Orleans. They had proven themselves to be of the same military mettle as their white compatriots. In the Old South, no other act more conclusively demonstrated masculinity than prowess on the battlefield, but the soldier who died in combat claimed a special place of honor among his nation's heroes as the embodiment of bravery and manhood. Captain Cailloux's death ensured him of immortal manhood and an honored place in the pantheon of black Creole martyr-heroes.[8]

Cailloux succinctly explained his death on the battlefield: "I fought, I succumbed." Early spirit messages from the fallen Union captain exhorted the séance participants to continue their gallant struggle for social and political equality, declaring in a communication dated July 17, 1863, that "Equality will come later it is true. To construct a building the first stone must be placed there. You will need victims to serve as steppingstones to liberty. We have been the first steps, we need others." Cailloux's optimistic view of Reconstruction would later fall apart in the face of determined white intransigence.[9]

Years later, in 1872, Henry Rey's séance circle received a spiritual message from André Cailloux, who identified himself as "the Black Captain . . . who represents the martyr who fell on the battlefield . . . with a sword in hand and facing the Enemy, which killed him under a rain of murderous balls." Death was not considered to be a deterrent to continuing the noble fight. "The man falls! The principle lives!" declared the venerated Andre Cailloux to Rey's Cercle Harmonique. The spirit of Captain Cailloux represented a towering, almost god-like, figure for the now beleaguered Creoles of color fighting a quixotic battle for equal social and civil rights in the 1860s and 1870s. His communications imagined a world in which the republican ideals of France were realized in a new egalitarian society in New Orleans and throughout the South.[10]

Similar to Captain Cailloux, Second Lieutenant John Crowder, who also perished in the Battle of Port Hudson, pressed for the séance circle to be steadfast in their struggles. Crowder urged the circle to "be firm and stand on a platform of Equity! Do not feed vultures ready to suck your blood!" John

This is the original spirit communication received from Captain André Cailloux. René Grandjean added the top sentence and underlining. Grandjean Register 85-30, July 1863, 158. Grandjean Collection. *Courtesy of Special Collections, Earl K. Long Library, University of New Orleans.*

Crowder lied about his age when he enlisted in the first regiment of Native Guards, becoming at the tender age of sixteen one of the youngest officers in the Union army. Unlike Cailloux, a Creole of color, Crowder was part of the growing numbers of Anglo blacks who now served with distinction in the Native Guards.[11]

The inclusion of Anglo blacks within the ideal society of spirit messengers was a microcosm of the ever-expanding societal circle of the once insular black Creole elite. As the war years wore on and transitioned into the turbulent postbellum years, Henry Rey and other former free people of color enlarged their social and business contacts to include former slaves, Anglo free blacks, northern whites and southern Unionists, sometimes derisively labeled as scalawags.[12]

The Union objective of gaining full control of the Mississippi River was achieved when Vicksburg fell on July 4, 1863, and a few days later Port Hudson surrendered after a forty-eight-day siege. In New Orleans, Henry Rey was greeted with the deafening sound of a one-hundred-gun salute to celebrate the Union victories. The citywide celebration of Captain Cailloux's extraordinary valor was prolonged by a month-long flying of the Stars and Stripes at half-mast (July 29-August 29, 1863). Normally reserved for the passing of American presidents, this unprecedented gesture of honor for a black man must have struck a chord of patriotism and pride in such men as Henry Rey and his brothers.[13]

The Rey brothers were reunited in New Orleans after they had all experienced disappointing military service. Both Hippolyte and Octave Rey had resigned for reasons of prejudice. Second Lieutenant Henry Hippolyte Rey of the Third Regiment of the Louisiana Native Guards was the first to resign on February 19, 1863. Hippolyte was described in pension records as five feet six and "bright yellow with black eyes and black hair." The younger Rey brother could no longer endure the slurs of white officers who considered it an insult to be addressed by a black officer.[14]

Lieutenant Octave Rey had served in the Second Regiment of the Louisiana Native Guards on Ship Island—a seven-mile-long barrier island off the coast of Mississippi. The desolate, sandy island had initially been used as a staging area for the capture of New Orleans and was later employed as a jail for some of General Butler's hapless political prisoners. The soldiers of the Second Regiment were in a sense imprisoned as well. Instead of pursuing martial glory, they spent their time in the mind-numbing tasks of boring garrison duty on a tiny windswept island, far away from civilization and the ongoing Civil War. By March 1863, Octave Rey had had enough of boredom and the racial insults from white Union soldiers and resigned at Fort Pike, Louisiana. Within the short span of three months, all three brothers had resigned from the Union army, the same army in which just a few months earlier they had begged to be mustered.[15]

It is unclear what the Rey brothers did for employment upon their return to New Orleans, now occupied by Union troops and under military control. Octave may have found work as a cooper, his prewar occupation. Hippolyte probably found employment as a printer with the popular French New Orleans newspaper, *L'Abeille de la Nouvelle-Orléans* (*The Bee of New Orleans*). Henry Rey may have returned to Eugène Hacker's hardware store or he may have simply coasted on the money that he had earned in the army. Rey had received a rather large bonus of three hundred dollars for his recruiting efforts in enlisting men into the First Regiment Native Guards once General Butler had agreed to the mustering in of men of African descent.[16]

Henry Rey may have capitalized on his stature as a skilled medium to earn supplemental money with private spiritual communications. No longer an officer in the Union army, Captain Rey nevertheless commanded respect from fellow Louisiana Native Guards who had either remained in

New Orleans or had resigned from the Union army. Some white Union soldiers freed from prejudice accorded Henry Rey the respect that Union captains normally received. Rey combined this respect with his growing reputation as a gifted spiritual medium to give private communications to the influx of northerners who had arrived as part of the Union occupation. The presence of northern soldiers in New Orleans increased local interest in Spiritualism.[17] Union army officers such as Colonel Nathan W. Daniels sought out Rey and spoke glowingly of his mediumistic abilities. Nathan Daniels had been the white commander of the Second Louisiana Native Guards stationed on Ship's Island but was removed from duty and arrested because of some minor violations concerning the amount of lumber he used to build batteries at the post. Daniels believed that he had been arrested not because of what he considered to be frivolous charges, but because he had treated his black regiment with respect. While waiting in New Orleans for the charges to be resolved, Daniels was not incarcerated, and he sought solace with a bevy of girlfriends as well as with Spiritualism, which now became part of his daily life. In his diary entry dated Tuesday, September 22, 1863, Colonel Daniels wrote that he visited "Capt. Henry Rey who was excellent spiritual medium and gave me some good test communication." Interestingly, two days later Colonel Daniels consulted "old" Valmour, the renowned black Creole medium who was also a close friend of Rey and François Dubuclet.

Modern American Spiritualism provided spiritual balm for women in New Orleans on both sides of the sectional divide. Julia Ellen LeGrand, an upper-class southern lady, railed against Union occupation in her wartime diary, describing her angst and torment at seeing "the insolent faces of the Massachusetts mob which has been sent to rule over us." To sooth her anxieties, LeGrand read *The Great Harmonia* (1850), by A. J. Davis, even though such literature had been condemned by her friends as too radical and too northern. Davis was particularly anathematic to southerners because of his ardent support of the Union and abolition. LeGrand enjoyed long, leisurely talks in the evening with Spiritualists like Mrs. Waugh who, according to LeGrand, "converses upon the subject [Spiritualism] with an ease which familiarity alone can give. . . . My heart leaps to catch a ray from the light which she says is coming."[18]

On the other side of the sectional divide were northern women residing in New Orleans with their Union army officer husbands. The occupation of New Orleans in 1862–1865 was a particularly challenging time for the devoted wives who had followed their husbands. Besides the miserably hot and humid summers, northerners faced ridicule and disdain from the locals;

outrageous prices in the marketplace; and the fact that there were few fellow Spiritualists among the citizenry.

Laura de Force Gordon and her husband, Dr. Charles H. Gordon, moved from St. Louis to New Orleans in 1864 because of the doctor's enlistment in the Union army. As a young woman, Gordon had traveled on the trance speaker lecture tour, and it was while on one of these tours in 1862 that she met her future husband. Once settled in New Orleans, she expressed her dismay and disappointment in not being able to connect with other Spiritualists. In a letter penned on July 30, 1864 to the *Banner of Light*, Laura declared that she had not seen a single Spiritualist "excepting those from the North, who are with the Army, including several officers of high rank." Gordon rightly theorized that there were other Spiritualists in New Orleans, but that they were reticent to openly declare their spiritualistic sympathies. Because Spiritualism was associated "with being Yankee and [because of spiritual sympathizers'] knowing how obnoxious everything that savors of Yankeedom" was to southerners, these clandestine Spiritualists shunned the conservative public's critical eye. Spiritualism, nevertheless, gave solace and stability for women on both sides of the sectional divide during the turbulent Civil War years, especially in the occupied city of New Orleans. Laura de Force Gordon, like Julia LeGrand, welcomed the chance to connect to Spiritualism when she received issues of the *Banner of Light* "in the midst of wars and rumors of war," happy to read the periodical with "its glad tidings of joy."[19]

The occupation years witnessed the opening volleys fired in the bitter and acrimonious battle for African American suffrage in New Orleans. Because the Crescent City capitulated early in the Civil War—barely one year after the surrender of Fort Sumter—Louisiana had the earliest and most protracted struggle for civil rights in the South. As the Civil War raged during the years 1863 and 1864, the first passionate demands for suffrage rang out at packed meetings in Economy Hall on the 1400 block of Ursulines, the site of La Société d'Economie et d'Assistance Mutuelle. The purchase of the Economy Society's first meeting hall was notarized in February 1836 as a private transaction by Henry Rey's father-in-law, Pierre Crocker, and two other free men of color, Manuel Moreau and Pierre Duhart. Twenty years later, the Economy Society purchased a lot directly across from the original hall and began construction of a second meeting hall, finishing the work in 1857. According to Fatima Shaik, this second home to the Economy Society was "a large, two story building that towered over the neighborhood of small single- and double shotgun houses. It had a large ballroom, an auditorium, and several meeting halls. There was a separate kitchen building and a fence at the front of the property. On the hall itself was a copper cornice and a beehive for decoration, which was a symbol of organization."[20]

On the evening of November 5, 1863, an interracial crowd hotly debated the contentious question of franchise for men of African descent. Predictably, most of the white orators ridiculed the radical idea of black suffrage, but a black Creole and member of the Economy Society, François Boisdoré, rose up and spoke eloquently from his heart of the rationale for black male suffrage. He astutely observed that valiant black soldiers from Louisiana were fighting the bloody battles of the North and could potentially give their lives for the noble cause. Boisdoré reasoned that "if the United States has the right to arm us, it certainly has the right to allow us the rights of suffrage."[21]

Captain P. B. S. (Pinckney Benton Stewart) Pinchback echoed Boisdoré's sentiments. The Union captain boldly stated that "they did not ask for social equality, and did not expect it, but they demanded political rights—they wanted to be men." Pinchback, the eighth child of a white Mississippi planter and his manumitted black mistress, had—upon learning of the capture of New Orleans—moved to the Crescent City and raised a company of Union Native Guards. During Reconstruction, he climbed up the ladder of political success and became lieutenant governor and, briefly, acting governor. At the end of the meeting, the assembly approved a resolution requesting that General Shepley order the registration of free black voters. The former free men of color rejected all halfway measures and supported the radical political agenda of François Boisdoré.[22]

The end of the Civil War signaled a change in the black male suffrage debate in New Orleans. Returning black Union soldiers joined forces with white Union supporters from the South, such as northern-educated Thomas Jefferson Durant and Dr. Anthony P. Dostie along with carpetbaggers, most notably the young, handsome Henry Clay Warmoth. New Orleans's Creoles of color were heavily represented in this new contingent of black political leaders. More than 96 percent of the African American leaders had lived in New Orleans in 1860. The typical postbellum black leader was a young, light-skinned Creole, was literate, and had been freed prior to 1860. Many of these men had descended from the upper echelons of the free people of color in New Orleans, especially those of Saint-Domingue ancestry, and many had sterling military records with the Union Native Guards.[23]

The political strength of the former elite is particularly surprising when other demographics are considered. By 1860, the percentage of free people of color in New Orleans had diminished from a high of 28.7 percent in

1810, when it had been bolstered by the large influx of refugees from Saint-Domingue, to a low of 6.4 percent in 1860. The percentages are somewhat deceiving when actual numbers are considered. In 1810, when the total population was 17,242, the number of free people of color was 4,950; in 1860, with a total population of 170,024, the number of free people of color actually more than doubled to 10,939. So at the beginning of the Civil War there were more citizens in New Orleans that were free people of color, but they were now overshadowed by a large segment of the population (93 percent) that was white. Five years later the numerical strength of the Gallic black community had further declined with the addition of tens of thousands of anglophone blacks who flooded New Orleans looking for opportunities and an escape from the grueling plantation life of their former slave days.[24]

Henry Louis Rey was the quintessential postbellum black political leader. He was thirty-three years old in 1865, French-speaking, a lifetime resident of New Orleans, a Saint-Domingue descendent from an elite Creole family, literate, fair-skinned, and a man who had honed his leadership skills as captain in the Union Native Guards.[25]

The first evidence of Henry Rey's political activism appeared in 1865 with the formation of the Friends of Universal Suffrage, a precursor to the Republican Party in Louisiana. The Friends' platform was threefold: universal education, universal suffrage, and distribution of land by the states to heads of families. The president of the Friends of Universal Suffrage was Thomas Durant, and Henry Rey was the recording secretary and a member of the Central Executive Committee. On the rainy evening of September 13, 1865, Rey resigned his position, explaining that he was "about to leave the city for a long time." If Rey did indeed leave the city, it was only for two months, because in December 1865 he resumed his first séance register in New Orleans after a hiatus of two years.[26]

The black Creole séance venues from 1865 until 1867 shifted from the homes of Rey's neighbors to Valmour's home. His healing abilities and mediumistic skills were legend in New Orleans and the surrounding region during the 1850s and 1860s. As with Henry Rey, there are no surviving drawings or photographs of Valmour. The closest thing to a written description of Valmour was Dubuclet's comment that "he was of small size."[27] Since the average height of a man was shorter in that era than now, "small size" possibly meant around five foot three or less.

Valmour's residence/blacksmith shop faced the Carondelet Canal, which connected Bayou St. John to the Basin, hence the name of the street on that side was Basin Street. In 1794, the two-mile canal was cut through the cypress swamp at the rear of the city under the orders of Baron de Carondelet, then the Spanish governor of Louisiana. The thirty-foot-wide canal could not accommodate heavy cargo boats, so the typical canal traffic consisted of sloops and schooners, some laden with onions, turnips, collards, oysters, and shrimp and many others carrying lumber from Mississippi and Northern Louisiana via Lake Pontchartrain. Because of the lumber cargos, the banks lining the canal and the turning basin were the sites of planing mills and lumber dealers like the Jouet Lumber Yard. The adjacent German brewery, called the Old Canal Steam Brewery, further augmented the heavy marine and street traffic. It was a massive structure, even by New Orleans standards. A three-story icehouse with a cold-storage cellar faced Villere Street, and a tall iron chimney capped by a coronet marked the boiler house and its sixteen-horsepower steam engine.[28]

This vibrant area was the setting for the revered Valmour's return to public séances. François Dubuclet described the house as having a central door leading to the courtyard. The forge was to the right, and to the left was a "healing" room that he had used for fourteen years.[29]

The entries in Rey's second register are sporadic during the Valmour years (1865–1869). This may have been because spiritual communications had been recorded in Valmour's register. René Grandjean explained in the second register's margin notes that Valmour kept a large register, which was full of communications from various mediums, especially those of Paulin Durel. French Creole séance circles meticulously recorded spirit communications, which they considered to be sacred. Valmour's wife, Dianah, retained her husband's register after his death. Regrettably, the Valmour register was lost many years later when it was passed on to her daughter and son, Johnny Valmour.[30]

François Dubuclet and Valmour were close friends, and decades later Dubuclet recounted to his son-in-law, René Grandjean, many fascinating anecdotes about Valmour. Perhaps the most interesting one involved Valmour's infamous cousin, Marie Laveau, the Voodoo Princess of New Orleans, whom Dubuclet described as "*la sorcière*" (the witch). This would be the younger Marie Laveau, sometimes called Marie the Second by modern biographers to differentiate her from her mother with the same name. Her full legal name was Marie Heloïse Euchariste Glapion. It is unclear how they were related because Valmour's parents were from Saint-Domingue, and the younger Marie Laveau did not have any direct relatives from that island, according to her biographers. Possibly they were related indirectly by marriage through Valmour's wife, Dianah, who was a free woman of color from New Orleans, or perhaps it was just a fictive kinship. According to Dubuclet, one day Marie

Laveau was crossing the street when she encountered Valmour. "Ah, hello cousin," she greeted him on the banquette, "I have learned what you have done to help the sick." Valmour replied, "Alright, why don't you do like me?" Marie Laveau sighed, "Oh! Too late. I am lost! I know that we both have the same power [to heal the sick]."[31]

Valmour at one time was very involved in Voodoo but transitioned to Spiritualism when the movement appeared in New Orleans in the 1850s. Joseph Barthet's Spiritualist periodical, *Le Spiritualiste de la Nouvelle-Orléans*, documents Valmour's impressive healing powers, helping both whites and African Americans. Sometimes the healing process involved specially mixed potions, and sometimes just a touch of his hands would cure a bedridden patient. Constant Reynès, a friend of Henry Rey and later a spiritual messenger, recounted to Barthet how Valmour cured his young wife: "I declare with the greatest satisfaction. That my wife, age 23, has been cured of a stomachache, which has been very intense for five years and has resisted various cures The healer [Valmour] cured her instantly without using any physical agent."[32]

Dubuclet and other Creoles of color considered Voodoo (sometimes written Voudou) to be witchcraft that was used for evil purposes. A spiritual communication from Abner stated that people endowed with supernatural powers should use them for the good and not for the bad. Voodoo was sometimes alluded to in the spiritual messages but never directed named. The term *superstition* was occasionally used to describe Voodoo in the Grandjean Registers.[33]

It is tempting to analyze and connect these two belief systems that existed at the same time within the same geographical area and that attracted both races as devotees. Both of these belief systems rested on communication with a supernatural world, and both Voodoo and Spiritualism relied on the supernatural talents of an individual to act as a conduit between the earthly existence and the spiritual realm. Voodoo was "a fusion of ancient West African religious beliefs and Roman Catholicism." The black Creole séance circles were also heavily influenced by the Catholic Church, the most revered spirit messengers being members of the Catholic clergy such as Moni, Père Antoine, and Vincent de Paule. Caryn Bell observes that the "vibrancy of West African religious retentions in nineteenth-century New Orleans unquestionably proved hospitable to Spiritualism's emphasis on spiritual healing, herbal medicines, spirit possession and an egalitarian religious ethic."[34]

Besides Valmour, another of the early black Creole mediums and Couvent School instructor Nelson Desbrosses had Voodoo connections. Desbrosses visited Haiti for several years to study Voodoo. Upon his return, he received additional instruction from Valmour and developed into a healing medium. Rodolphe Desdunes notes that Desbrosses achieved widespread acclaim for his ability to heal with a simple touch of his hands.[35]

However, other hallmarks of Voodoo never appear in Spiritualism. Spiritualists in nineteenth-century New Orleans did not believe in amulets, gris-gris, or ritualistic dances. Furthermore, there were no special celebration days like St. John's Eve (La Fête de St. Jean) on June 24 for Spiritualists to congregate en masse and affirm their allegiance to their faith and their spiritual leaders. Conversely, the Voodoo practitioners did not believe that the supernatural world offered guidance toward a more perfect self and perfect world. The philosophy of progress so significant in the Rey circles was far too esoteric for Voodoo practitioners. Rey's Cercle Harmonique considered spirit communications to be guideposts to racial harmony and full social and political equality in the new postbellum era.

But what about the Voodoo devotees and leaders? Did they borrow some of the Spiritualistic protocols and beliefs and add them to their rituals? Because of the paucity of reliable sources and written accounts from within the Voodoo community, it is impossible to accurately gauge the influence of Spiritualism on Voodoo, a centuries-old religion founded on African spirit worship. Modern scholars point to connections between Voodoo and the twentieth-century Spiritual churches in New Orleans, although their spiritual leaders denied the link. According to Martha Ward, a biographer of Marie Laveau, the ghosts of Voodoo live in the Spiritual churches: "Both Zora Neale Hurston and the interviewers of the Federal Writers' Project recognized the connection between nineteenth-century Voodoo and the twentieth-century Spiritual churches; both passed through the prism of Creole Catholicism and African American or Afro-Creole music, dance, and ritual." There is also a link between Spiritualism and the Spiritual churches, so it may be that these two belief systems joined together in the twentieth century in a new reincarnation. Spiritualism and Voodoo paralleled each other during the mid-nineteenth century, but it does not appear that the two contemporary alternatives to mainstream religion significantly influenced each other's practices and traditions.[36]

Rey's surviving spirit messages during the early postbellum years reveal an optimistic frame of mind for the black Creoles, despite the uncertainty of their evolving social, political, and economic status. On December 1, 1865, August Dubuclet—older brother of François Dubuclet and son of

Antoine Dubuclet—the state treasurer of Louisiana from 1868 to 1878, acted as the medium at Valmour's house when he contacted his deceased mother. Claire Pollard advised the circle members not to occupy themselves with the past because their future was so brilliant and to always be devoted to the cause of justice. She predicted that past oppressors would beg for forgiveness of their errors in the afterlife. This was a common theme at the Rey séances: offenders of the black Creoles would later regret past transgressions in the afterworld.[37]

The initial euphoria in the early postbellum years dissolved into bitter disappointment and disillusionment. In 1866, one year after the Civil War, the highly coveted goal of black male suffrage remained elusive, and former Confederates made consistent inroads into the volatile political arena throughout the South. For the conservative southern whites, the three pressing postbellum issues were the continued federal military occupation, the presence of the Freedmen's Bureau, and state governments controlled by a tenuous coalition of carpetbaggers, scalawags, and African Americans. Of these three issues, the occupation by Union troops was the most offensive, according to historian John Hope Franklin: "Nothing offended the warriors of the Lost Cause more than the presence in their towns and villages of companies and regiments of the victorious army—including blacks, many of them former slaves—to remind them of their humiliation. . . . For many, military occupation was worse than defeat on the field of battle." Actually, the demobilization had been rapid, and relatively few troops remained stationed in the South by the end of 1866. Additionally, most of these troops were located in or near urban areas, leaving the countryside more open to virulent and violent racism.[38]

In Washington, the strained relationship between President Andrew Johnson and Congress became progressively more divisive and acrimonious. Johnson, a Democrat from Tennessee, lost several key legislative battles in 1866. His imprudent vetoes of the Civil Rights Act and the renewal of the popular and largely successful Freedmen's Bureau Bill were overridden by Congress. In April and May 1866, as a newly invigorated and more radical Congress considered what was to become the Fourteenth Amendment, the first of many violent confrontations in the South occurred in Memphis.

Three days of rioting occurred, from April 30 to May 2, growing out of conflicts between black soldiers and white peace officers. White vigilantes joined the police in an indiscriminate and fatal assault on the black community. Federal troops under the command of General George Stoneham were dispatched to quell the riots and to reestablish order. Before the rioting subsided, at least forty-six African Americans had died, five women had been raped, and hundreds of churches and schools had been pillaged or destroyed by fire.[39]

Twelve weeks after the Memphis riots, a similar violence occurred in New Orleans. The large population of former Confederates and their younger supporters in the Crescent City wanted to restore the antebellum social order and reduce African Americans to a state of neoslavery. The despised carpetbaggers, scalawags, and burgeoning population of freedpeople were odious obstacles that they were determined to obliterate.

On the other side of the political spectrum were the black suffrage activists who accelerated their demands. In 1866, Governor J. Madison Wells from Rapides Parish, bowing to local and national political pressures, issued an urgent call to reconvene the Constitutional Convention of 1864 for the dual purposes of disenfranchising former rebels and giving African Americans the right to vote. The Convention was to be held on July 30, 1866, at the Mechanics' Institute in New Orleans, a hideous, three-storied red brick structure near the corner of Dryades (now University Place) and Canal Streets. The structure was being used temporarily as Louisiana's capitol building. What transpired on that hot, muggy, summer day made the day one of the most horrific in American history.

Prior to the July 30 Convention, Mayor John T. Monroe and Police Chief Thomas E. Adams plotted to gather a formidable group of armed policemen. Monroe had recently returned to the office of mayor after serving time as Benjamin Butler's political prisoner in Fort Jackson and later at Fort Pickens. Two-thirds of the new police officers were former Confederates. Precinct captains organized their officers into squads and gave specific orders that when the city's fire alarm sounded a special signal of twelve taps, the police would converge on the meeting. The situation did not bode well for the Convention delegates.[40]

On a sweltering Monday morning with the mercury climbing into the 90s, a milling crowd of Convention supporters—mostly blacks, but some whites—gathered in front of the Mechanics' Institute. Agitated anti-Convention whites mingled as well outside the hall. Across town former Native Guards—ready to lend their moral and physical support to the cause of male black suffrage—formed and marched through the French Quarter. As they approached at noon, insults were exchanged, bricks were thrown, pistol shots rang out, and a bloody melee began. At this point, the general alarm sounded, and the police quickly converged along with armed vigilantes. The police were ordered to rush the marchers, and blacks were shot on the spot.

The police then entered the Mechanics' Institute. A few desperate delegates pushed back the doors and frantically barricaded them with tables, chairs, and their own bodies. The police shot through the doors and eventually battered the doors down. At this point, some delegates attempted to flee through the windows, others sought refuge under desks, still others futilely waved the white flag of surrender only to be brutally shot down. A witness before a select congressional committee later testified that "some were cruelly beaten and even killed by their captors after they had surrendered. Some were murdered whilst they were begging for mercy."[41]

The enraged mob singled out well-known white leaders for special attention. Dr. A. P. Dostie, a vocal supporter of the suffrage movement, was shot in the back and a sword was thrust into his stomach. Then the frenzied mob grabbed Dostie by his legs and dragged him down the street as his head repeatedly bounced on the cobblestones. According to Colonel Nathan Daniels, who later wrote a report on the incident for the *National Anti-Slavery Standard* in 1867, "Let the good work go on" were the last words uttered by the martyr as he fell. Later in the hospital, a friend described his face as all cut and swollen and barely recognizable. Dr. Dotsie died several days later.[42]

Another white defender of black suffrage—John Henderson, a lawyer from Mississippi—was mortally wounded as well. As Henderson exited the building, the police hit him repeatedly "and continued to beat him after he fell flat on his face on the banquette." Henderson was followed by former governor Michael Hahn, who was on crutches because of a club foot. Two police officers beat him up as well, but he managed to escape the angry mob in a carriage thanks to the timely intervention of Chief Adams, who by this time was frantically attempting to quell the mob and even some of his own policemen.[43]

The official congressional report of the Select Committee on the New Orleans Riots (1867) stated that "there has been no occasion during our national history when a riot has occurred so destitute of justifiable cause, resulting in a massacre so inhuman and fiend-like, as that which took place at New Orleans on the 30th of July last." A contemporary account noted at least fifty deaths, although the official inquiry set the number at thirty-eight. Cyrus Hamlin, the son of former vice president Hannibal Hamlin, described the grisly scene as wholesale slaughter and an instance of the least regard to human life that he had ever witnessed, surpassing anything he had seen on the Civil War battlefield.[44]

There is no evidence from primary sources or from the Grandjean Collection that Henry Rey participated in the ill-fated Convention or was a supporter in the streets, but many of his friends, relatives of friends, and champions of black suffrage did participate and suffered grievous wounds or died. July 30 became known as the Day of Black Independence, and some of the victims, like Dr. Dostie, John Henderson, and Victor Lacroix, each of whom obtained the status of martyr-heroes, frequently visited Rey's séance table. Victor Lacroix was the son of the wealthy real estate tycoon and former president of the Couvent School, François Lacroix. The younger Lacroix had been cut from head to foot, butchered, and mutilated in the Mechanics' Institute street battle. On the day of the massacre, Lacroix had worn an expensive watch-chain and was carrying a "great deal of money." The watch-chain as well as the money were stolen from the murdered Lacroix.[45]

Years later, the spirit of Victor Lacroix encouraged the Rey circle to focus on the present, noting that "nothing can obscure the road of Progress" and compared the opposition to "a house of cards that would cave in under the breath of the Will of the people." Within the same message, Lacroix lamented the fate of blacks who were forced to work like a flock of sheep and who had been abandoned by their brothers of the North; he further stated that "their only crime was being black." The message ended on an optimistic note: "Our blood flooded the streets of the Bloody City [New Orleans]. Your blood ... that of the martyrs has not been shed in vain. Because of the tragedy Congress responded to the atrocity."[46]

On November 18, 1871, John Henderson, a white martyr of the July 30 massacre, denied having regrets dying for a cause: "In my new world, I am satisfied to have been a victim of the cruelty of fanatical enemies of Human Rights, for it has given me Light, and I am going forward toward Eternal Progress!" This was a common theme in the Cercle Harmonique: a martyr did not die in vain. In fact, the death of a martyr was something positive, a steppingstone toward obtaining racial equality for African Americans.[47]

Ironically, the Mechanics' Institute Massacre (sometimes called the New Orleans Race Riot), instead of being for the former Confederates the hoped-for return to the antebellum social order, actually paved the road for congressional Reconstruction throughout the South. For many Radical Republicans in Washington, it was the last straw, and presidential Reconstruction came to an ignominious end. The obvious excess of violence pushed the US Congress to replace the Confederate-friendly policies of President Andrew Johnson with a congressional Radical Reconstruction that would temporarily protect the civil rights of African Americans in the South and prevent the return of the old regime in which moneyed Democrats controlled every aspect of both society and politics in the South.

Despite newly enacted Reconstruction legislation and changes in the national government, stormy days lay ahead for both the white supporters of a new egalitarian order and the resolute black Creole defenders of liberty for all African Americans. The postbellum years in New Orleans were a time of contentious political struggles, pitting the nascent Republican Party against the conservative Democratic Party and were also a time of vicious internecine strife within the Republican Party. As events turned more violent and civil liberties were threatened, Henry Rey and his revitalized séance circle members drew closer to weather the political storm.

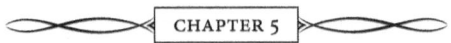

Stormy Days in Louisiana

On a Wednesday afternoon in 1867, a young couple and their eight-month-old baby daughter disembarked from the steamboat *Ruth* in New Orleans. The family had just completed the last leg of an arduous journey from Washington, DC, and the attractive mother was surprised by the pleasant weather as she descended the gangplank to the wide wooden expanse of the New Orleans docks. A heavy shower on Tuesday afternoon had lowered the temperatures for the following day, and a refreshing breeze on the riverfront provided a welcomed momentary respite from the heat and high oppressive humidity so typical of New Orleans in late May.[1]

The busy dockworkers, and the arriving and departing passengers who scurried around the busy wharf, paid no particular attention to the young woman, other than to notice her striking blonde beauty. Cora L. V. Hatch, a celebrated Spiritualist of the North, now the wife of Colonel Nathan W. Daniels, had arrived in the Crescent City without any fanfare or prior notice.[2]

Cora L. V. Scott Hatch Daniels was born in 1840 near the oddly named village of Cuba in Allegany County, New York, and became involved in Spiritualism at the tender age of eleven when she began delivering trance lectures in Lake Mills, Wisconsin. Her father, David W. Scott, had recently moved his family to Wisconsin hoping to build a utopian colony, that type of colony being so popular then; his young daughter's newfound celebrity as a medium resulted in the Scotts returning to western New York. A few years later, fourteen-year-old Cora was engaged as a regular trance lecturer in Buffalo, where she met her first husband, Dr. Benjamin Franklin Hatch.

Despite a huge age difference—Dr. Hatch, a dentist, was a much older man, in his forties—Cora married him in Attica, New York, during the summer of 1856, when she was only sixteen. Dr. Hatch assumed the role of his young bride's stage manager/mentor. During the late 1850s, under the tutelage of her husband, Cora Hatch achieved national notoriety as a celebrated Spiritualist, traveling the lucrative lecture circuit and packing in large, enthusiastic, paying audiences. She carried New Yorkers by storm with her trance lectures delivered with supernatural eloquence.[3]

The marriage did not last, and six years later, after an acrimonious and very public divorce, Cora Hatch met Colonel Nathan W. Daniels—the former commander of the Second Regiment of the Louisiana Native Guards—at Ship Island while on the lecture circuit. Daniels, a handsome young widower, had at long last met his soul mate—a stunningly beautiful woman who was both a Spiritualist and an abolitionist.[4]

During his tour of duty in New Orleans during the Civil War, Colonel Daniels kept a diary that documented his strong Spiritualist beliefs. He consulted various mediums, including Henry Rey, Valmour, and other local mediums. Upon returning to the North after a disappointing military career derailed by his support of black Creole officers, Daniels continued his Spiritualist activities, "attending séances and making friends with local believers." In March 1865, Daniels was invited to the White House in the company of a noted medium, W. P. Anderson, to attend a séance in the Green Room for the purpose of communicating with Willie Lincoln, Mary Todd Lincoln's youngest son, who had died three years earlier. (The First Lady was there, but the president was elsewhere in the White House.)[5]

Nine months later, at the residence of George Bacon in Washington, DC, on the evening of Friday, December 8, 1865, Colonel Nathan Daniels and Cora L. V. Hatch were married by the Reverend John Pierpont, the poet and Spiritualist, with a handful of friends in attendance.[6] In 1866 a baby girl, Henrietta, arrived; the doting parents affectionately called her Etta and Rosebud.[7] The Daniels moved first to Cora's home in western New York and then back to the nation's capital soon after Henrietta's birth, where Colonel Daniels became actively involved in the turbulent political scene and sought a government position in Louisiana. On his thirtieth birthday, May 10, 1867, he received the joyful news that he had been confirmed as "Register under the Bankrupt Act for the 4th District of Louisiana." The Daniels made hasty preparations for their departure.[8]

And so, on May 29, 1867, the delightful weather was for the Daniels family a harbinger of wonderful things ahead—politically, personally, and professionally. Nathan Daniels was hopeful "that health and prosperity may be accorded us." Little did the young couple know that stormy days in Louisiana were ahead for them and for the entire state of Louisiana.[9]

Colonel Daniels plunged ahead into his new bureaucratic duties and meanwhile was also very involved with the nascent Republican Party. Because of Daniels's political and social connections to former Native Guard officers and prominent black Creoles, Cora Daniels was invited to participate in marking the first year anniversary of the New Orleans Massacre at the Mechanics' Institute. On July 30, 1867, the interior columns of the Mechanics' Institute were draped in black, and at the entry stood the same flag that had been displayed on the day of the Convention of 1866, now bloodstained by the "blood of the martyrs of that day." At nine o'clock, Father Claude Paschal Maistre, the radical white priest who had celebrated the requiem mass of Captain André Cailloux in 1863, officiated at the crowded memorial service. After a speech delivered by Rufus Waples, Cora Daniels recited in a sonorous voice a poem she had composed to commemorate the solemn occasion. The lengthy poem, "In Memoriam—July 30," was printed in its entirety in the *New Orleans Tribune*. The poem began,

Toll, toll, toll!
Oh, ye solemn—sad'ning bells
We have need of mournful knells[10]

The brief, exhilarating glory days in Louisiana came to a sudden and tragic end in October 1867, when both Nathan Daniels and his beloved baby daughter succumbed to yellow fever. On October 1, Colonel Daniels died at his Jefferson City home, and tragically, Henrietta passed away two weeks later on October 15. A former Union Native Guard officer, Captain Louis A. Snaër, reported the death of Henrietta Daniels to authorities. It was his last service for his Civil War commander. By 1867, the vigilant sanitation measures of Generals Butler and Banks had fallen by the wayside, and New Orleans returned to being a dirty, unsanitary city with annual epidemics of yellow fever and cholera.[11]

The *New Orleans Tribune* published a lengthy obituary—highly unusual in those days—which eulogized Colonel Daniels for his military efforts and his ardent campaign for black male suffrage. The obituary included a reference to Cora Hatch, saying that Daniel had brought with him to Louisiana "his talented wife, Cora Hatch, well-known in the literary world, who is now afflicted with the great bereavement." Cora Daniels returned to the North, first stopping in Ohio where her deceased husband's family lived and then resuming her Spiritualist activities, which would extend well into the twentieth century.[12]

There is no direct evidence that Henry Louis Rey reestablished personal relations with Colonel Daniels in 1867, but considering how both men were so actively involved in politics and Spiritualism and given their common friendships with others, more than likely their paths did cross. Unfortunately, the primary sources do not provide positive proof of such a relationship.

During the same month as the arrival of the Daniels, the Afro-Creoles achieved a landmark departure in social relations. In May 1867, Eugène Chassaignac, a French émigré and the head of Scottish rite Masonry, opened the doors of the city's French lodges to black members. Now that antebellum restrictions on assembly were gone, it was easier for Afro-Creoles to found clubs and societies. Prominent black Creole leaders such as Paul Trévigne, the Rey brothers, Louis Nelson Fouché, and Arnold Bertonneau founded new, racially integrated lodges. On June 16, Chassaignac installed Henry Rey as the first secretary of the Fraternité #20, one of the French Freemasonry's new affiliates. Henry Rey was a member and an officer of the lodge from 1867 until at least 1873. His brother Hippolyte was a member and officer as well during the same years. Octave was a member for two years: 1867 and 1868.[13]

Henry, no doubt, enjoyed the camaraderie and took pride in the ritual and spiritual teachings of Freemasonry. He was uplifted by the brotherhood in an order claiming great antiquity and lineage to grand French republican luminaries like Victor Hugo and American presidents such as George Washington and Andrew Jackson. The Masonic lodge was also an outlet for Rey to further hone his blossoming leadership skills and make contact with white French émigrés as well as other groups whose members overlapped with the lodge.[14]

The year 1867 also heralded a diminution of the political dominance of the radical black Creole leaders who had steadfastly agitated for black male suffrage and equal access to public schools for their children. According to Joseph Logsdon and Caryn Bell, the leaders "who had so brilliantly maintained their agenda of revolutionary demands found it more difficult to exert the same dominance in the more normal electoral politics.... They increasingly found it more difficult to win elective offices."[15] Still, the former free people of color were well represented at the Constitutional Convention when it convened in New Orleans on November 23, 1867. By March 1868, the Convention had completed its work, which resulted in a new, liberal Constitution guaranteeing all blacks their civil rights.

Henry Clay Warmoth was elected governor in April 1868 and inaugurated on July 13, 1868. The handsome, gregarious Warmoth was just twenty-six years old when he took the oath of office. Warmoth was born on May 9, 1842, in McLeansboro, Illinois, and arrived in New Orleans in 1864 as part of the Union occupation force. He, like other Union soldiers stationed in New Orleans, decided to remain in the South after the Civil War because of promising business and political opportunities. Those referred to in Reconstruction history as carpetbaggers were generally men like Warmoth who were already in the South, not northerners who quickly tossed a few personal items in a cheap carpetbag and rushed to the South after the Civil War ended, seeking political office and ill-gotten riches.

Charles W. Boothby, who later became the superintendent of the interracial Orleans Parish Schools in the 1870s, was stationed in New Orleans in 1863 when he made the same decision to remain in Louisiana instead of returning to his home state. Boothby wrote to relatives in Maine explaining his decision: "[New Orleans] is a good place to make money and after this war, there will be good chances for smart Yankees to go into business and get rich."[16]

Making money was definitely on Henry Clay Warmoth's postbellum agenda; he earned the epithet of "Prince of the Carpetbaggers." Warmoth's remarkable, meteoric rise to power in Louisiana can be attributed to a combination of luck, intelligence, good looks, political savvy, and chaotic postbellum politics. Radical Reconstruction operated in a political power vacuum. Most of the local white male elite was temporarily ineligible for elective office, and once-powerful politicians were reduced to the unmanly situation of watching helplessly as former slaves and former free men of color assumed their coveted political positions.

The office of lieutenant governor went to Oscar James Dunn, a former free person of color from New Orleans. Warmoth's, Dunn's, and Rey's paths must have crossed in the mid-1860s because of their common involvement in the nascent Republican Party of Louisiana. François Dubuclet described O. J. Dunn as a *"griffe bien capable et très corpulent."* A *griffe* was a phenotype meaning a person with one parent of pure African ancestry and one parent who had a combination of African and European ancestry. Sometimes the definition of *griffe* included people of mixed African and Native American ancestry.[17]

The first session of the Louisiana state legislature under the new, liberal state constitution convened in the Mechanics' Institute, and Henry Louis Rey represented his district in the house of representatives. Antoine Dubuclet was elected state treasurer and appointed two of his sons—François and August—as his assistants. It was perhaps during the early days of the new constitution that François Dubuclet and Rey became friends and séance participants. The elder Dubuclet was a wealthy, black sugar planter at his Dubuclet-Durand plantation, ninety-seven miles upriver from New Orleans in Iberville Parish. He owned ninety-five slaves in 1850, making him one of the largest slave owners and richest planters among the free people of color in Louisiana. Antoine Dubuclet held onto his post of Louisiana state treasurer for ten years, which was an incredible achievement for an African American during the turbulent years of Reconstruction.[18]

Rey's Cercle Harmonique made a venue change in March 1867. No longer was Valmour's home the séance site. Now Valmour was the visitor to Rey's new residence on St. Louis Street, and the atmosphere and protocol of the séance circle had changed. Grandjean noted that the new circle achieved greater progress under the guidance of Henry Rey's closed meetings; however, interested people could still attend the séances if they received permission in advance. "Progress" meant a regular group of participants and a calmer atmosphere without interruptions from people seeking medical assistance.[19]

Henry Rey, now independent of the Valmour mediumship, dubbed his Spiritualist group Le Cercle Harmonique (the Harmonious Circle), harmony at the séance being the all-important ingredient in successfully contacting the departed. "Circle" had a dual meaning: first, as the configuration around the circular séance table, and second, as a term designating a small, but cohesive group united in common goals. According to historian Brett Carroll, it was not uncommon for Spiritualists who met regularly to give their group its own name, as this practice cemented group ties and gave the séance participants a sense of belonging. Rey, now empowered with leadership within his local community and on the state level as a state representative, was in the vanguard to radically change an archaic society. The emphasis on harmony recalled A. J. Davis's Harmonial philosophy of the 1840s, which was still popular in the North during the 1860s. Rey often referred to the séance as *séance harmonique*.[20]

On January 8, 1869, State Representative Henry Rey visited François Dubuclet at the Louisiana state treasury on the corner of Royal and Conti Streets, then the heart of the New Orleans banking district. Rey demanded some paper and wrote a communication addressed to Valmour. That evening "Petit," as François Dubuclet was known, delivered the spiritual message to Valmour, who smiled as he calmly read the announcement of his own death. The spirit messenger was Nelson Desbrosses, a family friend and business associate of the Henry Rey's father who became a celebrated medium after studying Spiritualism with Valmour. Desbrosses informed Valmour in his communication that he and Valmour's deceased friends were preparing a chariot of triumph in anticipation of his beautiful hour of departure.[21]

That hour arrived early Saturday, February 6, 1869. Henry Rey and François Dubuclet were summoned that night under the dim flickering gaslight to Valmour's house. Assembling family and friends around the deathbed was part of what was known as the Good Death of the Victorian era. It was important for the loved ones to witness the death because the last few minutes on earth would epitomize the departed's spiritual condition and would carry him across the Spiritual Divide. Mirrors were shrouded with white sheets because people believed that if a dying person looked in a mirror, his soul would be trapped in the mirror for all eternity. This was Valmour's final chapter on earth, and Henry Rey wanted to witness its conclusion. At four o'clock in the morning, Valmour crossed over to the world of the dead. Rey and François Dubuclet stopped the clocks in the house and hung black ribbons, death notices, and an immortelle on the front door and gate. Death notices included the age of the deceased, the names of the parents, and when and where the funeral would take place. An immortelle was a black wreath made of black ribbons which signified that someone had died in the house. As Valmour's body lay exposed in the same room, Henry Rey conducted a séance. Valmour, now a spirit messenger, comforted his bereaved family and friends, declaring, "Don't cry; . . . my spirit is being carefully lifted towards beautiful regions . . . a magnificent and grandiose panorama of the eternal life is unfolding. . . . Valmour is triumphant. Oh! My brothers, continue to combat the error, the injustice and the superstition, and you will have the satisfaction of the heart."[22]

On the following day, François Dubuclet filed the death certificate and made arrangements for a civil burial without priests. The death certificate did not give a cause of death, but in conversations with René Grandjean, Dubuclet partially attributed his death to stress caused by a flood in early October 1868. Street flooding was common in that era, and the nearby Carondelet Canal overflowed its banks, inundating Valmour's house with several feet of water.[23] On February 7, a death notice framed in black was prominently placed on the front page of the *New Orleans Tribune*: "Dead yesterday at

4 AM, VALMOUR (medium). The body is exposed at his last residence, St. Louis Street, between Galvez and Tonti. Friends and acquaintances are invited to attend the burial, which will take place today at 3 PM."[24]

On Sunday morning, Valmour's body was prepared and laid out. The clock was still stopped at four o'clock and would not be restarted until after the burial. The house was filled with the aroma of food brought by neighbors and the smell of strong chicory coffee brewing in tall urns near the doorways. After a brief solemn civil ceremony, the pallbearers transported the casket to nearby St. Louis Cemetery No. 2.

As the funeral procession slowly proceeded down the earthen street along the Carondelet Canal, crowds gathered on the wooden banquettes to pay their last respects to the great healing medium. Valmour had come to join the Creole spirit messengers he had conversed with for so many years.[25] His passing did not mean his disappearance at the séance table. He now appeared as a spirit guide who frequently communicated with Rey's circle, giving encouragement, solace, and advice for personal, social, and political problems and dilemmas. From 1869 to 1871, the circle occasionally gathered at the Valmour residence, as Valmour's widow, Dianah, continued her relationship with Spiritualism until her death in April 1871.

Valmour's death coincided with the acrimonious debate in the Louisiana state legislature concerning public schools in Louisiana. Henry Rey, as chairman of the Education Committee, was in the vanguard of legislators advocating free, integrated public schools, an extremely radical idea in those days. Universal integrated schools had actually been incorporated into the 1868 constitution under Article 135, which decreed that "all children of this state between the ages of 6 through 18 shall be admitted to the public schools without distinction of race, color or previous condition. There shall be no separated schools established for any race." Despite the objections of the more conservative legislators who declared that the Article was "unjust to the white people of the State," Article 135 was adopted as state law on March 7, 1868.[26]

Governor Henry Clay Warmoth refused to enforce the legislative mandate for integrated schools, and conservative district boards stymied the attempt to integrate schools. Warmoth was playing a shrewd political game by supporting white conservatives. The fickle political winds were now blowing in the direction of the disenfranchised planter elite and former Confederates. Much to the dismay of the black Creole intelligentsia, Warmoth distanced himself from the Afro-Creole progressive political agenda, which had helped to elect him governor.

For educational reform leaders like Henry Rey, the solution was to totally revamp the district boards, thus circumventing Warmoth's skullduggery and the recalcitrant district school boards. To many African American delegates, statewide integrated public schools were as important as the issue of universal suffrage. It had been one of the three critical objectives of the Friends of Universal Suffrage in 1865. Now it was up to more assertive legislators to sidestep entrenched boards of education. The boards and directors were certainly not model leaders in the field of education. State Superintendent Thomas Conway described the utter worthlessness of the old system in a committee meeting on August 21, 1868: "Generally, the teachers are scholastically bad and morally worse—the Directors [Superintendents] are uneducated and consequently incompetent to judge the requirements of applicants. If you could only see who have for Directors half of whom make their crosses to signatures."[27]

As chairman of the Committee on Education, Henry Rey's first attempt in August 1868 to ensure integrated public schools in New Orleans failed because the act gave the authority to appoint school board members to the governor with the advice and consent of the state senate. Rey reasoned that a new system of appointing board members would "correct the glaring defects heretofore existing in the prejudice and injury of one class of citizens and to the special benefit of another."[28]

On January 11, 1869, Henry Rey introduced an act to abolish public school boards and replace them with boards more amenable to integrated schools so as not to violate the spirit and intent of the constitution of the state of Louisiana.[29] The boards of directors (school boards) were going to be new slates of directors appointed by the state board of education. After several legal skirmishes, the old district boards were disbanded in December 1870, and schools were ordered to integrate within one month. Thus began a six and a half year experiment in integrated schools in Orleans Parish.[30]

Henry Rey waged the battle for education in New Orleans on another front. This time the battle was fought at his father's beloved Couvent School, which had deteriorated physically and academically after the death in March 1867 of its revered director, Armand Lanusse. In December 1869, a visiting committee declared the Couvent School to be in a state of miserable disrepair and without books and everything else necessary for a school. The girls' classroom did not even have windows. Enrollment had declined to eighty-five boys and forty-one girls. In February, Rey used his influence in the legislature to obtain operating funds, and in April 1870 the Board of Directors sent a letter to Representative Rey thanking him for saving the school.[31]

The following year, Henry Rey took a more active role in the Couvent School when in July 1871, he attempted to wrest control from its president, Canon J. Adolphe. According to Rodolphe Desdunes, Adolphe was

> *guilty of many fraudulent operations in the management of the school affairs between 1870 and 1885. . . . [Adolphe] obtained permission from the board of directors . . . to be the sole agent in all transactions relative to the school. . . . Mr. Adolphe could and did collect all the moneys for rent and otherwise, and could and did keep the money by him received, without rendering any account either to the board . . . or to the clergy.*[32]

The attempt to unseat the crafty opportunist Adolphe failed, as his minions continued to support him. However, Rey retained his position as board member. From 1871 to 1873, Rey was generally absent for board meetings, apparently acknowledging his own powerlessness in the face of Canon Adolphe.[33]

The Grandjean Registers contain just a few spirit messages related to the subject of education. One message received on June 10, 1871, from Eugène Sue (1804–1857), a French novelist, reveals a rather surprisingly modern outlook for public education. The spirit communication said that the most important question concerning public education was whether or not public schools would include high schools. This message came after public schools were integrated in early 1871.[34]

A more popular topic of Henry Rey's spirit world messengers concerned the Catholic Church, which after the Louisiana Purchase brought significant changes in the religious life of the black Creoles. Increasingly the Church leadership adopted the rigid binary racial system order that was dominant throughout the South and moved away from the more fluid, three-tiered system inherited from the French and especially the Spanish that set Louisiana apart from the rest of the nation. The free black community in the waning antebellum years turned to alternative, anticlerical outlets such as Spiritualism, which challenged the Church's traditional authority. The nemesis of Spiritualism in New Orleans during the 1850s was Abbé Napoléon Joseph Perché, the fiery editor of *Le Propagateur Catholique* who criticized Joseph Barthet and his Creole séance circle.[35]

The popularity of the Catholic Church further faltered during the postbellum years as newly freed slaves for the first time had the opportunity to decide their religious affiliation. Protestantism was particularly attractive to the African American community, and the Church leaders on both the local and national levels tried to guard their religious flocks against the many flourishing sects.[36]

The Catholic Church's continued adherence to racism and unabated demands for money from the parishioners earned disdain and frequent diatribes from Rey's spirit guides. The pope was a favorite target for many diatribes. "Your robe hides the vermin that covers your people in rags, suffering, while so much gold is hidden in your coffers. Oh! Miserable hypocrite!" was how one spirit guide lanced his vitriol against the Catholic leader. At another séance, the leader of the Haitian Revolution, Toussaint Louverture, vented, "A Pope! He's both the political and religious despot."[37]

Spirit guides targeted corrupt priests. In a message from Père Chalon, a deceased priest at St. Louis Cathedral, he lamented the fact that excessive amounts of money were constantly demanded for baptisms, pews, masses, funerals, and marriages. He further stated that "the Black is at the back of the church, but his money is white, his 'greenbacks' come from the Yankees that the priests hate, but they bless any and all 'greenbacks.' They blessed the Confederate flags."[38]

Another message, this from the French Romantic writer Rabelais, warned the séance participants that the priest "wants to be your master and that of your wife's and children, who would like to know all the family secrets." The reference to wives indicates that the mainstays of the Catholic Church were the women who clung to at least the perception that the priests were instruments of God and their protectors in their religious lives; the reality, according to Rabelais, was that priests were disingenuously using black Creole women to further their avarice and control over the black Creole community.[39]

The anticlericalism of the Rey circle is certainly significant, but not unique in Modern American Spiritualism. One of the major reasons for the rapid rise of the new faith was the failure of mainstream religions to connect with the spiritual needs of their congregations. Spiritualism was a compelling, nonsectarian alternative, which offered a philosophy of progress and harmony without the direction of a formal clergy. As Protestantism and the Catholic Church floundered on the slippery rocks of ideology and social issues, so Spiritualism profited by their weaknesses and gained more adherents from the moral multitudes. Spiritualism provided the balm for suffering souls injured by decades of poor sectarian leadership.

Despite the diatribes against the Catholic Church, the most frequently channeled spirit guides in Rey's séance circles were four Catholic figures. Especially popular was St. Vincent de Paule (1576–1660), a French Reformer known for his pious work with the impoverished and uneducated masses. For the Afro-Creoles, de Paule epitomized the Christian ideal of a pastor's unselfish and unconditional love for his religious flock. His relentless work in freeing slaves in the hulls of the French navy and other humanitarian works resonated with black Creoles who, in the early postbellum days, were battling former Confederates seeking to restore at least a semblance of the antebellum order. Two centuries after his death, Vincent de Paule's "mystical piety, fraternal charity, and egalitarian spirituality proved to be an irresistible model ... for a truly 'catholic' church."[40]

A second notable Catholic Church spirit messenger was the revered Spanish Capuchin friar, Fray Antonio de Sedella, who was the pastor of St. Louis Church (later St. Louis Cathedral) from 1787 until his death in 1829. De Sedella—better known by his French appellation, Père Antoine—was a devout friar who took his Franciscan vow of poverty seriously. His coarse brown monastic dress tied at the waist with a thick cotton cord, large broad-brimmed black hat, and plain sandals endeared him to generations of black Creoles. However, some of the Catholic clergy ridiculed the good father for his simple clothes and strict adherence to the solemn vow of poverty. Père Antoine was the only priest to wear monastic dress, and his rejection of worldly goods seemed to be old fashioned and out of sync with what other priests earned in their parishes. His home was a simple hut that he had erected himself to the rear of St. Louis Cathedral.[41]

The Catholic Church was viewed as a shelter from the storm. Literally from birth to death, the free people of color had the support of the Catholic Church. Their babies were christened in the Church; they received the holy sacraments; free people of color were married with the Church's blessings; and when they departed from the world, the priests officiated at their funerals.

When Père Antoine passed away on January 29, 1829, the city closed down for three days. Flags flew at half-mast, and thousands paid their respects. The passing of Père Antoine marked a turning point in the history of the Catholic Church and for the black Creoles. The death of this much-beloved friar marked a new era for the Catholic Church, now more American than Latin.

The Americanization of the Catholic Church brought significant changes in the religious lives of the Creoles of color. By the late 1830s, control had shifted to Anglo-Americans who were committed to southern social and political agendas. The Church was no longer a haven in times of trouble, and its influence suffered a slow, but steady decline. As the status of the free people of color deteriorated from 1830 to 1860, they fondly recalled the kind, pious Père Antoine. Over the decades, his legacy cast a long shadow, and the special rapport with him was reflected in Henry Rey's séance registers.

A third popular Catholic messenger was Père Antoine's successor, Father Aloysius Leopold Moni. In the face of growing opposition from the Anglo-American conservative faction, Father Moni perpetuated the liberal, Latin-European tradition for another decade. As a spirit messenger, he was simply known as "Moni."

Père Ambroise, a Benedictine monk and Catholic reformer of the seventeenth century, completes the quartet of Catholic clergy who frequently appeared at Rey's séance circles. Ambroise, as the Cercle Harmonique knew him, was a relatively obscure monk who was also frequently channeled at Joseph Barthet's circles.[42]

Altered relationships with the Catholic Church were just one change in the total reorientation of the black Creoles' society after the Civil War. Amicable business relationships with white Creoles and Anglo-Americans quickly soured, and whites distanced themselves from the Afro-Creole elite which had lost its luster as a privileged group. As the social leveling continued in the postbellum world, the once-privileged Afro-Creoles were considered no different from former slaves. The old, three-tiered racial caste system collapsed, and with each passing year it became more and more evident that the former free black population no longer retained its old advantages in society and business. The polarization of the races into simply black and white dealt a heavy blow to the black Creoles' social status, once at the antebellum pinnacle of the social order of the free black and enslaved communities, now rapidly declining in the late 1860s.

There must have been smug satisfaction within the Cercle Harmonique when a white Creole died and visited the séance table to repent and beg forgiveness for his errant ways and maltreatment of the black Creoles. Such was the case with the French-born Pierre Soulé, ambassador, senator, orator par excellence, lawyer, Confederate provost marshal of New Orleans, Barthélemy Rey's old business associate, and former friend of the oppressed. Soulé experienced a precipitous decline economically, socially, and politically during General Benjamin Butler's strong-handed occupation of New Orleans. Pierre Soulé returned to New Orleans after the Civil War; his wife had died in 1856, and his only son had become insane. His final two years were spent seated in front of a mirror having long conversations with his reflected image.[43] Pierre Soulé died a broken and ruined man on March 28, 1870. Two months later, Soulé's spirit apologized to Rey's Cercle Harmonique, saying "I used to be the friend of the oppressed, my heart beat for Liberty, but soon pride and ambition took over, I forgot my sacred aspirations and I loved the lamb of gold. I sacrificed my republicanism on the altar of slavery. Forgive me, forgive me! Brothers![44]

Experiencing the seismic societal changes of Reconstruction, the black Creoles pragmatically sought new political alliances with black Anglo-Americans. One early leader was Oscar James Dunn, who first entered political life in 1865, serving with Henry Rey on the same executive committee of the Friends of Universal Suffrage. Dunn later became America's first black lieutenant governor.[45]

Harmonious relations between the governor and lieutenant governor transformed into bitter internecine strife as Governor Warmoth courted conservative Democrats to expand his shaky and dwindling political base. Warmoth turned his back on African American reform demands. By the fall of 1871, Lieutenant Governor Dunn openly challenged Warmoth and actively worked to start impeachment hearings, calling him the party's "first Ku Klux Klan Governor."[46] Oscar Dunn's attempt to dislodge Warmoth as governor was cut short by his sudden and suspicious death on the morning of November 22, 1871. The official cause of death was listed as "congestion of the brain," but many skeptical Afro-Creoles believed that powerful enemies had poisoned him, probably by arsenic added to his meals by a paid house servant. The prime suspect was Governor Henry Clay Warmoth. Many thought that Warmoth wanted to eliminate Dunn because of the former's complicity in the Custom House faction, but there were others who could gain political dividends from Dunn's untimely demise.

Nowhere in any of Dunn's numerous communications does the spirit of Dunn mention being poisoned. However, François Dubuclet reported to René Grandjean that Dunn had indeed been poisoned, but not by Governor Warmoth and not by arsenic. The culprit, Dubuclet said, was the jealous and conniving P. B. S. Pinchback, who later succeeded Dunn as lieutenant governor. Decades later, Warmoth recalled Pinchback as "a restless, ambitious man . . . a free lance and dangerous," perhaps thinking of Pinchback's ostensible role in Oscar Dunn's murder.[47]

According to Dubuclet, P. B. S. Pinchback paid one of Dunn's house servants to poison Dunn. Marcus Christian investigated his death in a 1945 article titled "The Theory of the Poisoning of Oscar J. Dunn" and described his symptoms as hoarseness, vomiting, muscular spasms, shrunken and pallid face, feeble pulse and coma. Pinchback's *Weekly Louisianian* soundly quashed any rumors of foul play, citing "three eminent physicians united in giving a certificate testifying to the character of Mr. Dunn's disease, and vouching for the natural causes of his death." We will never know who was responsible for Dunn's death or even if there was foul play involved. The suspicious death of Oscar J. Dunn remains a curious historical "whodunnit." Interestingly, Governor Warmoth was one of the pallbearers at Dunn's funeral, which attracted thousands of mourners who lined the sidewalks and neutral ground from Claiborne Avenue to Tchoupitoulas Street near the Mississippi River.[48]

One week after Oscar Dunn's sudden death, Henry Rey's twelve-year-old daughter, Lucia, requested him to appear. Her deceased grandmother, Rose Gignac, appeared instead and explained that "Dunn could come, but at the moment he is deep in thought about his past life. Later, he will understand his position, and I believe he will come near your father."[49] The following week, Dunn delivered his first communication to the circle, advising its participants that "dividing a house is ruinous to all. For the sake of harmony and for the freedom of all, don't shatter to pieces the great work already done. United we stand, divided we fall." Most of the communications in the registers are written in French, but those of Dunn are consistently in English. The use of English indicates that Dunn only spoke English, and it also indicates that Rey's circle was bilingual.[50]

In the same vein, Oscar Dunn consoled Rey's Cercle Harmonique, saying that its "duty is not in fighting the wrong of your opponents. You are to work in harmonizing the two elements in a solid phalanx, to be able to vanquish your real political enemies. . . . I did not want to divide our ranks, I was wrong."[51] Again, the séance table provided a forum for the departed to repent and apologize for their mistakes. Dunn's communication demonstrates that some black Creoles realized in retrospect the political folly of abandoning Governor Warmoth. It also indicates that Henry Rey and Oscar Dunn collaborated at the highest levels of the state government.

On the first anniversary of his death, Oscar Dunn issued this command: "Tell the boys! Do not Despair! Hold on together. I am in the light."[52] Messages from Dunn appear frequently in the Grandjean Registers, mostly encouraging the circle to continue its noble struggle against adversity and not to give up. Dunn's communications never mentioned foul play being involved in his mysterious death.

After serving in the Louisiana House of Representatives for two years (1868–1870), Henry Rey was appointed to the lucrative position of Third District assessor in New Orleans on April 13, 1870. There appears to have been a political connection with Henry Clay Warmoth. The governor appointed a new mayor, Benjamin Franklin Flanders, on April 4, 1870, and Rey became the new assessor the following week. The new post raised Rey's social and political status, and he also received a much higher salary than what he had earned as a hardware store clerk. Henry Rey worked in room 21, 18 Royal Street, less than a block away from the Henry Clay Circle. The building was an architectural masterpiece designed by famed architect James H. Dakin; it was erected in 1836 and was later known as the Merchants' Exchange. The building also housed a post office and the Federal District Court.[53]

Henry Rey was now financially able to move from his small Creole cottage on Columbus Street to a spacious new home at 341 Villere Street. The new house was actually less than a block away from his Columbus Street home.

On March 5, 1872, after two years as Third District tax assessor, Rey's commission expired, and Governor Warmoth did not reappoint him.[54] The complex, hardscrabble world of postbellum politics in Louisiana may have been the reason for Rey's abrupt departure. Henry Rey initially supported Governor Warmoth in 1868 but changed his allegiance when the governor lost interest in the Afro-Creole elite's progressive political agenda and embraced a broader political base, which included some of the more moderate white Louisianans. Being a pragmatist, Warmoth realized that remaining isolated from the Democrats would be political suicide and that the days of Republican Party ascendancy in Louisiana were numbered.

Henry Rey and other African Americans attempted to gain control of the Republican Party in party elections held on August 7, 1871, incurring the wrath of the carpetbagger governor. Rey, as president of the Seventh Ward Radical Republican Mother Club, was in charge of an election for his district delegates to the Republican State Convention. The Warmoth faction claimed that there were improprieties in the electoral process. Congressional hearings were held in Washington to investigate the volatile political situation in Louisiana and used Rey's deposition taken in September. The governor waited until March 1872 to allow Rey's appointment as tax assessor to expire and then appointed a replacement.[55]

The Grandjean Registers do not indicate the reason for Rey's departure from the tax assessor's office, but the sympathetic spirits consoled Henry Rey, assuring him that "your loss of employment is for your Good."[56]

As the Afro-Creoles ventured out in the 1860s on treacherous political terra incognita, they discovered the duplicity of some of the Republican carpetbaggers as well as the strident racism of former Confederates and their younger supporters. As a way to articulate their hopes and dreams, some black Creoles banded together in séance circles. Spiritual communications mirrored the struggles of the black Creoles during the 1860s and early 1870s: the betrayal of Governor Henry Clay Warmoth; the loss of a promising Anglo-black politician, Oscar J. Dunn; the fight to establish integrated free public schools; and personal losses such as the death of the charismatic Valmour. Stormy days in Louisiana for the black Creoles and their supporters continued throughout the 1870s.

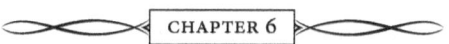

Windows of the Soul

Spiritualism entered its third decade of existence in the 1870s, and the number of disciples and followers declined significantly. In its first decade in the 1850s, Spiritualism burst upon the American scene as a fascinating and intriguing novelty. The public was captivated by its religious fervor; the independence from mainstream religions; and the intellectualism, showmanship, and mysticism. Attractive women mediums who spoke so eloquently in a trance-induced state enthralled even the male disbelievers.

The second decade was marked by the horrific losses of the Civil War. The unprecedented number of war casualties generated interest in communicating with the departed loved ones who had died hundreds of miles away from their homes without the comfort of loved ones gathered around the deathbed at the moment of departure. For many relatives, this was perhaps the worst aspect of death. A young soldier's death on a distant battlefield without the comfort of family members attending his last minutes on earth made acceptance of the untimely demise unfathomable. Spiritualism offered one way to reconnect the deceased soldier with living family members and friends, who were unwilling to wait until their own deaths to be reunited with their loved one. Séances and the use of the planchette were common ways to communicate at home with the departed. The planchette, a precursor of the Ouija board, consisted of a heart-shaped piece of wood, which was believed to move in response to spiritual forces as one or more people placed their fingers on it. When used in combination with a copy of the alphabet, the tip of the heart would point to letters to spell out communications. Sometimes, a pencil was inserted in a precut hole, and the spirits would use the pencil to write messages on paper placed underneath the planchette.[1]

The *Banner of Light* offered free thrice-weekly séances in its offices on Washington Street for relatives and friends to communicate with their deceased loved ones. The departed were able to communicate through the mediumship of Jennie "Fanny" Conant. The Boston periodical printed the communications in a popular weekly column, The Messenger, beginning with the journal's premier issue on April 11, 1857. Many spiritual messages received by Conant provided solace and closure to the living family members. The departed often reported that they were happy in the afterworld, and they were apparently still their definable and particular selves.

During the Civil War and for a decade after, most of the communications in The Messenger were responses to the families and friends of fallen soldiers, Confederate and Union. The communications began with the departed identifying the military unit that he was with at the time of death. Next, the spirit typically communicated some information about where and when he died, the amount of sufferings he endured prior to death, his age, and some words of consolation. Occasionally, the spirit would express his regret for dying so far from home. Such was the case of Richard Isallis of the 11th Vermont Heavy Artillery, who said, "I want the folks to know I feel sorry I couldn't be with 'em when I died, but I died like a soldier." The Good Death that soldiers were denied on the battlefield was somehow accomplished through Spiritualism.[2]

In the early 1870s, Spiritualism was approaching its first quarter century of existence, and it began to show its age at the national level. But while interest in Spiritualism waned in other parts of the country, the black Creole Cercle Harmonique entered into its heyday with Henry Rey's adept leadership and skillful mediumship. His dedicated circle continued to meet regularly at the homes and shops of neighbors. The Grandjean Registers reveal a sophisticated and mature approach to meticulously documenting the political and personal messages received from the spiritual world as the circle considered the spiritual messages to be sacred. The use of spiritual registers was sui generis to the French Creole séance circles in New Orleans. René Grandjean documents in his margin notes that Valmour, the charismatic blacksmith medium, kept registers of spiritual messages, which unfortunately were lost by his children after his death. Now, Valmour's friend, fellow medium, and successor, Henry Rey, continued the French Creole tradition of transcribing spiritual communications in ledger books and journals.

In 1874, an investigative reporter for the *New Orleans Times* described the use of registers among the French population. According to the reporter, there were "large French creole circles that had been in existence for nearly

Séance circles were advised by Spiritualist newspapers to evenly divide the participants between men and women, seated around a table with their hands either joined or laid on the table. *Bettmann Archive.*

twenty years" and the circles "kept a careful record of all its sittings, and of spirit writings received, until their records number many volumes." The reporter further stated, "It is said these volumes contain many interesting incidents, the séances having all been carefully written up and preserved. As for mediums, there are many, but very few of such are rated professional." The article cited the almost nightly occurrence of séances in which "Friends—believers and unbelievers—gather in houses in a social way simply, and prosecute the investigations with unflagging zeal."[3]

The references to the séance registers, mediums, and venue details correspond perfectly to Henry Rey's circle; however, the reporter failed to identify any of the participants or mediums. He could have been documenting another French circle in New Orleans that has long since disappeared from the historical record. Nevertheless, information gleaned from the *New Orleans Times* article demonstrates the visibility and viability of Creole séance circles in New Orleans and the defining hallmarks of those circles, so different from those of the city's Anglo-American circles.

The reporter estimated the number of Spiritualists to be "not less than five or six thousand," but many of them were careful to hide their devotion to Spiritualism because of its unpopularity in New Orleans as well as the continued resistance of the traditional churches. The newsman, who described himself as Doubting Thomas, investigated some of the Anglo séance circles and reported chilling and harrowing nights among the spirits.[4]

Some of these séances took place in the uptown area of New Orleans at George W. Kendall's home on Carondelet Street. His teenage daughter Mabel was chosen to contact the dead. Kendall, an attorney and son of the founder of the *Daily Picayune*, reported that spirits of both sexes had visited him for a period of two years. The method of communication was slate writing, often used in northern séances. As the fifteen-year-old Mabel held a slate in a darkened room under the table, the spirit wrote a simple message on the slate.[5]

Other séances featured musical instruments laid on the floor for the spirits to either play or throw helter-skelter in the darkness, leading to chaotic and noisy sessions. The instruments included tambourines, trumpets, bells, harmonicas, and guitars. As the spirits appeared, a cold chill rushed into the room, and "trumpets were frequently caught in the air far above the head of the tallest man." Sometimes the flying instruments shattered the chandelier glasses, and sometimes the spirits were content to play a perfect bedlam of discordant sounds.[6]

The following week a rival newspaper, the *Daily Picayune*, published its own investigative article and reported a larger number of Spiritualists, giving the figure at over fifteen thousand and "growing at rapid strides." At the observed séance, there were about thirty-six participants of both sexes seated around the room. Most of the participants at the New Orleans séance were French speaking, and a bucket of whiskey was provided as the only refreshment.[7]

When the gaslights went out, phosphoric lights appeared, and the spirits entered the parlor conversing in French and English and making their presence known with random rappings. The session became violent as the chairs and table began to shake. Suddenly, the table lifted itself and darted rapidly across the room, overturning half a dozen séance participants. An armoire waltzed around the room and chairs were uplifted as the participants watched the strange, unearthly scene. The medium calmly explained that the spirits were in a bad mood because the living had disturbed their eternal repose. Finally, the room became silent and the ill-humored spirits departed, only to return a few minutes later. The apparitions vented their anger by lancing a large flint boulder through the window that smashed a dozen panes of glass. Another boulder descended from out of nowhere and fell in the middle of the room, breaking into a thousand pieces with a flash of light and the sound of a pistol. Minutes later, according to the reporter, "every lamp, chair and table in the room was smashed."[8]

The following year, the *New Orleans Times* continued its investigation of psychic phenomena in a second article, disclosing similar details but adding additional frightening new features of the nocturnal psychic extravaganza. A reporter described the silent pitch black darkness of the séance as ghostly white, glimmering gossamer clouds glided into the newly chilled room in ill-defined outlines. Three raps on the cabinet signaled the willingness of the spirits to communicate, and then music was heard from instruments that had been placed on the floor, this time playing a perennial favorite, "Home, Sweet Home."[9]

A second séance involved slate board writing as seen in the earlier Kendall séance. A spirit materialized and wrote short sentences on the board with "the flourish of a skilled penman." Later, another medium held the slate board, but changed the chalk from one hand to another, apparently angering the spirit. The offended apparition dashed the board on the floor. At the same séance, the spirits placed a large chair on top of a cabinet and then pushed the chair off and the gaslights came on, effectively ending the séance, since spirits shun light.

The two-decade tradition of Spiritualist lectures continued in New Orleans among the Anglo-American community, but now at new venues. Minerva Hall on Clio Street between Prytania Street and St. Charles Avenue became the premier location for lectures and social gatherings of the Spiritualists.[10] This section of the city was in what was then called the American section, which was across town from the homes and séance venues of the black Creoles. Articles and advertisements in the New Orleans newspapers document the ongoing interest in Spiritualism. Some lecturers were local, and others had traveled to New Orleans from the North to spend several months lodged at a downtown hotel. They lectured at Minerva Hall, usually on Sundays.

The most famous of these peripatetic lecturers from the North during the 1870s was the Reverend James M. Peebles, who made at least two hibernal trips to the Crescent City. Known as the Spiritual Pilgrim, Peebles was a world traveler based in Baltimore. In 1871 and 1876, Rev. Peebles spent two pleasant winters in the warmer climate of New Orleans, lecturing on Spiritualism. Peebles's most consulted and revered spirit messenger was Black Hawk, the famed warrior of the Sauks, who in the spiritual world had washed the war paint from his face, broken his arrows, and converted to the ways of peace. Black Hawk later became a favorite spirit guide for the ministers of the eclectic twentieth-century Spiritual churches described in the Epilogue.

James Peebles was an impressive figure. He was tall—over six feet—and had long brown hair and a huge full beard. Peebles reported his successes in *The American Spiritualist*, stating "there are many Spiritualists in New Orleans" and mentioning the Reverend J. W. Allen as being the president of the Spiritualist society.[11]

Rev. Allen also delivered lectures at Minerva Hall, the nerve center of Anglo-American Spiritualism in New Orleans. A newspaper article dated March 13, 1876, reported on one of the reverend's trance lectures on Sunday morning. Between fifty to a hundred people were in the hall when Allen appeared in a simple suit of gray cloth. "His hair, which was a shade lighter than brown, was worn long and unparted." Rev. Allen took his place at a desk and proceeded to read a poem followed by several hymns, and then a lecture on the nature of Spiritualism. The reverend rhetorically asked, "Is Spiritualism a science, a religion, or a philosophy, or does it embody all three within itself?" As the Reverend Allen went into a trance, a spirit from within his body answered the question, informing the audience that Spiritualism appeals to man by "opening the windows of the soul and affording glimpses of the world beyond."[12]

By the mid-1870s, self-appointed truth seekers were exposing the tricks and chicanery of Spiritualism in a series of performances at the Academy of Music and other locations. Professor Cooke demonstrated the methods used in slate writing, pellet reading, and "spirit bride" tests. As the years went by, the fabric of Spiritualism became frayed, faded, and torn apart by relentless truth seekers and their convinced multitudes.[13] At the same time, Rey's black Creole séance circles began to feel similar aging pains as those experienced by the Anglo-American Spiritualists in New Orleans. In addition to the movement's loss of popularity on the national and local fronts, Henry Rey and his circle participants confronted political and economic problems, which hastened the demise of the Cercle Harmonique.

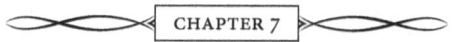

CHAPTER 7

Le Cercle Harmonique

Henry Rey's abrupt dismissal as Third District assessor in 1872 marked the beginning of his downward political and economic spiral, which paralleled that experienced by other Creoles of color. The typical demographic characteristics of the free people of color in a three-tiered racial hierarchy of Louisiana—light-skinned, French speaking, Catholic, freed prior to the Civil War, and well educated—no longer garnered special economic dividends among the white Creoles and Anglo-Americans in the postbellum years. The ongoing polarization of the races was perhaps a factor in Rey's long-term unemployment; it was years before Rey found work again in 1877, and this time as an entry level "first clerk" in another hardware store, G. Pitard & Brothers.[1]

As a young man, Henry Rey had entered into an apprenticeship around 1857 with another Saint-Domingue descendent, Eugène Hacker, in his Tremé hardware store. Rey was unable to return to his former job because Hacker died on May 13, 1871. René Grandjean noted that he committed suicide, but an official city inquiry placed the cause of death as apoplexy.[2] A spirit relative of Hacker's appeared six months after his death and explained that Eugène wanted to visit his family at the séance table because he was worried about the financial stability of his hardware store and his struggling family. Hacker's French-born widow, Agathe, had attempted to manage the store but failed to keep it solvent. In 1872, Eugène Hacker's store closed, and his nephew, Gustave Pitard, took it over and later moved it to the Central Business District on Canal Street. Henry Rey worked at G. Pitard's Hardware Store until his death in 1894.[3]

Another event adversely affected Henry Rey's financial situation. In 1873, Rey and his wife Adèle invested their money in the Freedman's Savings and Trust Company, but the bank failed in 1874.[4] The failure of the Freedman's Bank was related to the national depression of 1873 that was especially serious in Louisiana, which was still recovering from the devastating economic damage related to the Civil War. Once the Queen City of the South, New Orleans struggled in the postbellum years to regain some of its past glory and economic strength.[5]

In the watershed year of 1877, Reconstruction officially ended. However, the first cracks in Radical Reconstruction had appeared earlier in Louisiana and throughout the South. Despite their reduced numbers, the Union troops managed to protect black suffrage in the cities and helped to suppress coup d'états against the new liberal state governments. For the conservative whites, the Union troops were obstacles to recapturing their state governments and recreating the antebellum status quo; for African Americans, the troops were the guardians of their newly acquired civil and political liberties and their tenuous bond with scalawags and carpetbaggers. The bloody New Orleans street battles of the 1860s and 1870s demonstrated the futility of relying on the thinly spread Union troops against an opposition so intent on overthrowing the carpetbaggers and their allies. In battle after battle, the troops were called in after the fact and were unable to prevent the loss of life. Their main role was to return order to the city and to keep the Republican-supported state government in place.

Rey's séance circles and his registers reflect some of this chaotic political era. Initially, the tone of many spiritual messages was cautiously optimistic. But as the years went by, the tone changed to a begrudging acceptance of what Rey referred to as "the oligarchy" and a new lower status for the former free people of color, now facing a devastating leveling of their coveted antebellum status as a superior caste when compared to enslaved blacks, now freedpeople. The circle discussed social reform as something that would happen in the distant future, not as an impending remedy to societal problems. Historian Robert Cox characterized the spiritual communications received by the Rey circle as "more and more removed from daily life, and more and more restricted to heavenly, rather than earthly, concerns and compensations." Gone were the strident calls for immediate radical changes and the almost exhilarating visions of a utopian future where the races would be equal socially, economically, and in the eyes of the government. Safely ensconced in their homes, Rey's séance circles drew closer and more insulated from the ongoing political turmoil raging in the streets and in the halls of the state legislature.[6]

The topics discussed by the spirit messengers covered a wide range. Some communications gave political advice or apologized for lapses of moral judgment. Spirits frequently returned from the Great Beyond to give their living friends and relatives words of encouragement. "Don't fear the Future," "*En avant!*" (Keep going), "Continue your Route," and "The Banner of Light is flying" were just a few of the spirit aphorisms designed to inspire the black Creoles to doggedly pursue their reform agenda.

The Banner of Light was a recurring image and more than likely connected to the eponymous Boston periodical. François Dubuclet informed René Grandjean of the periodical and its contents, which by this time had ceased publication. A banner is symbolic of an allegiance to a particular belief or group. Similar to a flag, those who march behind the banner, whether literally or figuratively, are declaring their firm commitment to that belief or group represented by the banner. Light is symbolic of truth, purity, civilization, and justice. Putting together these symbolic meanings, the Banner of Light was an appropriate symbol for Rey's circle to rally behind.[7]

The Route was another recurring image in the Grandjean Registers and was symbolic of the long and arduous journey to obtain an elusive but highly valued goal. The Route is beset by Herculean obstacles and unforeseen, dangerous detours that would deter less determined individuals. The sympathetic spirit friends' role was to help realize the black Creoles' aspirations by encouraging them with slogans and advising them to stay focused on the prize as they traveled on the perilous Route. Vincent de Paule reminded the Cercle Harmonique to be firm and dedicated, because "as Spiritualists, your task is to surmount all of the obstacles that present themselves before you" on the Route.[8]

Other sympathetic spirit friends extolled Spiritualists as leaders of change and persons in the vanguard of an idyllic future society. Montesquieu, a French philosopher, defined a Spiritualist as a "philosopher who walks with the flame of Truth in his hands lighting the Route of humanity, the protection against errors! He is the Free-Thinker who has broken down the obstacles that block the Route. His feet touch the ground, but his thoughts open Heaven's Gates, and he shows his brother the luminescent Ladder that leads there."[9]

The Ladder of Progress/*L'Echelle de Progression* was another of the séance circle's reoccurring images. Life, according to Moni, was "a long rocking ladder on which you climb and fall at the moment you least expect it."[10] The imagery of a precarious ascent up an unwieldy ladder could also apply to the movement of society away from slavery and prejudice to a time of harmony between the races. Second-class citizenship rested at the bottom of the ladder, and an egalitarian society existed on the top rung. As the postbellum black population attempted to make the difficult transition, there was the distinct potential for failure. The black Creoles still clung to this goal, possibly believing northern rhetoric, which assured them of racial equality, and they pursued their quixotic quest of a progressive political and social agenda.

A third symbolic meaning of the ladder is the spiritual ascension to heaven, the continuum between the earthly world and the celestial world, between the living and the dead, between moral imperfections to the attainment of perfection. Helping the celestial ascent are the faithful spirits who serve as guides and remind the living and the recently deceased of the importance of humanitarian missions and charity. Included in one of Grandjean's Registers is a two-page image of The Ladder of Progress/L'Echelle de Progression, which depicts a deceased man on the floor with a medium seated nearby at a round table in what appears to be a trance state. The spirit of the man rises up the ladder as well as the spirit of a woman, while a Christ-like figure waits at the apex of the spiritual ladder. The drawing visualized A. J. Davis's philosophy of Harmonialism, which rested on the belief that the more spiritually advanced individual would later be rewarded by entering a more advanced sphere after death. Because the mortal world represented the lowest of these spheres, there was a spiritual continuum between the living and the dead. The artwork is unique within the Grandjean Collection, although there are a few other simple drawings within the pages of the registers.[11]

Other popular discussions included the status of women, diatribes against the Catholic Church, the mission of Spiritualism, the meaning of progress, and panegyrics for the fallen martyrs/heroes of the Battle of Port Hudson and the Mechanics' Institute Massacre. Most messages were not political. In fact, the vast majority of the communications were banal messages from the departed to living loved ones, assuring them that they had arrived at a better world and were no longer suffering from their illnesses. Such was the case of Henry (Henri) Broyard, who on February 28, 1875, belatedly appeared at the séance table three years after his death, explaining his absence and providing soothing words. The hereafter was represented as a halcyon existence. Broyard, who died on February 5, 1872, explained, "I have not manifested [myself] to others because you haven't looked for me. Here! I am happy.

There aren't any tears shed for me! The hours of torment have disappeared for me! You that I have loved, look for me!"[12]

Intense suffering from illness was common in an era without modern painkillers. Myrtile recounted in a communication how much he suffered from an illness: "Who am I? A young child who succumbed to a cruel sickness that made him suffer horribly. Now, we two [Myrtile and mother] are united, and we are gliding happily in space."[13]

Happy and fulfilling days in the hereafter were a common theme for other deceased Afro-Creoles. A decade after his death in Rome, Eugène Warbourg reached out to Rey and assured him of his joyful state, exclaiming, "I am happy, because I am working without stopping. Your world today seems like a nightmare. Henri, do you remember when my pencil one time drew your face? I have not lost my artistic genius."[14] Warbourg had been a famous sculptor in New Orleans who received commissions for busts of generals, magistrates, and other notables. He also accepted contracts from the clergy and sculpted masterpieces for New Orleans cemeteries. Warbourg departed for Europe in 1852 because of increasing racial hostility and a tightening of legal restrictions on the free people of color in Louisiana. Henry Rey and Eugène Warbourg must have been good friends as young men because the communication mentioned a portrait of Rey that Warbourg had drawn before Rey was twenty-two. What happened to the Warbourg drawing is a matter of conjuncture.[15]

Nelson Desbrosses, a friend and business associate of Barthélemy Rey, also reached out to the black Creole séance circle, describing the exciting and fulfilling existence that awaited them in the spiritual realm. He assuaged their trepidations to cross over the spiritual divide by assuring them that the afterworld was a better world and saying he would be waiting on the other side to welcome them.[16]

The living were ruefully reminded of the ephemeral nature of their bodies, which was an exterior that flattered but would one day wither away and disappear. The Spirit was the intellectual part of Being that never dies, and it enriches a new light forever after death. Moni directed the circle members not to be concerned about their physical body that ultimately perishes and disappears, but rather to be focused on the Spirit that lives eternally.[17]

By the early 1870s, the séance venues had shifted from neighborhood homes and Valmour's home/blacksmith shop to Henry Rey's home and Joseph Vignaud Lavigne's cigar shop at No. 162 Esplanade at the corner of Esplanade Avenue and St. Claude Street (now Henriette Delille Street) in Faubourg Tremé. According to René Grandjean, Lavigne's business was located "to the left going to City Park." It was here at the Lavigne shop that most of the séances took place. Joseph Lavigne and Henry Rey had been childhood friends, and their friendship had extended into adulthood. Lavigne taught at the Couvent School and had been mustered into Captain Henry Rey's First Regiment of the Native Guards (both Confederate and Union). Now, in their forties, the two men remained close friends as well as séance circle participants and members of the Economy Society.[18]

Cigar making was one of several occupations in which the free men of color excelled. Émigrés from Saint-Domingue may have learned the trade while living in Cuba before the secondary migration to New Orleans. Afro-Creoles worked in other of their traditional occupations as tailors, coopers, plasterers, shoemakers, masons, and furniture makers, and so on. In 1860, cigar makers numbered 171; by 1870, the number had increased to 397; and in 1880, there were 534 black cigar makers in the city. The large increase may be at least partially explained by stricter enforcement of licensing and taxing after the federal occupation of New Orleans. For many, the actual manufacturing of cigars was done at home. According to one tax collector, cigar makers would buy a few pounds of tobacco, roll cigars, and then sell the cigars "under the table," thereby avoiding the expense of a license and the monthly tax.[19]

The Louisiana Bureau of the Treasury was another venue for séances. The séance registers were stored in the office of François Dubuclet, who assisted his father, Antoine Dubuclet, the state treasurer. The younger Dubuclet acted as a curator of the registers. The French Quarter building on Royal Street, with its sturdy brick walls and vaulted ceilings over the main banking room, had originally been constructed for the Louisiana State Bank in 1820, the state's first purpose-built bank.[20] Rey even used one of the old bank's ledger books dating from 1822 for one of his séance registers. The spiritual communications began in 1871, making the ledger book almost fifty years old at the time of the séances, a fact proudly noted by Henry Rey.[21]

Many of the communications detailed a specific protocol for the conducting of séances. Punctuality was essential because latecomers "destroyed the already prepared harmony," and séances began promptly at either seven o'clock or eight o'clock in the evening, depending on the season. The change in hours was related to the need for darkness. As with the Davis liturgy, the séance room had to be darkened and quiet so that the participants could concentrate and so spirits would be more receptive to conversing with the living. At the appointed hour of the season, the doors were closed, and the previous séance's communications were read. After the readings, latecomers were admitted, and the doors once again were closed. The precise instructions were in essence rituals that produced a calm, harmonious atmosphere and reinforced group allegiance to the Cercle Harmonique.[22]

Details of the actual séance proceedings are scarce, despite the voluminous registers. François Dubuclet did make a special addendum to a Vincent de Paule message because of the manner in which the communication was written. On that particular night, there were nine participants, and after the communications from the previous séance were read, a butterfly extinguished the gas lamp. Despite the darkness, the medium quickly wrote the first paragraph, and then the lamp was relit. The medium asked the circle what to write next. Lucien Lavigne replied "Perseverance." The pencil flew across the page, pushed by supernatural forces. Another circle member, Maitre Prion, added "Victory," and still another said "Fidelity."[23]

In many spiritual communications, the medium was referred to as "the apostle giving the evangelic and angelic world." The medium acted as a conduit between the earthly world and the spiritual world, posing questions collected from the circle and then relaying the responses. Moni emphasized that such a procedure resulted in keeping the all-important harmony within the circle. Questions such as "Where were you born? In what year? When did you die? In what sphere do you belong?" were considered to be "foolishness" and "stupid questions" that slowed down the march toward progress. Rey admonished his circle to "never call any Spirit, for often he cannot come and another then, could take his name.... Have a great respect for Spirits; for you must be like them one day." The spirits who called themselves vigilant friends advised the séance participants to stay focused on matters that would ultimately lead to *l'amélioration spirituelle*, spiritual improvement.[24]

In an 1872 communication, the Swedish seer Swedenborg played homage to the medium's role, defining the medium as "the architect who gives plans.... The medium is the electric wire which transmits to Humanity the results of discoveries from the Spiritual Science.... He prepares the route of progression ... leading to the Temple of Truth and Happiness." Father Moni observed that the good medium abandons his body to the spirits and becomes "a machine that makes us [spirits] appear, without restriction." Thus, Henry Rey elevated his status as a gifted spiritual leader within his séance circle and within the black Creole community.[25]

Some black Creole mediums crossed the spiritual divide and became spirit messengers who echoed the Swedenborg depiction of the medium's role. Nelson Desbrosses praised the medium in his 1870 communication explaining that "the medium is the soldier of the army of Progress, like the Phoenix, is reborn from the ashes. The medium is the guardian of the Idea marching to the Objective. The medium is the avant-garde, the advanced sentinel of Progress; he is the light illuminating the route of Humanity." The medium played the crucial role at séances; however, a core of serious and devoted participants was also essential for a progressive and successful circle.[26]

Rey did not list the attendees at the séance circles, but the indexes, the use of French, Grandjean's margin notes, and the texts of the communications all indicate that those in attendance were generally men from the black Creole elite and to a lesser extent black Creole women. White guests were occasionally admitted to Rey's séances. Most of the registers included a list called an Index in the front of the register with names of the spirit messengers alphabetized and the page numbers on which their communications appeared. Occasionally, François Dubuclet informed René Grandjean who the guest participants were, and Grandjean noted the information.

Adolphe Duhart and George Herriman Jr. were mentioned as guest participants. Duhart, like Henry Rey, was of Saint-Domingue descent. He began his professional life as a mason but found his true vocation in teaching and writing. Like so many of Rey's friends and participants in his Cercle Harmonique, Duhart taught at the Couvent School and acted as principal upon the death of Joanni Questy in 1869. As historian Caryn Cossé Bell notes, "In accordance with their belief in individual perfectibility, Spiritualists advocated education and education reform as an accompaniment to religious regeneration. Not coincidentally, Rey's circle of black Creole Spiritualists included prominent members of the Couvent School's teaching staff."[27]

Duhart is also known as an author of short stories and, additionally, penned articles for the *New Orleans Tribune*. Because Adolphe Duhart's sister, Adeline, married Hippolyte Rey, Henry Rey and Duhart were indirectly connected by marriage.[28] Some of Henry Rey's séances in the late 1850s took place at the Duhart home. George Herriman Jr. was a neighbor of Rey's on Villere Street. The elder George Herriman and his half-brother, Alexander Laurent Chessé, ran a tailor shop on Royal Street in the French Quarter, his occupation and residence being similar to Barthélemy Rey's in the 1830s.[29]

François "Petit" Dubuclet explained the composition of Rey's circles as being two circles with different regular members that met on two different days of the week. Interestingly, Rey's regular séance participants were all males, the opposite of northern circles, which advocated an equal number of men and women around the séance table for the purposes of the all-important element of harmony. Even Joseph Barthet's French/Anglo-American circle of the mid-1850s included an equal number of women.[30]

On Mondays, the circle included Joseph Alexi, a cooper; Romain (no other name given); Donatien Déruisé, a shoemaker; Emilien Planchard; Joseph Lavigne, Rey's close friend from the Couvent School and the Native Guards; François Dubuclet, who sometimes acted as a medium; and Rey himself. On Fridays, the circle included Jules Mallet; Emile Luscy; Maitre Prion; Nelson Desbrosses, the famed poet and teacher at the Couvent School; Lucien Lavigne, a Cuban; and Dubuclet and Rey. The regular members numbered seven, an important number for preserving the harmony within the circle. Neither the spiritual communications nor the margin notes explain why seven was important for harmony, but for centuries going back to ancient Egypt, the number seven has symbolized a connection to the cosmos and eternal life. In the nineteenth century, there were seven known planets, and cosmos cartographers often drew seven concentric spheres representing different stages of progressive perfection within the spiritual world. The actual number at the séance was likely to be greater than seven because of invited guests. Only the serious were admitted, the curious and the disbelievers being likely to upset the harmony needed for communing with the departed. The role of the circle participants was similar to that of the medium. Père Antoine depicted them as "vigilant sentinels, reliable guardians, devoted brothers who defend the entrance to the Temple of Spirits."[31]

Regular members who attended once or twice a week strengthened the cohesiveness of the Cercle Harmonique. This helped to cement the participants' sense of belonging. Such practices were similar to weekly church attendance. The fellowship engendered by common goals and séance rituals provided a harmonic environment in which Rey could progress in his spiritual development and promote rapport with the cosmos, ultimately benefiting his circle in their spiritual development.

The spirit messengers were more racially diverse than the séance members. Political figures, martyrs/heroes of the black Creole world, French Romantic writers, philosophers from the Enlightenment, deceased Creole friends and mediums, Catholic Church leaders who adhered to the Latin-European traditions, relatives, white friends, and former business contacts, plus a few Native American spirit guides such as Pocahontas, descended from the spiritual world to the séance table. The sympathetic and diverse spirits shared a common obligation to assist the living with their earthly lives and spiritual development.

When gender is considered for the spirit messengers, the difference between the sexes was sizable and significant. Men dominated the Creole spirit world; women spirits were relegated to an inferior role, similar to what was actually experienced in mid-nineteenth-century life. Using three indexes, I have calculated the percentages of female and male messengers in each register.

Register 85-31	July 5, 1865–July 6, 1870	Women 15%	Men 85%
Register 85-46	Oct. 17, 1872–Nov. 5, 1872	Women 14%	Men 86%
Register 85-53	Dec. 20, 1873–Mar. 16, 1874	Women 28%	Men 72%

More noteworthy than the paucity of female spirit visitors is their backgrounds and connections to the séance circle members and guests. Most female spirit friends were departed black Creole relatives—sisters, mothers, aunts, wives, and grandmothers. Only a few were women who had some other connections with the séance circle such as Madame Justine Couvent, the benefactress of the Couvent School; Virginie Girodeau, an actress; and Soeur Louise, a black Creole medium. The lack of female spirits reflects the Afro-Creole world, in which women were primarily viewed for their value as mothers and wives.[32]

Soeur Louise was the only female black Creole medium Rey mentioned in his séance registers when in 1858 Rey participated in his neighbors' séances as part of his early forays into Spiritualism. François Dubuclet admiringly characterized Soeur Louise as "an apostle with black skin but the soul of a diamond. Her entire life was devoted to healing without charge and producing good advice to those in need." It is not exactly clear who Soeur Louise was because no last name was ever given, and "Louise" was a very common first name of the era. She first appeared as a spirit messenger in July 1870, which means that by this time Soeur Louise had crossed the spiritual divide. In her maiden communication, Soeur Louise explained, as many other spirits had done, that she "had left earth after cruel physical suffering." In a positive light, the good sister assured the circle participants that she had received the immortal crown, and they would receive their crowns upon departing from the earthly realm.[33]

François Dubuclet mentioned other female mediums in the margin notes in the Grandjean Registers. Typically, they were northern traveling mediums such as Emma Hardinge Britten and Mrs. Rice. Britten had passed through New Orleans in December 1859, and Rice was in New Orleans in early 1872. Although it can be concluded that women played only a small leadership role in black Creole séance circles, the value of women as mediums was more recognized in the North.[34]

Henry Rey's Cercle Harmonique valued women as members of black Creole society, albeit in a diminished capacity. The spirit of a French Enlightenment luminary, Jean-Jacques Rousseau, lamented the role of women in the nineteenth-century, observing that, "For many men, a woman is a pastime, a piece of furniture, a beautiful jewel that they love to show off. Often she is a Doll with which they adorn themselves; but alas, too often, she [evolves into] a servant, a scapegoat, a neglected plaything." Sister Louise in her living role as a medium communed with a departed Creole and declared marriage to be either "the peace, the good luck or the pain, the trouble and disorder." In order for a marriage to be successful, the spirits advised men to develop "an immense respect for their wives who have confided in you their future."[35]

A rare female spirit who was not a black Creole relative or an educator—Marie de Rabutin-Chantal, Marquise de Sévigné—directed the circle to respect women's rights. Sévigné recognized the subordinate position of women within nineteenth-century society but predicted with great foresight that "the woman will have her rights, and man will be amazed at his errors engendered by pride. He will understand morality" and then correct his past mistakes.[36]

Sometimes the female spirits, unlike the male counterparts, would act as if in a chorus; one spirit would communicate a short sentence, and then another would pick up the theme and issue a brief communication only to be quickly joined by more female spirits. Such was the case with an 1874 communication from a trio of Jeanne Dastugue; Assitha, a relative of Assitha Grandjean; and Claire Pollard, mother of François Dubuclet. Often five or more spirits are listed as spirit messengers at the end of a communication, as if the message gained importance when multiple spirits acted in unison.[37]

The Grandjean Registers offer another intriguing clue to the position of women within the Spiritualist community and the Afro-Creole society. The consistent use of the word *frères* (brothers) in the spiritual communications when addressing the séance table participants acknowledged male dominance within the circle and also verbally conceptualized a universal brotherhood among the participants. Possibly the Cercle Harmonique was echoing Andrew Jackson Davis's Harmonial philosophy, which envisioned men and women united in one common brotherhood in the pursuit of societal advancement and placed Spiritualism outside the realm of mainstream Christianity.[38]

The Grandjean Registers provide a rare window into the status of the black Creole woman. For Afro-Creole women in the 1870s, New Orleans society was a patriarchal world that eschewed the value of women in leadership roles and rigidly circumscribed women into the roles of devoted mothers and wives. However, messages from the spiritual world occasionally communicated modern themes and envisioned a society more like the early twenty-first than the mid-nineteenth century. In regards to equality for women, a careful reading of the Grandjean Registers reveals some surprisingly accurate prophecies and radical missives that would be fulfilled a century later.

Henry Rey's circle was a fusion of séance Spiritualism from the North, Afro-Creole radicalism from the Caribbean and France, A. J. Davis's Harmonial philosophy engendered in the Burned-over District, and Latin-European Catholicism developed in New Orleans during the eighteenth and nineteenth centuries. The intersection of these philosophies and religions from various points in the world created a unique séance circle in the French faubourgs of New Orleans with its own protocols, venues, hallmarks, and progressive social and political agendas. Communications and messengers from the spiritual world reveal the widening ideological chasm between the Americanized version of the Catholic Church and that of a bygone era which had previously supported a fluid tripartite order of races, an era that respected and valued the lives of the Afro-Creoles, an era that no longer existed except in the minds and souls of the former elite free people of color. Deceased Catholic figures descended from the spiritual realm to console and advise the black Creole intelligentsia who gathered weekly at the séance table. The popularity of spirit messengers such as Vincent de Paule and Père Antoine indicated the deep and profound attachment that the black Creole elite still held for the Catholic Church, despite its support of a polarizing American racial order. Paradoxically, other messengers issued stinging criticisms of the Catholic Church.

A. J. Davis's Harmonial philosophy provided the atmosphere and set the precise protocol for Henry Rey's séance circles. Harmony was considered to be the essential ingredient when communing with the dead, and Rey admonished his circle to conform to strict codes of punctuality, procedures, and appropriate séance behavior. The harmony within the circle was necessary to duplicate the harmony of the cosmos and to facilitate communing with the dead.

Afro-Creole radicalism, with its Saint-Domingue and French roots, abetted the former free men of color as they attempted to transform the antebellum order into a new egalitarian postbellum order. Many of the circle members and guest participants were of Saint-Domingue ancestry and fiercely clung to the noble French Revolution's traditions of liberty, equality, and brotherhood. It is noteworthy that many of the spirit messengers were philosophical figures from the Enlightenment and many others were French Romantic writers. Rey's black Creole séance circles set their moral compass with French ideals to navigate the ever-shifting cultural and political currents.

The French language had been on a slow but steady decline for decades by the 1830s. But according to historian Paul Lachance, that decade marked the linguistic turning point for New Orleans as a huge influx of Irish and German immigrants overwhelmed the Gallic population. Lachance further states that "in the last two years of the decade, creoles and the foreign French together made up only one-third of the white Catholic spouses in the city and by 1840 they may have slipped to less than one-fourth of the total white population, including Protestants as well as Catholics." In the last two antebellum decades and the first two postbellum decades, the decline of French accelerated, once again because of the heavy influx of immigrants but also as a result of Americans migrating from other sections of the country and an ever-burgeoning number of Anglo blacks flooding the city, especially after the Civil War. Newspapers transitioned to English as the dominant language. *L'Union* began in 1862 as a French-language newspaper published for the free people of color. Its successor, the *Tribune/La Tribune*, began in 1864 and was bilingual. Legal documents increasingly were written in English. Fatima Shaik notes that the minutes of the Economy Society were initially kept in French, but that from the 1870s onward various English words were inserted into the minutes and the organization's constitution was translated into English in 1874.[39]

The francophone black community found support from the Catholic Church in its now-dying effort to preserve French as a viable language in New Orleans. The Catholic Church continued to conduct services in French, even though the congregations were mostly English-speaking. Despite opposition from the growing number of English-speaking clergy, francophone priests considered New Orleans to be "*une annexe*" of France and refused to speak anything but French to their English-speaking congregations. This coalition of French clergy would remain firmly entrenched in the New Orleans church hierarchy until after World War I.[40]

Even though Rey and his circle members were fluent in English, most of the spiritual messages were written in French. Henry Louis Rey exuded the air of a French Romantic writer as he penned countless spiritual communications in superbly crafted writing. It was a type of marriage: writer and medium bonded together to produce the beautiful prose that bespoke of the cosmos and a celestial existence without pain and sorrow.

Henry Rey's world was part of the Atlantic francophone world—a world that celebrated the accomplishments of the republican upheavals of the French Revolution of 1848 and relished its ancestral roots and familial ties to Haiti and France. It was a world that was fast fading away from the collective memory of the African American population in New Orleans but was nevertheless still the focus of the black Creole elite during the 1860s and 1870s.

The French Romantic literary movement of the 1830s captured the imagination of the Creole intelligentsia, which then created its own unique black Creole literature, starting with a short-lived literary journal, *L'Album litteraire*, in 1843 and culminating two years later in the seminal anthology of poems, *Les Cenelles*, edited by Armand Lanusse. Romanticism's use of literary art to attack injustice held enormous appeal during the decades of increasing oppression prior to the Civil War. Romanticism continued to be a strong literary force and heavily influenced Henry Rey's Spiritualist circles and its written communications.[41]

The medium had a dual role: first, to convey messages from the departed, and second, to be a poet guiding his brothers with his visionary powers to a better earthly world and celestial happiness in the spiritual world. As the spirit of Nelson Desbrosses explained, "The medium is the soldier of Progress ... which like the Phoenix, will be reborn from the ashes.... The medium is the avant-garde, the sentinel to advance Progress; he is the light showing the route of humanity."[42]

French Romanticism found a powerful expression in the writings of Henry Louis Rey and other black Creole writers who rallied to the cause of liberty, equality, and fraternity. Spiritualism was one of several literary forms to convey their belief in universal brotherhood and republicanism. As northern mediums exerted their influence upon the Spiritualist community in New Orleans, this political activism continued, but the circles were pulled more into the national orbit.

The French Creole séance circles followed the national leadership of celebrated mediums from the North such as Emma Hardinge, Thomas Lake Harris, and the *Banner of Light* editors. These traveling emissaries of Modern American Spiritualism provided the spark, enthusiasm, support, and framework for séance Spiritualism among the French Creoles, who molded northern Spiritualism to fit their linguistic and cultural ethos.

Engaging and dealing with seismic societal changes, Henry Rey and his circle relied on religious and philosophical leaders as spiritual messengers who upheld their cherished visions of a society without prejudice. But the visions and the reality were two different things. The Fourteenth and Fifteenth Amendments, which were designed to make African Americans the equals of white Americans, were being systematically dismantled during the mid-1870s. It was just a matter of time before Reconstruction was officially over and a new postbellum order directed by the Redeemers assumed control of Louisiana.

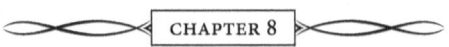

Transitions

Henry Louis Rey continued his civic duties, and judging from the increased number of spirit communications during the early 1870s, the séance circle moved at a quick pace. In 1873 Rey was appointed for a two-year term as a director (school board member) of the revamped interracial Orleans Parish School Board, which resulted in the integrated school system that he had so diligently worked to establish during his tenure as a state representative, despite the duplicity of Governor Henry Clay Warmoth and the conservative Democrats. The New Orleans public schools became integrated in 1870. Initially, Afro-Creole children enrolled in the previously all-white schools, but soon the sons and daughters of former slaves enrolled as well. By the end of the year, almost a third of the city's schools had desegregated, and the school system was regarded by the national press as an example of racial progress and harmony. An examination of the Orleans Parish School Board minutes reveals a dedicated director who seldom missed meetings and volunteered on visiting school committees as well as standing committees such as School Supply Purchases and New Schools. The visiting school committees were committees of three who visited schools within a district and reported back at the school board meeting about the conditions of the schools. It was on a revolving schedule, and each month the district and composition of the committee changed. According to Donald DeVore and Joseph Logsdon in *Crescent City Schools* (1991), good management and substantial new funding helped the public schools prosper until 1877, when the Orleans School Board replaced Rey and most of the directors.[1]

Prominent moderate white southerners, including General James Longstreet, occupied most of the twenty school board positions as directors.

Longstreet was originally from Georgia. But he moved to New Orleans like many other Confederate officers who were attracted to a major southern city that had escaped the widespread destruction of the war. Whereas other Confederate generals like John Bell Hood and Jubal Early actively kept the spirit of the Lost Cause alive in the Crescent City, James Longstreet recognized the political reality of the new postbellum social order and regarded any attempt to replace slavery with second-class citizenship for African Americans as a flawed and doomed policy. Longstreet's surprising metamorphosis from Confederate General to Republican leader sent hard-line southern conservatives into a state of apoplexy, but nevertheless he remained firmly entrenched within the new Republican majority. The politically astute Longstreet adroitly climbed up the ladder of success in his adopted city, using connections with his old West Point classmate, President Ulysses S. Grant. The generals were indirectly related by marriage through Longstreet's cousin, Julia Dent, who was Grant's wife. The generals had been Civil War adversaries and met in combat at the Battle of the Wilderness (May 5–7, 1864); but now that the war was over, friendship and family trumped the Civil War sectional divide.[2]

After being turned down by President Andrew Johnson for a presidential pardon, Longstreet easily obtained one from President Grant in 1869 and was appointed deputy customs collector at the US Custom House in New Orleans. General Longstreet received another political plum when Governor Warmoth appointed him commander of the new Louisiana State Militia, an organization designed to strengthen the governor's shaky political base. The Louisiana State Militia continued to maintain a tenuous hold of the carpetbaggers on the embattled state government during the tenure of the next governor, Governor William Pitt Kellogg.[3]

James Longstreet, like Henry Rey, was a dedicated school board director and attended the monthly meetings on a regular basis. He and Rey were frequently on the same school visiting committee and on some of the same standing committees as well. Longstreet's alliance to the Afro-Creole progressive agenda was more than a matter of simple political expediency as evidenced by a careful reading of the Orleans Parish School Board minutes.[4]

Charles W. Boothby, a carpetbagger from the small town of Saco, Maine, was the superintendent of the interracial Orleans Parish Schools (Sixth District in Louisiana). Boothby had been a private in the Twelfth Regiment, Maine, and was stationed in New Orleans (1862–1864). He later obtained the rank of lieutenant and then captain, commanding Company D of the First Louisiana Regiment, New Orleans Infantry. Boothby remained in the South after the war because of potential business opportunities in New Orleans and also to avoid the brutal Maine winters. He worked as the assistant assessor of internal revenue of the First District of Louisiana and then in 1871 was appointed to membership on the school board while still working at the federal Custom House with James Casey, President Grant's brother-in-law. In April 1873, Charles Boothby was appointed superintendent of Orleans Parish schools. Boothby's conservative Democratic critics begrudgingly commended him for a well-run school system. Boothby had come from New England, an area of the country that historically valued education, and he himself was a product of excellent free public schools.[5]

A special type of camaraderie must have prevailed among the twenty board directors. Most had participated in the Civil War—some on the side of the South, some on the Union side, and some, like Henry Rey, participated on both sides. Despite the sectional and racial divides, the Orleans Parish School Board appeared to work in harmony for the most part, and the board's directors shared common educational goals.

Superintendent Boothby's office was located in room 20 in the New Orleans City Hall (now Gallier Hall), across from Lafayette Square. Each workday, Boothby would arrive at City Hall, climb the imposing eighteen blue Quincy-granite steps, walk past the ten Ionic columns, and enter into a long marble-floored hallway. He would make his way to his private office in the rear and work through the day on reports, budgets, letters to principals, and occasionally a personal letter to his family in Maine.[6]

On a warm Monday afternoon, Boothby was in his office quietly writing a long-overdue letter to his family. The opened office window allowed the muffled street noises of St. Charles Avenue and nearby Lafayette Square to enter his office. He could hear the familiar and soothing sounds of the cadenced clanging of the St. Charles streetcar bells, the clip-clop of horses, and the gentle grind of carriage wheels over the granite block street. The shouts and laughter of noisy school children playing in the square during their lunch hour dissolved to a few hours of welcomed afternoon silence. But the afternoon's calm of September 14 would be punctuated by the disconcerting sound of an unruly street mob about to stage a coup d'état. A legion of enraged White Leaguers brandishing outdated Civil War muskets, pistols, and swords abruptly stormed into Boothby's office and brusquely ordered him to leave. Shaken by the unexpected entry of the insurgents, Superintendent Boothby boldly asked by what right they had to take over his office. "We are the government!," snarled the angry men in unison. The takeover of New Orleans City Hall was just the first step in a long day of death, destruction, and mayhem.[7]

In his letter of September 25, 1874, Boothby recounted that there were three thousand men in New Orleans with muskets and many more with pistols. At four o'clock in the afternoon, he and two friends strolled to Canal Street from City Hall, thinking that there would be no further armed conflict. There he witnessed the legendary street battle of Liberty Place at the end of Canal Street by the Mississippi River. The White Leaguers staged a coup to end the rule of the despised carpetbaggers, to reestablish their control over state government, and to retrieve shiploads of guns that they had ordered but which had been commandeered by the state government.[8]

The New Orleans chapter of the White League was an urban extension of the newly formed rural organization. By the end of 1873, the protracted struggle over civil rights for African Americans was basically over, particularly in rural Louisiana.[9] White opposition had taken a tragic, violent turn with the formation of the White League, a paramilitary organization similar to the Ku Klux Klan. In April 1874, the first chapter of the White League appeared in Opelousas (St. Landry Parish), and the chapters spread like wildfire throughout rural Louisiana.

Two months later a chapter was founded in New Orleans with former Confederate General Frederick Nash Ogden as its president. The White League's chief target was the carpetbagger governor, William Pitt Kellogg. With four thousand federal troops still stationed in New Orleans, it was not going to be an easy task to employ the same scare tactics used so successfully in the countryside. Nevertheless, events culminated in another historic, bloody New Orleans street battle.

The main impediment to further White League victories was the lack of modern weaponry. To solve this problem, a huge shipment of modern rifles was ordered, and on Saturday, September 12, 1874, three shipments of guns destined for the White League arrived on the steamboat *Mississippi*. It was Governor Kellogg's worst nightmare. The leader of the state militia, General James Longstreet, decided to take a stand against the White League and together with Algernon Sydney Badger, the superintendent of the mostly black Metropolitan Police, set up a position barring the way to the waterfront on Canal Street. Earlier in the week, incendiary local newspaper articles railed against what the editors perceived to be an infringement on one of their most basic constitutional rights: the right to bear arms.[10]

On Monday morning at eleven o'clock, a hastily arranged meeting at the Henry Clay Statue on Canal Street brought a hysterical call to arms for the men who attended the meeting. Makeshift barricades were erected at intersections reminiscent of a Parisian street battle, but with the distinctive New

Orleanian touch of turned-over streetcars. At four o'clock, the two opposing sides clashed at the US Custom House near the steamboat *Mississippi*, where the shipment of guns was still stored. In the opening salvos, the Kellogg forces had the distinct advantage of modern weaponry.

The rapid firing of a Gatling gun and the loud discharge of Remington rifles echoing against the downtown buildings startled the White Leaguers. However, eagle-eyed White League snipers stationed in the windows of nearby buildings managed to pick off many of the artillerists. A crowning blow came when both General Longstreet and Superintendent Badger were wounded in the midst of the street battle. Algernon Badger sustained severe wounds to his hand, arm, and leg. Surgeons amputated his leg, and for the rest of his life he used a prosthetic limb.[11]

At this point, it was a rout, and the Kellogg forces beat a hasty retreat. Octave Rey, a captain in the Metropolitans, was stationed on the Chartres Street side of the US Custom House, and as the rout commenced, his force collided with the White Leaguers. Eventually, most of the demoralized Kellogg forces fled into the Custom House with the governor, anticipating correctly that the street mob would not dare trespass on federal property. Safely ensconced, Governor Kellogg telegraphed President Grant, pleading for federal troops to restore order.[12]

Emboldened by their unexpected successes, the frenzied mob fanned out into the French Quarter. This time their objective was the state capitol, then housed in the old Saint Louis Hotel.[13] According to Superintendent Boothby, "the building could not be defended against the men. The insurgents could have set the building on fire, and were preparing to do so." The state officers abandoned the state capitol with the exception of one person who handed over the keys to the insurgents the next morning at 2:00 a.m. Federal troops entered the city two days later, and order was restored.[14]

The death toll for the Battle of Liberty Place was eleven for the combined forces of the Metropolitans and the militia; the Ogden forces lost twenty-one men. The US Army quickly quelled the coup, and Governor Kellogg resumed his duties as governor the following day. But the street battle graphically displayed how fragile the carpetbag government was and how dependent it was upon the military might of the federal government. The Republican Party in Louisiana knew that its days were numbered, and the Creoles of color were even more apprehensive about their bleak futures.

Unfulfilled promises, crushed hopes, and failed laws lay in the wake of the catastrophe, turning New Orleans into the city of broken dreams. The spiritual communications reflected the ongoing political turmoil: "For Rey's circle the frustrations of repeated political failures and the exposure to recurrent violence showed in changes in the style and content of the messages they received from their departed friends, revealing a reluctant, and forced accommodation to the new social order."[15]

Rey's Cercle Harmonique received a flurry of spiritual communications on the night of the battle and in the weeks following the debacle. The spirits advised the mortals on September 14 not to dwell on their sorrows and vanquished dreams of equality because the "pitiful Despots will lower their heads and kneel before you." Those who suffered at the hands of the despots had the satisfaction of knowing that they would receive the "crown of Martyrs with patience and resignation, without hate." Valmour and other spirits praised the Cercle Harmonique for marching proudly toward a brilliant star.[16]

Still, some spirit messages remained guardedly optimistic. Vincent de Paule lamented the loss of life in the Battle of Liberty Place: "The blood spent yesterday shows how much hate there is in the hearts of men looking to subjugate their Brothers! ... You will see Civil Rights proclaimed and they will be maintained. Fear nothing! You will see a rainbow of Peace.... Don't worry about Political troubles that are going on now, stay firm in your liberal opinions and march with the National Party."[17]

The Battle of Liberty Place had its martyrs, and the apparitions appeared at the séance table detailing their last moments: "Some victims have fallen recently under murderous balls and they have come to you and others.... Monatte lying on a bed of pain was the martyr of an acute pain, he cried out for Deliverance from his body."[18]

The reverberations of the attempted coup continued long past September. In December 1874, three days of school riots occurred in the racially mixed schools of New Orleans. High school boys coached by White Leaguers ejected students whom they determined to be "colored." Some of those ejected were in reality white, and some students not ejected were light-skinned African Americans. Teachers were insulted, and Superintendent Charles Boothby was threatened with hanging. Despite the turmoil, schools reopened after the Christmas holidays.[19]

Valmour cautioned the séance circle against retaliation: "Resist with force the temptation to retaliate; and with courage, march in the path of Good! You are in your body, but this isn't a reason to believe that you can't control your passions.... With good luck you will be the victors in the struggle against evil.[20]

After the initial flurry of spiritual communications in the aftermath of Liberty Place, the Rey circle began to disband. The Grandjean notes indicate that the Battle of Liberty Place made séance participants wary of meeting. The right of assembly was hindered by the fear that White Leaguers might persecute the black Creoles for meeting for séances. So for reasons of prudence, the number of séances was greatly reduced after 1874, and they were stopped completely a few years later.[21]

The worst economic and psychological setback for Henry Rey came on December 3, 1875, when his Villere Street home was destroyed by fire. The Grandjean séance notes indicate that the fire started around Claiborne Avenue and moved toward St. Claude, aided by a strong north wind. The *Robinson's Atlas of the City of New Orleans* (1883), which was used for insurance purposes, shows eight adjoining vacant lots on the block where Rey's house was located and vacant lots in the neighboring two blocks, all indicating that there was a fire just as François Dubuclet described. Rey's magnificent house burned down, and he was only able to salvage a few of his possessions. Unfortunately, Rey had let the insurance lapse just two days prior to the fire. The Reys returned to their smaller home at 95 Columbus Street—the home that the Reys had lived in prior to his appointment as the Third District tax assessor.[22]

The end of New Orleans's largely successful six-year experiment with integrated schools coincided with the end of Reconstruction. In March 1877, Rutherford B. Hayes was inaugurated as president after a hotly disputed election, and in April he withdrew federal troops from Louisiana as part of the infamous Compromise of 1877. A panel named the Special Congressional Committee had settled the disputed election by giving to Hayes all of the contested nineteen electoral votes from Louisiana, Mississippi, and South Carolina plus one from Oregon to Hayes, who thereby won the election by one electoral vote, even though the Democrat, Samuel Tilden, had won the popular vote by three hundred thousand votes. In return for Democratic acceptance of the dubious electoral results, Hayes and the Republican Party abandoned the South. The Republicans no longer needed the support of the South to control the White House, and the North had become weary of supporting carpetbag governments with federal troops.

At the local level, the month of April 1877 was a pivotal one for Henry Rey and the African American community. The entire Orleans Parish School Board disbanded and was replaced with a new, conservative board. State Superintendent of Education William Brown was replaced with the rabid segregationist Robert M. Lusher. There is no indication from the last meeting's minutes on February 7, 1877, that the board would be terminated. (These minutes were never recorded in the official journals, but were published in the local newspapers.) Sometime between March 7 and April 4, 1877, the new school board took over and gained possession of the journal in which the minutes were written. Henry Rey was ousted as a director of the Orleans Parish School Board.[23]

After the Compromise of 1877, the black Creoles in New Orleans no longer held any significant political power, and their economic power had been seriously eroded as well. Ironically, the incoming flux of Anglo-blacks had in some ways hurt their social and legal status. Now, black Creoles were competing with freedmen for scarce jobs that the former slaves had previously been unable to obtain. There was racial amalgamation: Creoles of color—even light-skinned, well-educated black Creoles from the elite families—were considered to be of the same social and political status as former slaves.

The advantages that the black Creoles held at the beginning of Reconstruction vanished. No longer were they the only literate and politically ambitious African Americans, and no longer were Gallic connections impressive assets. The triple whammy of the national recession of 1873, the pitched bloody street battles in New Orleans, and the return of former Confederates to power along with a new generation of young aspiring white men combined to squash the tenuous political power of the once proud and prominent black Creoles.

Henry Louis Rey was part of the second generation of the Saint-Domingue immigration. As a child and as a young man, he had lived in a close-knit community that tenaciously clung to its French Caribbean roots by the interaction of family relations, benevolent associations, Masonic connections, the Couvent School, social exchanges, the *New Orleans Tribune*, the Native Guards, and the French language. Thus, the Saint-Domingue diaspora of the free people of color was able to thrive and transform the cultural and political landscape of New Orleans during the first half of the nineteenth century. The Civil War and its aftermath diminished the diaspora's social standing in New Orleans and Louisiana. Henry Rey and other black Creoles had to adjust to the total reorientation of their society and the new postbellum normal.

The following pages display an index typical of those in the Grandjean Registers. This index is taken from Grandjean Register 85-34, which covered the period from July 4, 1871, until December 11, 1871. The indexes are extremely valuable tools of research into the black Creole community. Not only are the names of the spiritual messengers listed with the page numbers where the communications can be located, but also René Grandjean often

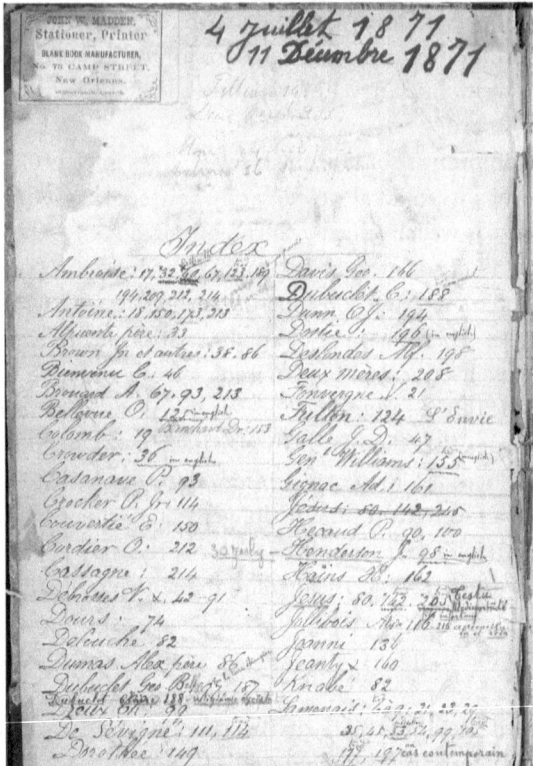

Page one of an Index from Grandjean Register 85-34. Grandjean Collection. *Courtesy of Special Collections, Earl K. Long Library, University of New Orleans.*

added helpful notes to explain who the messengers were and sometimes included information about the contents of the messages. The spirits were often relatives such as Pierre Crocker, Adèle Gignac, and Claire Pollard Dubuclet; French luminaries such as Lamennais; revered French Catholic clergy like Pères Antoine and Ambroise; martyr/heroes like Dr. Dostie, John Brown, and John Henderson; former mediums gone to the afterlife like Nelson Desbrosses; or Anglo-blacks such as Lieutenant Governor O. J. Dunn. The indexes were usually in the front of the registers, and not in the back.

On April 24, 1877, Reconstruction officially ended in Louisiana when the federal government withdrew its troops.[24] At this point, the Republicans and the nation abandoned the carpetbagger governments as well as their roles as guardians of African American civil rights. The nation had entered

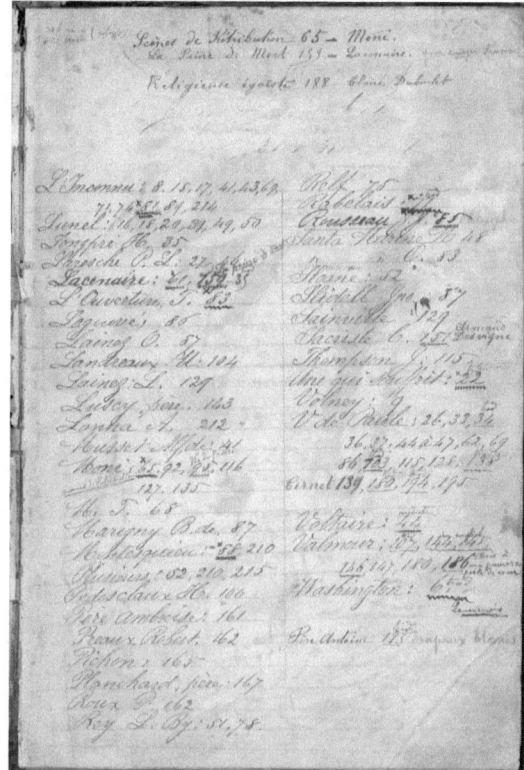

Page two of an Index from Grandjean Register 85-34. Grandjean Collection. *Courtesy of Special Collections, Earl K. Long Library, University of New Orleans.*

the Gilded Age, and there were higher priorities—namely, making lots of money and settling the Wild West. The Civil War had been over for twelve years, and for a new generation it was time to move past old rivalries and sectional divisions that no longer seemed relevant. Gone from the halls of Congress were the Radical Republican firebrands, Charles Sumner and Thaddeus Stevens, and there were certainly no replacements forthcoming.

The exit of federal troops heralded the arrival of a new political era in Louisiana. The Redeemers, also known as the Bourbons,[25] now controlled the state government and easily deposed the Republican governor, Stephen Packard, and his African American lieutenant governor, C. C. Antoine. Taking their places were a former Confederate brigadier general, Francis T. Nicholls, and a former mayor of New Orleans, Louis Alfred Wiltz. Nicholls had lost his left arm at Winchester and his left foot at the Battle of Chancellorsville.

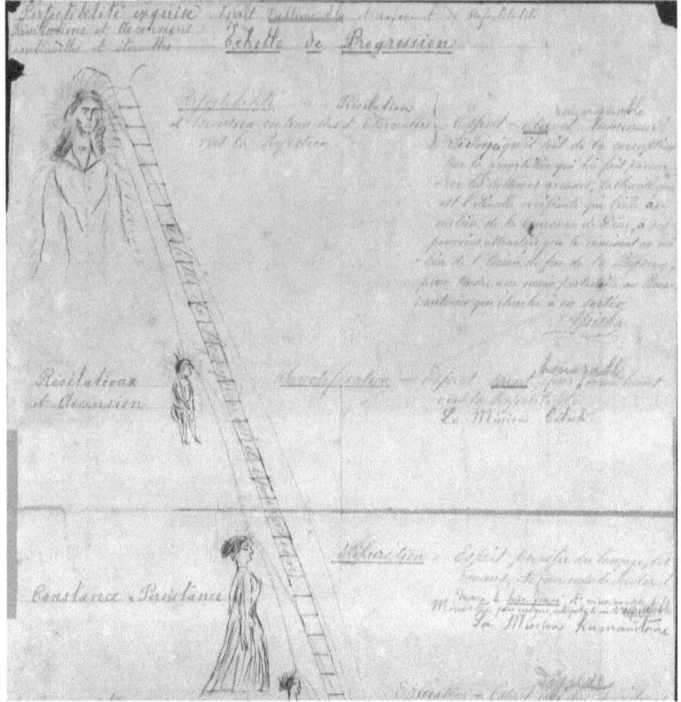

Echelle de Progression/Ladder of Progress from Grandjean Register 85-40, pullout page. Henry Rey's Cercle Harmonique believed that individuals ascended a ladder of progress to obtain perfection. The darker writing is that of of René Grandjean, who wrote copious margin notes, and the other handwriting is that of Henry Rey. The spirit Assitha was Grandjean's deceased mother-in-law. There were just a few drawings in the voluminous registers. Grandjean Collection. *Courtesy of Special Collections, Earl K. Long Library, University of New Orleans.*

When he was nominated for governor, the delegate proudly proclaimed, "I nominate what is left of Francis Tillou Nicholls."[26]

Similar to the antebellum state government, the Redeemers were dominated by an alliance of large planters from rural Louisiana and wealthy businessmen from New Orleans. The spirits that Henry Rey had channeled in his séances referred to them as the "oligarchy." The Redeemers proceeded to dismantle the hated Reconstruction government by reducing rural blacks to a state of neoslavery and excluding most blacks from political power. Property taxes were slashed and state budgets plummeted, thereby severely reducing basic state services and drastically cutting aid to public education. The cuts for public education affected not only African Americans, but the poor and middle-class whites as well. In fact, Louisiana became the only state in the

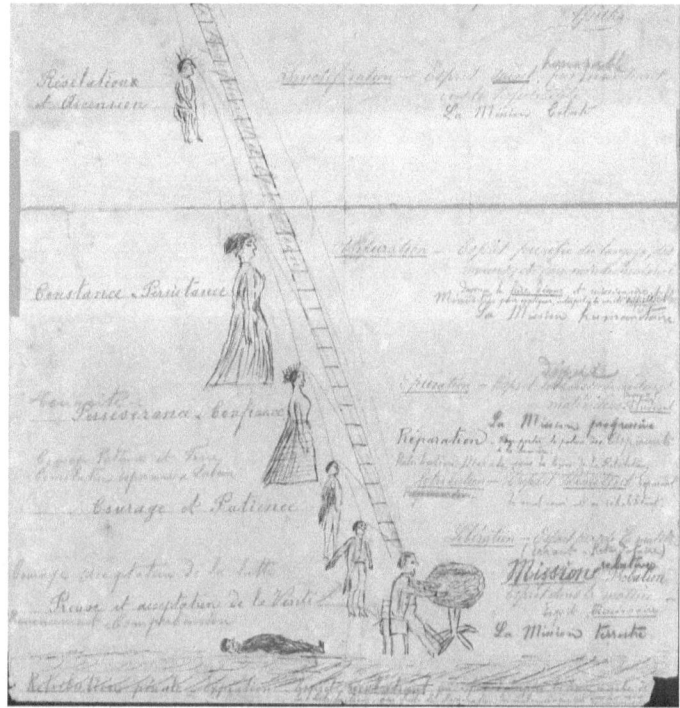

Part II – Echelle de Progression/Ladder of Progress from Grandjean Register 85-40, pullout page. Grandjean Collection. *Courtesy of Special Collections, Earl K. Long Library, University of New Orleans.*

Union in which the percentage of illiterate whites actually rose between 1880 and 1900.[27] The ouster of the carpetbagger government gave Louisiana the dubious distinction of the state with the highest rate of illiteracy and poverty. The restoration of the oligarchy in Louisiana brought few economic benefits for the general public, but plenty of monetary benefits for the privileged few.

For the Afro-Creoles in New Orleans, the restoration of the Democrats was a disaster. Many realized the futility in attempting to dislodge the now-entrenched Redeemers and their regressive political agenda. But others banded together to aggressively fight the encroachment on their civil rights and the resegregation of the Orleans Parish Schools. Among these intrepid leaders were Aristide Mary, Paul Trévigne, and Arnold Bertonneau.

The first order of business for the revamped Board of Directors of the Orleans Parish Schools was to resegregate the schools. The board director who spearheaded the demise of the integrated school system was Archibald Mitchell, who had been a White League captain in the failed coup

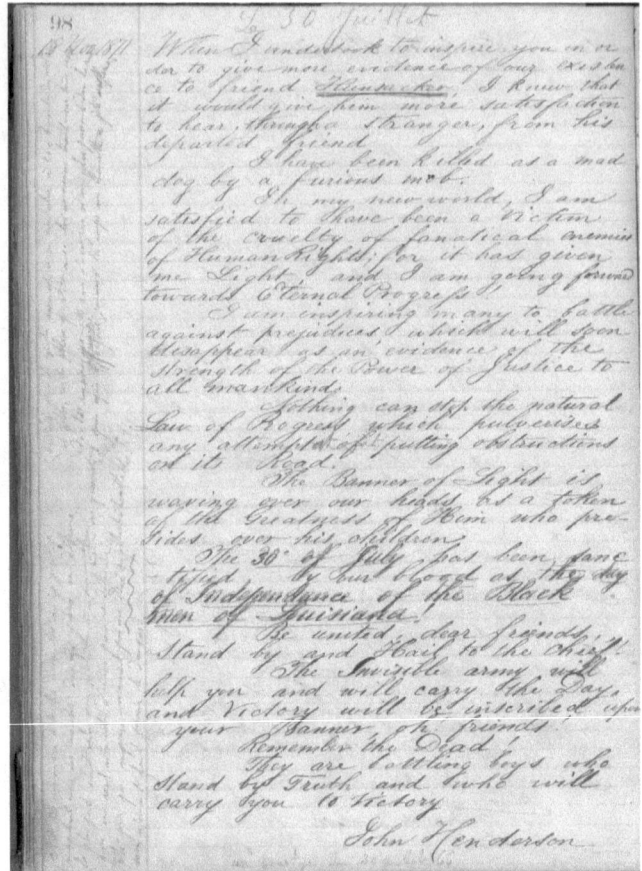

The above communication comes from John Henderson, a white martyr/hero of the Mechanics' Institute Massacre. Henderson encourages the séance circle to continue the noble fight against prejudice and to march behind the Banner of Light. The writing is in English, indicating that Henderson only spoke English. Grandjean Register 85-34, November 18, 1871, 98. Grandjean Collection.
Courtesy of Special Collections, Earl K. Long Library, University of New Orleans.

of September 14, 1874. There was no discussion of resegregation in the first two meetings of the new board of directors, but that changed in June 1877.

According to an ad hoc committee headed by Archibald Mitchell, "Public Education has greatly deteriorated since colored and white children were admitted indiscriminately into the same schools." In July, the Mitchell committee reported that the best possible education could only be "attained by educating the different races in different schools."[28] Aristide Mary appeared in person before the Board of Directors to plead the case for continuing

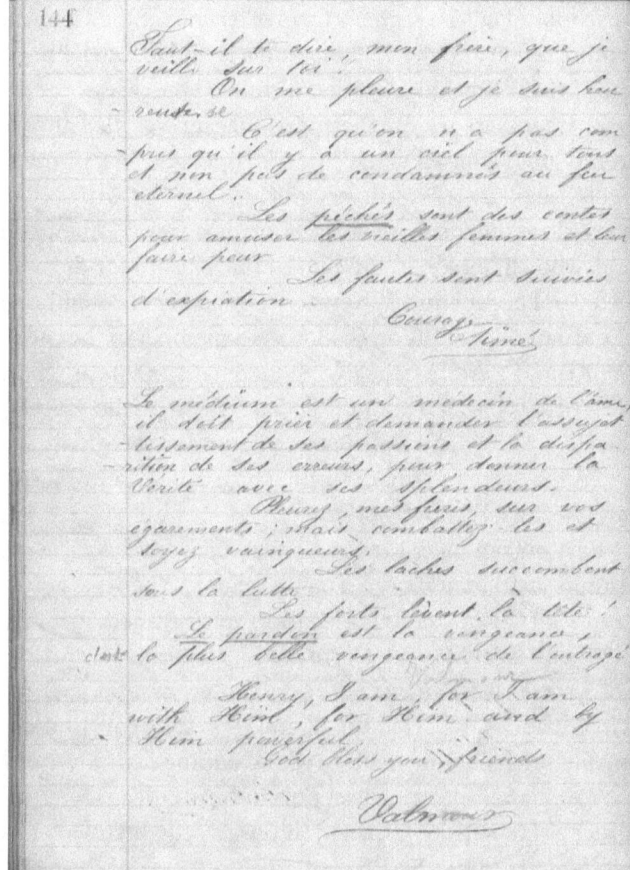

Page 144 from Grandjean Register 85-34. Valmour was a popular medium with a large following among Creoles. After his death in 1869, he frequently appears at Rey's Spiritualist Circles to console, advise, and encourage the black Creoles. This message is partly in English, which indicates that Valmour and the séance participants as well were bilingual. Grandjean Collection. *Courtesy of Special Collections, Earl K. Long Library, University of New Orleans.*

integrated schools, but to no avail. The vote was fifteen affirmatives and three nays. Among the nays was Louis A. Martinet, a prominent black Creole who would later be in the vanguard to challenge the Separate Car Act of 1890, which culminated in the landmark Supreme Court decision, *Plessy v. Ferguson* (1896). When school opened in the fall of 1877, all schools were segregated; but for some black Creoles, the battle had just begun.[29]

The battlefield now moved from the boardroom to the courtroom with a former Orleans Parish Board director leading the challenge against the newly segregated schools. Paul Trévigne, a former teacher at the Couvent School, editor of both *L'Union* and the *Tribune*, and a friend and neighbor of Henry Rey, was the plaintiff. The judge quickly dismissed the case as Trévigne failed to show any personal injury. Furthermore, the suit was filed after the board had begun resegregation. Trévigne, like Martinet and Mary, would later be involved with the *Plessy v. Ferguson* case.[30]

Following close on Trévigne's legal footsteps was another well-known Afro-Creole, who championed the cause of black suffrage during the early days of the federal occupation of New Orleans and later co-authored Article 135 in the Louisiana Constitution of 1868. As a member of the constitutional convention, Arnold Bertonneau, a wine merchant, vigorously pursued the passage of Article 135, which guaranteed integrated public schools in Louisiana. Later, Henry Rey—as a state representative in the legislature—aggressively pressed the state to adhere to the spirit and letter of Article 135 to establish an interracial school system.

Arnold Bertonneau filed a second suit, which used Article 135 as a legal justification for reopening interracial schools. The state court reached a decision in February 1879. Resegregation was justified, it ruled, because segregated schools existed in the North, and federal courts sanctioned them. The issue of Article 135 was never addressed. A few months later, a new state Redeemer constitution replaced the liberal 1868 state constitution, thereby eliminating the provisions of Article 135 and ending definitively the unique six-year experiment of integrated schools in New Orleans.[31]

The unsuccessful battle to return to the largely successful interracial public school system in Orleans Parish was just a warm-up for the more grueling court battle of *Plessy v. Ferguson* fifteen years later. Many vocal opponents to segregated schools in the late 1870s would later be actively involved in the *Plessy* legal fray. But as far as the historical record shows, Rey was not directly involved in any of the court battles. In addition to his political setbacks, Rey suffered some personal ones when several close friends passed away within a relatively short period of time. The first was real estate mogul and longtime family friend, François Lacroix.

François Lacroix in his later years was shadowed by the violent death of his son, Victor Lacroix, who perished in the Mechanics' Institute Massacre. The Grandjean Registers indicate that Lacroix was a participant at some of the séances and attempted to communicate with his deceased son. Years after the 1866 tragedy, Victor in a spirit communication told his father, "I have left the earth after suffering cruel injuries!" Somehow, it may have comforted François Lacroix to be assured that his son Victor no longer suffered. This

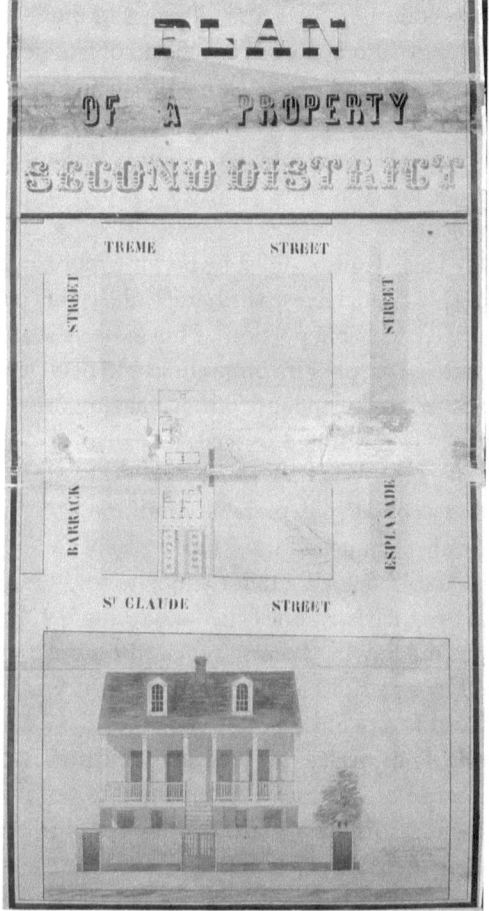

Many of the Rey séances were held at Joseph Lavigne's cigar store, located at the corner of St. Claude (now Henriette Delille Street) and Esplanade Street (Avenue). The Notarial Archives Research Center does not have records of any plans of the Lavigne business; however, this plan does show a house a short distance away on St. Claude Street. *Tourné F. Nicolas and de l'Isle Plan, Book 44, Folio 50, April 21, 1858. Courtesy of Dale N. Atkins, Clerk of Civil District Court, Parish of Orleans.*

was another common theme in the séances. The departed who suffered grievously on earth were relieved of their earthly pains and assured their living relatives and friends of improved conditions in the spiritual world.[32]

François Lacroix and Barthélemy Rey had been close personal friends and cofounders of the Couvent School. Their lives were closely intertwined on other levels: both were born in Cuba and were part of the Second Emigration of 1809–1810, both were among the upper echelon of free people of color, and both were highly regarded and respected within their close-knit community. Lacroix and Barthélemy Rey began as tailors in their younger years and later worked in the lucrative field of real estate. Lacroix had accumulated a huge amount of real estate and was widely regarded as one of the richest men in Louisiana in the 1850s.

But as François Lacroix grew older, he became more and more despondent and neglected his financial responsibilities. Two years prior to his death, the civil sheriff seized a sizable portion of his massive real estate portfolio to pay past due taxes. Lacroix's incomprehensible negligence in failing to pay property taxes led to the collapse of his amazing financial empire. His physical appearance deteriorated as well. One year prior to his death in 1876, a journalist from the *New York Times* visited his Dumaine Street home, which he described as being in deplorable condition, with broken glass and old newspapers and rags pushed into the casement to keep out the wind and rain. When Lacroix owned a tailor shop, he sold the finest and most expensive fabrics from Paris. At one time, "the young French dandies of the city never thought of showing themselves on the streets unless their lean legs were encased in a pair of Lacroix's trousers." Once fabulously wealthy, Lacroix was reduced to a penurious existence.[33]

On April 15, 1876, François Lacroix died at his brother's home at 14 Frenchmen Street. The cause of death was determined to be "congestion of the brain." The death of Lacroix left a void in Henry Rey's life as he lost not only a close personal friend, but also a father figure.[34]

Diminished political and economic fortunes created a malaise that engulfed the black Creole community after Reconstruction ended. Clubs, Masonic orders, and fraternal organizations provided a welcomed respite from the reality of everyday life, now devoid of the opportunity for full citizenship. Fraternalism had existed for decades prior to the Civil War, but the 1870s brought renewed interest in organizations such as the Economy Society. The structure of the benevolent Economy Society resembled that of a family. The society itself was considered to be a mother, and its members were brothers who were all equal and who addressed each other as "brother." The symbol of the Economy Society was a beehive, symbolic of maternal reassurance and protection.[35]

The membership of the Economy Society had grown from 15 black Creoles in 1836 to over 160 members in the 1870s who met for regular bimonthly meetings. In the early days, the members lived in the creole Faubourgs Tremé

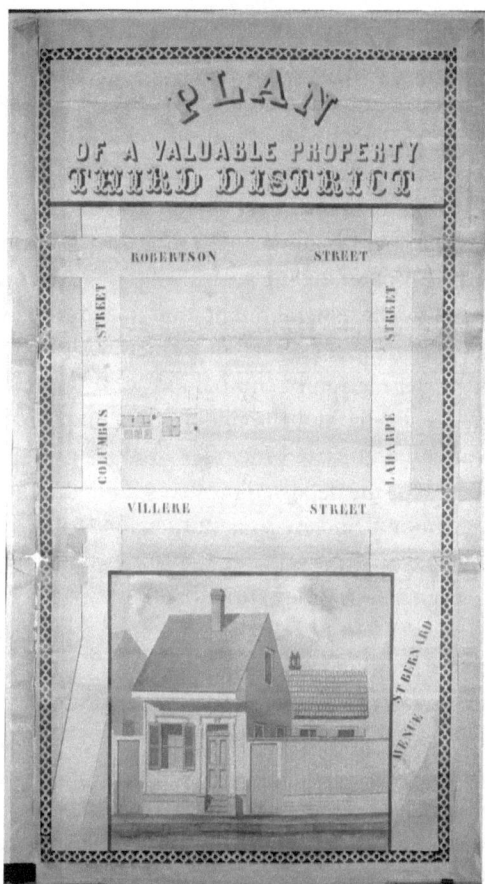

The Notarial Archives Research Center in New Orleans does not have any plans of Henry Rey's house at 95 Columbus Street. However, this plan shows a neighbor's home at 92 Columbus. Neither house exists today. *James Strehler Plan, Book 84, Folio 44. January 7, 1876. Courtesy of Dale N. Atkins, Clerk of Civil District Court, Parish of Orleans.*

and Marigny. Now, the area of the members' households had widened to other parts of the city, including Algiers, across the Mississippi River; no longer was the Economy Society an exclusive enclave for the Creole elite. According to one contemporary, the Economy Society "is composed of some of the oldest and most respected citizens and has truly at heart the welfare of New Orleans."[36]

The association's initial goals were to provide fellowship and to offer leadership opportunities, since the traditional avenues of leadership in church and government were blocked to free men of color. Social activities such as dances and Carnival balls had been mainstays of Economy Hall since at least the early 1840s and continued throughout the nineteenth century. During the turbulent 1860s, Economy Hall transformed itself into the cradle of African American suffrage as the frequent meeting place for men agitating for civil rights. The association was also known as one that helped during times of natural disaster—especially the seasonal flooding—with monetary contributions as well as other provisions. This relief during an era without government assistance did not go unnoticed by the general public, and in a local newspaper article a reporter applauded the "laudable zeal" of its members.[37]

Another important function of mutual aid societies was to assist with their members' medical bills, and the final obligation of Economy Society members was to attend a departed member's wake and funeral. A specific protocol was followed for the departed brother's funeral, which was detailed in Article 2 of the Economy Society constitution. A special committee called the Vigilance Committee watched over the body religiously and did not leave it alone for even one moment. The brothers who accompanied the deceased to the cemetery wore a sprig of cypress for a boutonniere, and for the following thirty days they wore a sign of mourning. After the religious ceremony, the president of the Economy Society performed a solemn Cypress Ceremony, and the fraternal brothers would disperse in silence. The president of the Economy Society at this time was Myrthil J. Piron, an undertaker who had a funeral parlor on North Rampart Street in the Faubourg Marigny. Piron would later be a member on the original Comité des Citoyens, a group that attempted to eliminate Jim Crow laws in Louisiana through legal challenges.[38]

As part of the solemn funeral protocol, the society's secretary wrote a condolence letter heavily bordered in black ink to the deceased's family in the name of the Economy Society. This last task fell to Henry Louis Rey, the newly installed secretary. Just a month prior to the Orleans Parish school board takeover, Rey had been elected secretary of the Economy Society on its anniversary date of March 1, 1877. As in the Cercle Harmonique séances, Rey played the role of a conveyer of sympathetic messages and a portal for the afterlife. His task was to offer solace for the living, who grieved for their departed loved ones.[39]

On June 13, 1877, Henry Rey as secretary wrote his first condolence letter. It was to the widow of Joseph Vignaud Lavigne, his childhood friend, Couvent School instructor, Native Guard comrade, medium, and faithful séance circle regular. Rey commended Lavigne for being "a model son, a faithful friend, a tender husband, a devoted patriot like his father, a person with great intelligence and an ardent propagator." Rey consoled his widow with his belief that Joseph was "now in a glorious place as a result of his work for the Triumph of Good."[40]

Joseph Lavigne's death meant that his tobacco shop on Esplanade Avenue was closed and would no longer be used for séances. The Grandjean Registers stop in November 1877, but in fact, the séance circles had ended two years earlier in 1875. The Battle of Liberty Place in September 1874 made séance members reluctant to meet on a regular basis. There was a suspicion attached to secret assemblies, and for safety reasons the séance circles were curtailed. Joseph Lavigne's illness was one more reason for terminating the Cercle Harmonique, but there were additional reasons.

One regular member, Jules Mallet, died in 1875. The Grandjean notes say that "Jules Mallet, former Circle member, departed for the world of spirits, returning to communicate." Another regular member, Emilien Planchard, quit the circle in the same year. The fire of 1875 that destroyed Rey's Villere house also adversely affected the Cercle Harmonique. For the last two years, Henry Rey continued the registers alone, just as he had begun the registers alone. In 1877, Rey finally found full-time employment with G. Pitard and Brother's Hardware Store on Canal Street, and the registers ended completely because of his heavy workplace demands.[41]

During the last two years of the registers, the zealous calls for political action and the euphoria over an anticipated change in the racial structure in Louisiana were replaced with melancholy communications that urged Rey to be patient and to be content with the present. Quiet resignation reigned.

The spirit guides informed Henry Rey that they were "happy to be able to call to your sides the luminous Spirit of glory and of Progression.... We are with you." The communications are filled with assurances that members of the circle were not alone in life. "Remember that we will be with you to protect you and to give you the force," Oscar Dunn, a frequent spirit messenger, assured Rey on November 22, the anniversary of his death. Dunn continued, "Truth must prevail and justice will come in all its glory. Do not fear anyone.... We are watching coming events." The final message in the René Grandjean Séance Registers was communicated on November 24, 1877, from *un ami* (a friend), who reminded Rey that "we are with you for an eternity."[42]

During the 1880s, African American activists negotiated for racial accommodation rather than demanding racial equality. Black leadership roles moved to such men as former governor P. B. S. Pinchback, who brokered a deal to accept the regressive Redeemer Constitution of 1879 in exchange for the founding of an all-black university, Southern University. He reasoned that blacks had to be realistic and pragmatic in this new world of second-class citizenship: "I have learned to look at things as they are and not as I would have them ... this country, at least as far as the South is concerned, is a white man's country. ... What I wish to impress upon my people is that no change is likely to take place in our day and generation that will reverse this order of things."[43]

Although the deal was made in 1879, the compromise brokered by Pinchback was similar to that of the Atlanta Compromise of 1895, in which Booker T. Washington advocated acceptance by blacks of an inferior economic and social status in exchange for limited educational opportunities and modest advancements within the black community. And like Booker T. Washington's black advocates, Louisiana blacks followed Pinchback's lead and abandoned their faltering struggle for political reform and social and economic equality.

However, key members of the Afro-Creole community continued agitating for full citizenship as they had done in the 1860s. The battle for civil rights had not ended for the Afro-Creoles. It had just entered a phase of uneasy truce during the 1880s and would later be revived in the 1890s. A new generation of Afro-Creole activists stood ready to assist the older generation in its battle to resist accommodation and to continue the tradition of Creole radicalism.[44]

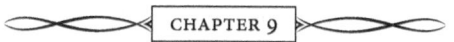

CHAPTER 9

The Spiritual Rubicon

Every workday in 1890, Henry Rey stepped down from the Claiborne streetcar at Rampart Street and walked across the neutral ground to his job at G. Pitard and Brother's Hardware Store at 207 Canal Street. The store had been his workplace since 1877, and some of his co-workers had been there for decades. Rey must have wondered for at least some of those days what had happened to his city. Canal Street was still a wide commercial street with many old familiar stores such as D. H. Holmes, Werlein's Music, and S. N. Moody's. Newer and larger department stores such as Maison Blanche and Mark Isaacs attracted more shoppers to the shopping Mecca of the South.

Instead of a few streetcars on a landscaped green neutral ground,[1] there was a sea of mule-drawn streetcars in the medium, now totally devoid of any vegetation. Every block had at least two towering telephone poles crowned with colored glass insulars with an intricate network of black lines extending across Canal Street to businesses lucky enough to have the resources for a telephone. Streetcar lines proliferated, and the city had over 173 miles of street railway. None of the streetcars were electrified in 1890, but that day was coming. The twentieth century was just a decade away, and already New Orleans was converting to electricity and adding more telephones with four-digit phone numbers.[2]

The daily hustle and bustle of pedestrian traffic on the sidewalks increased slowly in the morning and reached a crescendo by early afternoon. Ladies, dressed in their finest, would never think to go shopping on Canal Street without the appropriate hat and gloves. Men dressed a little more casually, but almost all wore a hat—wool in the winter and straw in the summer. As the shoppers and workers passed by the two large picture windows of the hardware store, some paused to see what was on display. Because it was typical hardware stock—saws, paints, varnishes, and small tools—that had not changed for years, no one lingered. The exception came on rainy days when some pedestrians would seek the protection of the overhang of Pitard's store and wait for a respite from the rain before venturing out again.

The best seasons for working at G. Pitard's Hardware Store were the fall and the spring. The windows, transoms, and double front doors could be opened wide to allow a refreshing cool breeze without the annoying, unwelcome entry of mosquitoes and flies that came in summer. When the winter arrived, the doors and windows were shut, and the fumes from the varnishes and paints within the tight confines of the store could be irritating. After decades of working in hardware stores, Rey was acclimated to the unpleasant odors and hardly noticed them. It was always a surprise when a customer commented on the offending odors.

The summer was the worst season to be in the store. The afternoon sun beat down unmercifully through the second- and third-story windows, and the mosquitoes that flew through the opened windows were huge, vicious, and abundant. But there wasn't much that could be done about the heat at a time before air conditioning. Just wait. Eventually, it would be fall again.

There was another reason to detest the summer. July 30 was an annual reminder of the grisly and horrific Mechanics' Institute Massacre of 1866. The massacre was still a fresh memory for Henry Rey, but for the new generation it was just history. Hardly anybody in New Orleans had the personal memories of what Rey called "The Black Independence Day" in his séance registers. The hideous red brick Mechanics' Institute had been sold in 1882 to the University of Louisiana, which later changed its name to Tulane University in honor of its benefactor, Paul Tulane.[3]

A few blocks away from the hardware store towered the Henry Clay Statue in the busy intersection of Canal Street at Royal Street and St. Charles Avenue.[4] The statute was a huge nuisance, obstructing the exploding streetcar traffic of the late nineteenth century. The streetcars had to negotiate a difficult turn around the statute, and eventually, in 1900, the statue would be moved to a more tranquil location in the leafy, green Lafayette Square opposite New Orleans City Hall, where it stands today.

But for now, the Great Compromiser stood tall and erect on his pedestal in the traffic circle, the former rendezvous for disgruntled former Confederates and their younger supporters in the 1870s. In the 1890s, the circle became a meeting place for shoppers and businessmen, and during the Carnival season, parades made the traditional turn around the statue from St. Charles Avenue. Less than a block away was the magnificent Merchant's Exchange, where Rey once held a prestigious and lucrative political position as tax assessor.

The St. Charles streetcar connected the business district with the Garden District and the growing suburbs. The streetcar line enabled the wealthy to move from the crowded downtown district and the deteriorating Faubourgs Tremé and Marigny, which experienced an influx of lower-income Italian and other immigrants and outright indigents. The French Quarter also suffered a downward economic decline. With the advent of public transportation, it was no longer necessary to live close to industry and business. The walking city was a relic of the past. The moneyed Anglo-American inhabitants of the neighborhoods serviced by the St. Charles line boarded the streetcars in the Central Business District and were transported to the bucolic surroundings of their sumptuous mansions.

At the end of Canal Street stood the imposing US Custom House where Rey and his Confederate Native Guard comrades first met General Benjamin Butler in 1862, declaring their allegiance to the Union and seeking to be mustered into the Union army. The massive granite structure was finally completed in the 1880s.[5] The building symbolized Republican power in Washington, which doled out coveted federal jobs as rewards to the faithful few in New Orleans. In late afternoons, Henry Rey boarded the yellow streetcar and returned to his Creole cottage on 95 Columbus Street. The Claiborne streetcar turned right at the intersection of Canal Street and Claiborne Avenue and passed by St. Louis Cemetery No. 2, where numerous friends, relatives, and Creole notables were interred. Behind the faded white brick wall lay the city of the dead with angels, crosses, and marble grave slabs to mark their tombs. It was here that the faculty and students of the Couvent School made their annual homage on All Saints Day, November 1, to honor their revered benefactress, Madame Justine Couvent. The students placed flowers on her tomb and collected donations for their school from people who visited the cemetery on All Saints Day to honor their loved ones.[6]

Onward the streetcar traveled under the shady green canopy of huge live oak trees, over the bridge at the Carondelet Canal, and past numerous simple shotgun houses, which featured rooms laid out in one straight line and no hallways. It was in one of these shotgun houses at 244½ North Claiborne (today 1108 Claiborne) that a twenty-seven-year-old shoemaker lived a rather uneventful life with his young wife. The black Creole shoemaker was Homer

Plessy, who would later be catapulted into American history with the *Plessy v. Ferguson* decision.[7]

Three blocks further was Rey's stop on Columbus Street. Henry Rey usually got off at Columbus Street, but occasionally he disembarked at the next stop, which was St. Bernard Circle, the streetcar turnaround. Rey bought fruits and vegetables from vendors at the open market before returning home. Henry Rey lingered at the stands, talking to the vendors and carefully selecting produce for the dinner table. While French had been the predominant language at the marketplace, now the prevalent language was English with a mixture of French and Italian.[8]

The political landscape had changed, and not for the better. As much as the Democrats complained about scandals and chicanery during the carpetbagger days, they proved to be the true masters of fraud and deceit in the Redeemer era. The most glaring example involved Edward Austin Burke, a veteran of the failed Liberty Place coup. Burke succeeded Antoine Dubuclet as state treasurer in 1878, the latter having held the office for ten scandal-free years. Burke also held the office for ten years, but they were hardly scandal free. In 1888, Burke absconded to Honduras with over $1 million of state funds. Because at the time there were no extradition treaties between the United States and Honduras, the state was powerless to recover the money.[9]

At the height of black political power during Reconstruction, African Americans held several top state positions, and many sat in the state legislature as senators and representatives. By 1890, there were just a few black state representatives, and in ten years there would be none. Until 1890, Jim Crow segregation was de facto, not de jure. That changed on July 10, when Governor Francis T. Nicholls signed into law the Separate Car Act, whereby railway companies were legally mandated to divide the races into separate coaches. Blacks who attempted to sit in the whites-only car would be sentenced to a twenty-five-dollar fine or twenty days in prison.[10]

Even more heart wrenching to Henry Rey than the political scene was the death of Adèle, his wife of thirty-three years, who passed away on July 22, 1890, of heart failure.[11] The séances had resumed for a few months just prior to Adèle's death. Old spirit friends reappeared and consoled Rey with their typical spiritual aphorisms of "We are with you," "Keep up the fight," and "The banner is flying." Soeur (Sister) Louise, the woman with the black skin and the soul of a diamond, and Valmour were channeled after so many years of noncommunication. It was like a reunion of old friends for a brief period of time.[12]

In the register titled "Séances Harmoniques," Soeur Louise sounded a happy note when she declared, "The number of believers has not diminished!" Valmour paraphrased the Bible when advising the circle, "By closing your eyes, you will be with the Spiritual World. Seek and you will find; ask and you will receive; look and you will see. I will not keep you long, but I tell each of you here at the Table of Truth: the Light can only shine on your soul, on what you are, on what you will be."[13]

On September 1 of the following year, eighteen African Americans formed a committee to protest the beginning of legalized Jim Crow in the form of the Separate Car Act (1890). Henry Rey's name does not appear among the members of the Comité des Citoyens (Citizens' Committee), but some members had connections with Rey either through the Economy Society, the state government, or the Couvent School.

It was a small world in the New Orleans Afro-Creole community, so there may have been other connections. Myrthil J. Prion, the president of the Economy Society, was briefly on the Citizens Committee, but he passed away shortly after the committee was organized. L. J. Joubert had connections with the Couvent School, as did Rodolphe Desdunes, who attended the school in the 1850s and 1860s. Desdunes authored *Our People and Our History*, which contained more than fifty literary portraits of black Creole notables, most with Saint-Domingue roots. Desdunes later corresponded with René Grandjean in the 1920s after he moved to Nebraska to live with Daniel, his son. C. C. Antoine was the vice president of the committee; earlier he had served as lieutenant governor (1872–1876) under Governor William Pitt Kellogg.[14]

The Citizens' Committee planned to challenge the Separate Cars Act with a test case. The committee's members decided to have Homer Plessy, an Afro-Creole with a fair complexion, to deliberately break the law and sit in the whites-only car. The members naively thought that the federal courts would exonerate Plessy and overturn the Separate Cars Act, thereby effectively preventing any further onerous Jim Crow legislation throughout the South.

On June 7, 1892, Homer Plessy boarded the East Louisiana Railroad on Press Street near the Mississippi River and informed the conductor that he was colored, even though by all accounts Plessy was light enough to have been considered white. He was arrested for violating the Separate Car Act, and the test case first went to Orleans Parish Criminal Court with Judge John Howard Ferguson presiding. Judge Ferguson rendered a decision against Homer Plessy, and the case was appealed to the Louisiana State Supreme

Court in New Orleans, which upheld the original Ferguson decision. The next legal battle took place in the US Supreme Court.[15]

The historical record does not show that Rey was active in the Citizens' Committee. Perhaps he realized the futility of pursuing its doomed goal and preferred to be a supporter but not a leader. The federal courts in this era were very conservative, and it was a foregone conclusion that the Supreme Court would not overturn the lower courts' decision. Nevertheless, the resilient Afro-Creoles continued their legal fight despite the odds. Rodolphe Desdunes reasoned that it was "more noble and dignified to fight, no matter what, than to show a passive attitude of resignation. Absolute submission augments the oppressor's power and creates doubts about the feelings of the oppressed." A final decision for the *Plessy v. Ferguson* case would not be rendered until after Henry Rey's death.[16]

The more critical battle for Henry Rey did not involve civil rights but rather economics. In 1892, he was sixty-one years old in an era that considered fifty to be elderly, and there were no social safety nets like Social Security to help retired people. What looked at first blush to be salvation for Rey was the Act of June 27, 1890, signed into law by President Benjamin Harrison after having been vetoed by the previous president, Grover Cleveland. The legislation granted pensions for veterans starting at eight dollars a month and going higher depending on the veteran's rank and his age. The major problem for many veterans was that the benefits were limited to those who had sustained a disabling injury from service in the Civil War. Furthermore, the applicant had to navigate through a mountain of federal paperwork, locate witnesses to verify the injury and their identity, and submit to medical examinations by three doctors.

To help him navigate through the legal paperwork, Rey—like many other applicants—hired a lawyer specializing in Invalid Pension claims. These lawyers charged high fees for their services, and some were unscrupulous in representing their clients, performing such unprofessional actions as advising the claimant and witnesses to commit perjury. So what originally appeared to be a prudent idea turned out to be one full of pitfalls and potential legal problems.[17]

Henry Rey claimed on his pension application, filed on August 27, 1892, that while marching with the Union Native Guard across the Lafourche Crossing in October 1862, he fell and injured his right and left ankles "and since then he has frequently fallen from the weak and crippled condition." In addition, the claim declared that Rey suffered from impaired vision and piles (hemorrhoids). The impaired vision and piles were injuries that pension seekers frequently claimed, and the Bureau of Pensions was particularly suspicious of such supposed injuries.[18]

The next hurdle—and probably the most formidable one—was the medical examinations by three doctors employed by the federal government. In Henry Rey's case, he was instructed to report to the Board of Examining Surgeons on October 10, 1892. However, Rey never reported for his physical. He may have realized that the doctors would not certify the injuries that he claimed to have suffered in the Civil War thirty years earlier, or perhaps he no longer wanted to deal with the paperwork. His pension application was filed "rejected" two years later, after his death.[19]

Henry Rey's two brothers had been more successful with their pension applications. Hippolyte Rey, who had been in the Third Regiment of the Louisiana Native Guard, applied for his pension on June 10, 1892, a few months before Rey filed for his. Hippolyte Rey claimed "impaired vision, general debility and an arm that was injured from a fall while on duty one night in Bayou Lafourche." The younger Rey managed to navigate the paperwork and received eight dollars a month until his death on August 18, 1902. Eight years after his original application, Hippolyte Rey had to once again provide depositions, this time proving that he indeed was the real Hippolyte Rey and not some imposter receiving monthly checks. Paul Trévigne and two younger men who knew him from working at the bilingual newspaper, *L'Abeille (The Bee)* filed depositions testifying that he indeed was the real Hippolyte Rey.[20]

Octave Rey had a more difficult time receiving the Invalid Pension. He filed his application two years after his brothers on May 15, 1894, claiming exposure to smallpox and an injury to his left knee, which was aggravated in 1871 by a buggy accident. The claim was rejected in 1895 and again in 1899. In 1900, however, it was approved, and he began receiving money the following year. In 1908, the pension was increased to fifteen dollars a month, which he collected until his death on October 4, 1908.[21]

It was a different world for Henry Rey and other black Creoles in the early 1890s as they struggled to come to terms with the new social and political landscapes. Their world was in disarray and unrecognizable. The once proud men and women who stood apart from the enslaved blacks were now amalgamated with African Americans in one homogenized, subordinate racial caste, shattering their dreams of social and political equality. The specter of future onerous Jim Crow legislation and total disenfranchisement loomed over them. Their slim hope for change rested on the Citizens' Committee, which was pursuing legal remedies.

The first generation of the Saint-Domingue émigrés had died out years ago, and now the second generation had entered the fifties and sixties, an age when men and women reflect on their lives, reliving their lifetime accomplishments, and asking themselves what could have been done better. For Henry Rey, his accomplishments in the fields of civil rights and education were impressive. He had played a pivotal role during the early postbellum years as a state representative in establishing the first interracial school system in the South. As a director on the Orleans Parish School Board, he had worked tirelessly to improve education in New Orleans for both races. Yet this progressive reform was nullified by the ascent of the Redeemers to political power and the end of Reconstruction in 1877.

Henry Rey fought for the continuation of a viable Couvent School. His efforts were stymied by corruption within the state administration and the dual loss of support from the community and the Louisiana legislature. What had begun in his father's time as a bright star in education for free people of color was struggling to survive in the 1890s.

In his personal life, Rey was more successful. His three adult children had done well within their community. His eldest child, Lucia Rose, was married to Victor Dorsin Martin. The oldest son, Henry Joseph, was a piano tuner at Grunewald's on Canal Street and the proud father of a daughter, Agnes, named after her grandmother. The youngest, Alfred Louis, was a cigar maker. Both Henry and Alfred were married and lived nearby.[22]

Henry Rey's professional life must have been a disappointment. Nearing the end of his career, Rey was still employed at the same hardware store and in the same position that he had begun with as a young man. Eugène Hacker hired Henry Rey in the late 1850s to work as a clerk in his Tremé store. After Reconstruction, Rey returned to a similar position with Hacker's nephew, Gustave Pitard, in the Canal Street hardware store that took over Hacker's store. He never advanced professionally despite his high level of education, intelligence, and dedication to his employer. Henry Rey's home was still the small Creole cottage on Columbus Street. With the exception of a few years in a house on St. Louis Street and later, a larger house on Villere Street, the Rey family had lived in their Columbus Street home since 1859.

What did Spiritualism mean to Henry Louis Rey? It certainly had been an important part of most of his adult life as evidenced by the voluminous communications that he and other members of the Cercle Harmonique meticulously copied in their spiritual registers. Thousands of pages in numerous registers over a period of almost two decades are a testament to Rey's unflagging belief in Spiritualism and Afro-Creole republican idealism, which had its roots in France and the Americas. Rey may have believed that his many years communing with the departed to have been just another defeat in his lifetime. He may have felt disappointment when his Cercle Harmonique disbanded and when the coveted but elusive and fleeting goals of civil and social equality disintegrated and transformed into second-class citizenship, now in the 1890s sanctioned and institutionalized by Jim Crow laws. But did he really abandon his firm beliefs in Spiritualism once his séance circles ceased meeting? It is difficult to say, as the historian cannot play the role of the medium. This author personally believes that Henry Louis Rey never lost his faith in communing with the departed and continued his Spiritualist activities in his home alone, just as he had done in 1852 when his father passed away. Now in his sixties, Rey remembered his sympathetic spiritual friends and their comforting aphorisms—"The Banner is flying," "Continue your Route," "Patience and Courage!"—which earlier in his life had strengthened his resolve to relentlessly advocate for the black Creoles and the freedpeople. Surely, he must have thought of the next phase in his existence . . . the phase that would lift him out of his physical body on the day of departure . . . the phase that would enable the eternal spiritual part of Rey to ascend the rungs of the Ladder of Progression in the idyllic afterlife . . . the phase where he could unite with departed loved ones and spend blissful and fulfilling days, freed of suffering and living in an unjust society.

The hour of departure arrived on the morning of April 19, 1894, when Henry Louis Rey crossed the Spiritual Rubicon. He died of anthrax at 9:30 a.m. in his Columbus Street home.[23] At Rey's request, he was buried in a civil ceremony without priests. Regrettably, François Dubuclet was not informed of his death and missed the funeral of his old friend. René Grandjean eulogized the séance leader decades later when he wrote, "Rey, the noble Apostle went to the world of spirits to find the apostles that had preceded him and with whom he had communicated their instructions to all." Thus ended a sad, long-forgotten chapter of New Orleans' history.[24]

The *Plessy v. Ferguson* decision rendered by the US Supreme Court on May 18, 1896, was the crowning blow for the hopes and aspirations of the Citizens' Committee. The majority of the Court stated that "if one race be inferior to the other socially, the Constitution of the United States cannot put them upon the same plane." The conservative court turned back the judicial clock to antebellum days by ignoring the Fourteenth Amendment.[25]

The decision encouraged other state legislation in the South to disenfranchise African Americans. At the Constitutional Convention of 1898, Louisiana enacted the grandfather clause, which limited suffrage to males who could have voted prior to 1867 or male descendants of those voters. Because African American males could not vote in 1867, they were prevented from voting, thus effectively eliminating almost all black males from the voter rolls. Black suffrage dissolved in one felled swoop by the combination of federal court approval and state legislation. The chairman of the Judiciary Committee of the Louisiana legislature, Thomas Semmes, explained that the supremacy of the white race had to be preserved. Governor Murphy J. Foster congratulated the constitutional convention on the invention of the grandfather clause, which circumvented the Fifteenth Amendment of the US Constitution. Additional onerous Jim Crow legislation beginning in 1902 decreed the resegregation of the New Orleans streetcars and separate water fountains for the two races.[26]

The onslaught of Jim Crow legislation pushed many black Creoles to change their race designation from "black" or "mulatto" to "white" and to turn their backs on their black Creole heritage. Declaring oneself as white became known as "*passe à blanc*" or simply "passing."

All three of Henry Louis Rey's children declared themselves and their families to be white on the US Census. Lucia Rey Martin was listed as white in the US Census of 1900; Henry Joseph Rey, who moved to his father's house on Columbus Street, was listed as white in the US Census of 1930, as was his younger brother, Alfred Louis Rey. Alfred moved to Chicago to join his son and his family. Information in the US Census of 1930 indicates that the Chicago neighborhood they were in was a white immigrant working-class area and that most of the neighbors were German.[27]

Chicago was a popular destination city for Afro-Creoles looking for a better way of life in an area free of virulent racism. The distance from New Orleans had the additional advantage that neighbors, co-workers, and friends in the faraway city were unlikely to realize that the newly arrived migrants had African ancestry. Relatives from Louisiana were discouraged from visiting in order to maintain the appearance of being white. Frequently, relatives were of a darker hue, and people in the destination city might conclude that their friend or neighbor was actually black. The black Creoles from Louisiana often turned their backs on their Creole heritage when they failed to disclose their true race and origins to their children and grandchildren, thus losing valuable oral history and family genealogical information.

The Dubuclets were another family that migrated to the Chicago area and changed their racial designation to white in the US Census. François Dubuclet's nephew, Laurent Dubuclet, moved to Chicago from New Orleans and enjoyed a successful career as a ragtime musician, composer, and teacher.

Henry Rey worked at G. Pitard's Hardware Store from 1877 until his death in 1894. The store was located near the corner of Rampart and Canal Street in the heart of the New Orleans shopping district. Years later the building was demolished, and F. W. Woolworth, the famous five-and-dime store, was built on the site. This photograph was taken in August 1916. *Photograph courtesy of Derrick Pitard, great-great-grandson of Gustave Pitard.*

Laurent married Leda Marie Chessé, another black Creole from New Orleans. Leda and her two sisters lived in Chicago and according to a descendent, "Creole heritage was never discussed." Laurent was the cousin of Assitha Dubuclet, who later married French-born René Grandjean in St. Andrew, Jamaica, on October 29, 1913.[28]

California was another popular destination for Creoles of color who wanted to start a new life with a new identity free of racial discrimination during the nadir of African American discrimination in the South. Such was the case of George Herriman Jr., who was a participant at the Henry Rey séance table and a neighbor of Rey. He and his family were part of the black Creole diaspora of the 1890s and moved to Los Angeles, where they were considered to be white. George Herriman's son, also named George, later gained fame as the Krazy Kat cartoonist and kept secret his black ancestry.[29]

Many of the artistic and talented Creoles of color who left New Orleans blossomed when racial barriers did not circumscribe them. Crossing the racial divide from black to white had both economic and social advantages. Anatole Paul Broyard, the great-grandson of Henry Broyard and Marie Bonée, moved to New York in 1927. Henry Broyard was a spirit messenger at the Rey séance table who was actually white but who declared himself to be a free man of color so he could legally marry a free woman of color in 1855. Anatole Broyard hid his African American ancestry and gained fame as the literary critic of the *New York Times*. His children did not learn of their father's ancestry until two months before his death. Bliss Broyard's *One Drop* (2007) chronicles her search to discover her father's hidden black Creole past and to reconnect with her father's family.[30]

For many Creoles of color, the journey from Saint-Domingue to Louisiana occurred in the early 1800s. For some of the descendants, a new journey began in the late 1800s in the wake of draconian Jim Crow legislation and the promise of a brighter economic and social future in cities hundreds of miles away. As they departed Louisiana, it must have been with mixed emotions, similar to the sentiments Pierre Clément de Laussat expressed in his memoirs. Upon completion of his duties in 1804, the French colonial prefect who transferred Louisiana to the United States sailed downriver past the ramshackle buildings of La Balize at the mouth of the Mississippi River. As he entered the open, dark blue choppy waters of the Gulf of Mexico, he wrote, "I will say no more of Louisiana; it is too painful to have known it and then to have been separated from it."[31]

Epilogue

Henry Louis Rey's Cercle Harmonique disappeared in 1877, coinciding with the official end of Reconstruction. Except for a brief period in 1890 when Rey once again channeled departed black Creoles, the spiritual messengers remained strangely silent throughout the rest of the nineteenth century. There is no evidence to indicate that other French Creole séance circles replaced those of Rey's in New Orleans, although there was Spiritualist activity in the Anglo-American community.

The demise of Spiritualism in the Crescent City mirrors the precipitous fall of Spiritualism at the national level. The heyday of séance Spiritualism occurred in the 1850s and continued through the 1860s; then the number of devotees and mediums subsided in the 1870s and 1880s. By the last decade of the nineteenth century, Spiritualism had suffered the fate that so many other reform movements and nonmainstream religions from the Burned-over District had already experienced: séance Spiritualism evolved into a historical curiosity.

What had been amazing yesterday was now ordinary, humdrum, and staid. What was once declared to be genuine by influential newspaper editors was now widely viewed as legerdemain, trickery, and chicanery.

Further hastening the decline of mid-nineteenth-century Spiritualism was the advent of new and compelling ideologies like New Thought, Christian Science, and Theosophy, all of which refigured its metaphysical aspects. The new religions offered new ways "to understand spirituality and to achieve oneness with the Cosmos." As séance Spiritualism waned in popularity, new forms of nineteenth-century spiritualism took its place throughout the United States.[1]

In New Orleans during the 1880s, Minerva Hall continued to be the premier venue for Spiritualist activities such as trance lectures, public séances, Sunday morning services, and the annual celebration on March 31 of the genesis of Spiritualism. Occasionally, Grunewald Hall was used for these activities and others such as slate writing, "reading the contents of sealed letters, reading from a book held by one of the audience, making tables and pianos perambulate, and playing instruments while bound hand and foot."[2]

The New Orleans Spiritualist Association was organized in 1882 with a membership of three hundred. The president was none other than Dr. J. W. Allen, who had consulted James Mansfield, the Spiritual Postmaster, in 1860 and who had so favorably impressed the famous northern medium, the Reverend James M. Peebles, ten years later. Dr. Allen held a dominant sway on Spiritualism for the next two decades after meeting Rev. Peebles. At different times, Dr. Allen acted in various capacities as president, secretary, and board member of the New Orleans Spiritualist Association.[3]

By 1891, the organization was solvent enough to purchase its own hall at 321 Camp Street, which served as a popular venue for Spiritualist activities and social functions as well. The New Orleans Spiritualist Association does not appear to have had any connections with the French Creoles. All of the last names of officers, members, and mediums, which were mentioned in local contemporary newspapers, were Anglo-American names.[4]

Spiritualism diversified and evolved in the 1890s, even as the number of its adherents, particularly the middle-class followers, declined. This was the period in which Spiritualists began to create effective, national-level organizations, established hundreds of Spiritualist churches, and founded camp meetings—rural communities where Spiritualists could spend their summer vacations relaxing and contacting their spiritual friends. Some of the better-known camps were located at Lily Dale, New York; Cassadaga Lake, Florida; and Harmony Grove, California. Spiritualism in the late nineteenth century became increasingly institutionalized, and the mediums less nomadic. The hallmarks of Modern American Spiritualism began to fade away and were replaced by a religion less antagonistic to orthodox Christianity and more traditional by virtue of its Sunday services, established ministry, and stable congregation. Indeed, the fifty-year-old movement would hardly have been recognizable to the followers of the Modern American Spiritualism that first appeared at the mid-nineteenth century. No longer was Spiritualism an "every man a prophet" religion. It was now a type of Christian Spiritualism that was congregation-based, not home-based. The soft warm glow of sunshine filtering through church windows replaced the darkened parlors of yesteryear.

In 1895 William Brodie, an officer of the New Orleans Spiritualist Association, attended the National Spiritualists Association in Washington, which had been founded by Cora L. V. Hatch Richmond in 1893. The Reverend Richmond, now in her fourth marriage, had moved to Chicago and started a Spiritualist church called the First Spiritual Church of Chicago. According to a *Daily Picayune* article, Cora Richmond's congregation was large and wealthy. The following year, she became the pastor of the Church of the Soul in Chicago. The aging disciple of nineteenth-century Spiritualism had forsaken her peripatetic lifestyle and adopted a more sedentary approach to spreading the word among her dwindling devotees.[5]

The celebrity mediums of the North crossed the spiritual divide with no new notable mediums to take their place. The founders of Modern American Spiritualism died within ten months of each other, both of causes related to alcoholism. Catherine (Kate) Fox Jencken died on July 2, 1892, while on a drinking spree. Eight months later, Margaret (Maggie) Fox Kane died penniless and alone on March 8, 1893, in a New York City apartment loaned to her by Henry Newton, president of the First Society of Spiritualists. Friends contributed money to bury the Fox sisters together in Cypress Hills Cemetery in Brooklyn, New York.[6]

On January 2, 1923, Cora L. V. Hatch Daniels Tappan Richmond, the matriarch and last of the famous nineteenth-century Spiritualists, died. Less than a year prior to her death, Dr. James Martin Peebles passed away at the last stop of his long spiritual pilgrimage: Los Angeles. Dr. Peebles had been looking forward to a one hundredth birthday party slated for March 23, 1922; sadly, he missed the century mark by just thirty-six days.[7]

François Dubuclet, the last surviving member of Henry Rey's Cercle Harmonique, moved from New Orleans to Jamaica, in the Caribbean, in 1913 with his daughter Assitha and his son-in-law, René Grandjean. Together, the three lived in St. Andrew, Jamaica, for seven years, and during that time Dubuclet continued his fervent association with Spiritualism by discussing the faith's basic tenets with his son-in-law and by corresponding with relatives. His letters were filled with expressions of his ardent love for Spiritualism and stories about his old Spiritualist friends from a bygone era, Henry Rey and Valmour. Thousands of miles away, the Dubuclets of Chicago also continued their association with Spiritualism by joining a Spiritualist church and by reading copies of Rey's spiritual communications as well as ones from

Paul Durel. The elder Dubuclet expressed his immense satisfaction with the younger generation's continuing association with Spiritualism: "I am happy, *very* happy indeed to learn that my example is followed by my grandchildren, with regard to Spiritualism. When I read your letters transmitting such glad tidings, I could not refrain from shedding tears of rejoicing to learn also that you are receiving and reading the beautiful spirits of what I cherish the most on earth—Spiritualism!"[8] (emphasis added).

Sidney Dubuclet assured his grandfather of his keen interest in Spiritualism, citing a figure of six million Spiritualists in the United States. However, there were enemies. The Illinois legislature passed in 1917 the Fortune Telling Law, which outlawed anyone "holding himself out as skilled in fortune telling by means of card reading, palmistry, . . . spiritual mediumship or any crafty science" (Section 1). The law also banned the publication and distribution of advertisements of any person's ability to offer "advice of any kind or nature by means of occult or psychic powers" (Section 2). Fines could be assessed for as much as five hundred dollars under Section 1 and two hundred dollars for Section 2. In addition, a papal decree prohibited Catholics from attending spiritual meetings and séances.[9]

Odette Dubuclet Gauthier, another grandchild, wrote her "Pape" and assured him of her active involvement with her Spiritualist church in Chicago, the Soul Circle Church. Odette described an Indian guide called Honto who talked like a little girl and gave "beautiful messages" and controlled the minister, Mrs. Williams. This story has some of the hallmarks of the New Orleans Spiritual churches in the 1920s: a matriarchal ministry and an Indian messenger in a church setting.[10]

François Dubuclet and the Grandjeans returned to New Orleans from Jamaica in 1920. After the death of François in 1924, the Chicago family members gathered for séances, attempting to contact their beloved relative. Across the spiritual divide, the deceased patriarch answered questions concerning his happiness, saying that he was once again united with Henry Rey and Valmour. When asked if he found things as he expected them to be in the spiritual world, Dubuclet responded, "Yes, exactly."[11]

Spiritualist churches similar to the ones founded in Chicago appeared in other American cities that had once been bastions of Modern American Spiritualism, including New Orleans. According to the *New Orleans City Guide* (1938) written by the Federal Writers' Project of the Works Progress Administration (WPA), in 1938 there were three such churches in New Orleans.[12] Oscar Lewis Clark, a twenty-seven-year-old minister from Plymouth, Massachusetts, founded the First Church of Divine Fellowship of

This is the original sign for the First Church of Divine Fellowship of Spiritualism, founded by Oscar L. Clark in 1920. The sign was refinished in 2009. *Photo by author.*

Spiritualism in 1920. That church was the only one of the three Spiritualist churches affiliated with the National Spiritualists Association, which had headquarters in Washington, DC. After a few years in temporary buildings, the church moved to its permanent location at 823 Spain Street, where it offered a variety of Spiritualist activities throughout the week, including healings on Monday, message circles and "developing classes" on Tuesday, trance lectures on Friday, and Sunday morning services. Occasional social events were added to the busy church calendar, and the requisite annual celebrations of the seminal Hydesville raps on March 31 were held. René Grandjean and his wife attended services regularly and were very involved with the First Church of Divine Fellowship of Spiritualism and the ministry of Rev. Clark. Judging from last names mentioned on a schedule of services and newspaper articles, the congregation was not connected with the French Creoles.[13]

The ministry of Oscar L. Clark ended when he died at the young age of thirty-five on September 7, 1929. The church was taken over by a series of temporary ministers, and in 1930 Dr. T. R. Rodgers assumed the role of pastor. It is unclear if and when René Grandjean stopped attending services after the change in ministry.[14]

In other parts of the city, the eclectic Spiritual churches of the 1920s and 1930s were established. Spiritual churches were a syncretic blend of nineteenth-century Spiritualism, Catholicism, Protestantism, and Voodoo. It was a matriarchal religion led by women called Mothers, who moved to New Orleans during this time. In an era when African American women were marginalized because of their gender, race, and class, leadership within the predominately black Spiritual churches provided a golden opportunity for them to empower and enrich themselves as well as to escape the traditional domestic occupations of housemaids and washerwomen.[15]

One of the most famous and popular Mothers was Leafy Anderson of Chicago, who arrived there in 1921. The cornerstone of her church, the Eternal Life Christian Church, was laid on Sunday, April 17, 1921, at 2719 Amelia Street.[16] While in Chicago, Mother Leafy had established a church in 1913 with a very similar name: the Eternal Life Spiritualist Church. Her religious dogma consisted of Christian beliefs plus a twentieth-century version of Spiritualism with the addition of a revered spiritual guide, Black Hawk, a tall Sauk who lived in the early nineteenth century and sided with the British against the Americans during the War of 1812.[17] Black Hawk had also been the favorite spiritual guide of Dr. James Peebles. According to historian Robert Cox in *Body and Soul*, the Spiritualism of Black Hawk became "enshrined as a symbol of and encouragement to the resistance to racial oppression."[18]

In New Orleans, African Americans and Native Americans had historically been linked as oppressed races with shared lineage that over the centuries had sought to resist marginalization. The addition of a Native American guide was an expression of racial pride and offered a non-European model of identity. It may have been related to the popular racial pride movement of Marcus Garvey during the early 1920s. A protégée of Mother Leafy, Mother Dora Tyson, explained to Robert Tallant, in his work for the Federal Writers' Project of the WPA, that Mother Leafy discovered and introduced the Native American to the South and only for the South. "Mother Dora did not know why this was so and when Black Hawk lived and received his power. But she was quite certain that he had power."[19]

The spiritual matriarchal clergy evolved from an almost totally female group to a mixed-gendered clergy but still more tolerant of female leadership than the mainstream African American religious denominations.[20] *The New Orleans City Guide* details eight Spiritual churches in the 1930s. Out of the eight churches listed, women were pastors in five.[21]

Catherine Seals, another protégée of Mother Leafy Anderson, ministered the Church of the Innocent Blood on Charbonnet Street, located in a working-class neighborhood. She had a highly unusual and entertaining way of entering her church—a rough red, white, and blue building resembling a circus tent. Mother Catherine, a large African American woman, was lowered from a hole in the roof of a side room, intimating that she descended from Heaven to preach the gospel. Upon arrival, she gave her blessing to the congregation, declaring, "Children, I've come here to do good, not evil!" The affable and charitable Mother Catherine appealed to both the black and white working classes, particularly the growing numbers of Italian immigrants. A few well-heeled uptown whites also attended the popular services, perhaps out of curiosity. Marcus Christian notes in "A Black History of Louisiana" (typescript) that the Spiritual churches were "accessible to residents of both races either in the uptown or downtown sections of the city."[22] This was in sharp contrast with Henry Rey's male-dominated séance circles. Rey's séances were usually conducted in French, whereas the Spiritual churches were strictly English speaking.

Spiritual churches were part of a religious movement that occurred in other major American cities such as Chicago, Detroit, New York City, Houston, Baltimore, and Philadelphia. During the Great Depression, Spiritual churches were the fastest-growing denomination among the small and intensely religious groups that arose throughout the black population. A large number of unchurched Spiritualists kept home altars or worked as Spiritualist advisors.[23]

For many Spiritual ministers, prophecy was an important aspect of their church. Spirit messages linked nineteenth-century Spiritualism to twentieth-century Spiritual churches; however, there were critical differences between the two belief systems. The Spiritualism that prevailed during the second half of the nineteenth century involved mediums that either led domestic séance circles or conducted public trance demonstrations. The early-twentieth-century medium conducted her trances and message sessions within the confines of services held at the Spiritual churches. In addition, the Spiritual medium often invoked Black Hawk as a Spirit guide. The New Orleans Spiritual churches disassociated themselves from the stigma attached to Spiritualism in twentieth-century American society. There was an even stronger denial of any association with New Orleans Voodoo.[24]

The denial of Voodoo by the Spiritual church ministers belies the reality. There were a number of similarities, including the ministers' clothes, the icon décor of the church, the ritual singing and dancing, and a matriarchal ministry. There is a curious link between the style of clothes and Voodoo. Mother Catherine and other ministers wore a long white gown with a blue cord at their waists, the exact same type of clothing that the Voodoo priestesses wore to distinguish themselves from her followers.[25]

The interior of the Spiritual church was decorated with countless candles, statues, banners, and pictures. Mother Catherine's altar was a motley array of religious artwork of the most puerile type. Grotesques statues made from burlap were cemented and painted by Catherine Seals herself. She also made crude banners and other primitive religious objects. Unfortunately, Mother Catherine had no artistic talent. Marie Laveau's house had a similar décor with numerous figurines of Catholic saints, dozens of burning candles, and amulets scattered helter-skelter near the altar.[26]

The emphasis on dancing and rituals was another similarity to Voodoo with its distinctive dances, the calenda, and the chica, brought from West Africa. The Voodoo dances were always done outdoors with a man and a woman dancing in the middle of a circle that was formed on a level piece of ground. One of the hallmarks of the Spiritual churches was the lively and enthusiastic movement as members entered a trance or spirit-possession stage. Claude Jacobs and Andrew Kaslow describe this as "violent seizures, long periods of dancing, dervish-like spinning, [and] writhing on the floor" with a pounding beat of a drum and organ in the background.[27]

In New Orleans, the Spiritual and Spiritualist churches of the twentieth century and the Spiritualism of the nineteenth-century were linked by their common belief in communication with the dead and because some mediums and pastors claimed healing powers. Otherwise, the three religions were very different. Spiritualism offered comfort and a feeling of closure to the bereaved who for a few precious minutes in a séance setting could once again communicate with loved ones across the spiritual divide. For the members of Rey's Spiritualist circles, there was an added dimension of the spirits' progressive and radical social and political agendas. The Spiritualist churches appealed to middle-class whites and some black Creoles and were more akin to mainstream Protestant churches, except for the emphasis on communication with the dead. The Spiritual churches eschewed any social and political agendas and appealed mainly to black workers, who desired a glimpse into the future and to make contact with the spiritual world. Modern American Spiritualism, the Spiritualist churches, and the Spiritual churches shared many commonalities, but there were significant differences in the demographics of their congregations, theological trajectories, and methods of communicating with the spiritual world.

The possibility of communicating with the departed has always intrigued the living. During the nineteenth and twentieth centuries, mediums from all walks of life in hundreds of American towns and cities, at different venues, espousing varying social and political agendas and with diverse participants sought to reach over the Spiritual Rubicon to achieve the impossible. Spiritualism has evolved from the nineteenth century and continues today in the twenty-first century. The religion of the dead never dies.

Notes

I have used the following terms to indicate sources of information from the Grandjean Collection:

Grandjean Séance Margin Notes: These were notes Grandjean added to the séance messages to give historical and biographical information pertinent to the message. Grandjean often explained who a certain person appearing in the spirit message was or what the historical background was. All of these insightful, detailed notes were written in French and are not included in the selected transcripts that Grandjean translated into English. The Grandjean Séance Margin Notes are all found within the thirty-five séance registers.

Grandjean Notes: Grandjean wrote a plethora of loose notes based on François Dubuclet's oral history. All are in French, and typically the information is not found in the séance registers. Occasionally, some of the information is duplicated in the séance registers. These notes are all located in folders 85-91 and 85-92 as part of the Grandjean Collection.

Grandjean Register: This is the particular volume where the spiritual communications are. The communications are generally dated at the beginning of the message, the medium's name is sometimes included, and the messenger's name(s) is (are) at the end of the communication—somewhat as in a letter. Most of the séance registers have pagination, so page numbers appeared in the footnotes, indicating where a particular message could be found as well as the date that the spiritual message was received and the particular register. Most of the registers have an index of spirit messengers, with the index usually located at the beginning of the register rather than on the final pages.

INTRODUCTION

1. Stephen J. Ochs, *A Black Patriot and a White Priest: Andre Cailloux and Claude Paschal Maistre in Civil War New Orleans* (Baton Rouge: Louisiana State University Press, 2000), 40–42.

2. "Spiritualism: Its Rise and Progress—Something of Its History in New Orleans. A Times Reporter Caught in the Toils of the Rappers—What He Saw and Heard," *New Orleans Times*, July 5, 1874. Creole refers to a person of Latin European ancestry, of any race, born in Louisiana.

3. Biographical information comes from the Grandjean Collection's Finding Aid. René Grandjean Collection, Earl K. Long Library, University of New Orleans (hereafter cited as Grandjean Collection).

4. Ibid.

5. The statements regarding the séances are not necessarily reflective of the author's beliefs. However, statements made by spirits and/or what transpired at the séances are stated as facts because the participants regarded them as facts.

6. Faubourg is a French term meaning suburb. Today the faubourgs mentioned in this book are completely integrated into the city of New Orleans.

7. Caryn Cossé Bell, *Revolution, Romanticism, and the Afro-Creole Protest Tradition in Louisiana, 1718–1868* (Baton Rouge: Louisiana State University Press, 1997).

8. Robert S. Cox, *Body and Soul: A Sympathetic History of American Spiritualism* (Charlottesville: University of Virginia Press, 2003).

9. Chris Michaelides, ed. *Paroles d'honneur: Écrits de Créoles de couleur néo-orléanais* (Shreveport, LA: Editions Tintamarre, 2004). Michaelides's introduction (in French) contains an excellent short history of the free people of color in New Orleans and fascinating biographical details about the ten Afro-Creole authors featured in the book.

10. Jill Lepore, "Historians Who Love Too Much: Reflections on Microhistory and Biography," *Journal of American History* 88, no. 1 (June 2001): 131, 133.

PROLOGUE

1. The description of La Balize is adopted from the memoirs of Pierre Clément de Laussat and Benjamin Henry Latrobe, who made similar voyages in 1803 and 1819, respectively. Pierre Clément de Laussat, *Memoirs of My Life*, trans. Sister Agnes-Josephine Pastwa (Baton Rouge: Louisiana State University Press, 1978), 1–15; Benjamin Henry Latrobe, *Impressions Respecting New Orleans: Diary and Sketches 1818–1820* (New York: Columbia University Press, 1951), 14–16.

2. Rebecca J. Scott and Jean M. Hébraud, *Freedom Papers: An Atlantic Odyssey in the Age of Emancipation* (Cambridge, MA: Harvard University Press, 2012), 60. The *Louisa* under the command of Captain Daniel MacDonald carried twenty-six men; twenty-eight women; six children; and seventy *criados*, a term that could mean either slaves or servants.

3. Laurent Dubois, *Avengers of the New World: The Story of the Haitian Revolution* (Cambridge, MA: Harvard University Press, 2004), 21.

4. Paul Lachance, "The 1809 Immigration of Saint-Domingue Refugees to New Orleans: Reception, Integration and Impact," *Journal of the Louisiana Historical Association* 29, no. 2 (Spring 1988): 110.

5. Nathalie Dessens, *From Saint-Domingue to New Orleans: Migration and Influences* (Gainesville: University Press of Florida, 2007), 14.

6. Dubois, *Avengers of the New World*, 61–64.

7. Ibid.

8. Dessens, *From Saint-Domingue to New Orleans*, 23.

9. Claiborne to Robert Smith, November 12, 1809, in *Official Letter Books of W. C. C. Claiborne, 1801–1816*, ed. Dunbar Rowland, vol. 5, 1–5 (Jackson: Mississippi Historical Association, 1917).

10. Joseph Logsdon and Caryn Cossé Bell, "The Americanization of Black New Orleans," *Creole New Orleans: Race and Americanization*, ed. Arnold R. Hirsch and Joseph Logsdon (Baton Rouge: Louisiana State University Press, 1992), 206, Table 1.

11. Genealogical information obtained from a marriage contract: Carlile Pollock, vol. 25, Act 43, July 1, 1829, Notarial Archives Research Center, New Orleans (hereafter cited as NARC).

12. The description of the marketplace is adopted from the memoirs of Benjamin Latrobe, who arrived ten years later. Latrobe, *Impressions*, 18–22.

CHAPTER 1

1. Carlile Pollock, vol. 25, Act 43, July 1, 1829, NARC. Natural child means that the parents were not married.

2. Succession papers of Henry Rey note that his mother was born in Saint-Domingue. Succession of Henry Louis Rey, May 3, 1894, City Archives, New Orleans Public Library (hereafter cited as NOPL), Certificate of Marriage, St. Louis Cathedral, M3, 98, July 2, 1829. Witnesses were Louis Carnon, Auguste Brouard, and Adolphe Duhart, who later was a teacher at the Couvent School and an important black Creole writer.

3. Dessens, *From Saint-Domingue to New Orleans*, 50–55.

4. The block on which Carlile Pollock's office was located was razed to make room for the Beaux Arts Louisiana Supreme Court on Royal Street, completed in 1910. Exchange Alley originally extended into the block.

5. Stephen E. Percy and Edward Augusta Michel, *New Orleans City Directory of 1832* (New Orleans: Stephen E. Percy, 1832); Richard Campanella, *Lincoln in New Orleans: The 1828–1831 Flatboat Voyages and Their Place in History* (Lafayette: University of Louisiana at Lafayette Press, 2010), 112–13. The Omni Royal Orleans Hotel now occupies the space where Hewlett's Exchange once stood.

6. Campanella, *Lincoln in New Orleans*, 112–13.

7. Joseph G. Tregle Jr., *Louisiana in the Age of Jackson: A Clash of Cultures and Personalities* (Baton Rouge: Louisiana State University Press, 1999), 13; Eliza Ripley, *Social Life in Old New Orleans: Being Recollections of My Girlhood* (New York: D. Appleton, 1911), 58–59.

8. John Chase, *Frenchmen, Desire, Good Children, and Other Streets of New Orleans* (Gretna, LA: Pelican Press, 2004), 25; Percy and Michel, *New Orleans City Directory of 1832*. Condé Street no longer exists; today it is part of Chartres Street.

9. Richard Campanella, *Bourbon Street* (Baton Rouge: Louisiana State University Press, 2014), 46–47, 35. According to Campanella, the old numbering system was replaced in 1894

with the present-day decimal system (53). Today 261 Bourbon would be in the 1100 block, between Ursulines and Governor Nicholls Streets.

10. Baptism of Louis Henry Rey, St. Louis Cathedral, vol. 29, Part 2: 1831–1833, 180, Act 1202, Archives of the Archdiocese of New Orleans, hereafter cited as AANO. The younger Rey later reversed the order of his first two names to "Henry Louis."

11. The children of Barthélemy Rey and Rose Sacriste were Elizabeth Rey (b. March 31, 1829), Louis Henry Rey (b. February 20, 1831; d. April 19, 1894), Henry Hippolyte Rey (b. March 22, 1833; d. August 18, 1902), Josephine "Octavie" Antoinette Rey (b. April 3, 1835), Felix Octave Rey (b. June 26, 1837; d. October 4, 1908), Georgine Scholastique Louise Rey (b. April 23, 1839), and Henriette Philomene Alphonsine Rey (b. November 13, 1842; d. July 30, 1915). Information obtained from ancestry.com and pension records of the Rey brothers.

12. Bell, *Revolution, Romanticism*, 124. For more on the definition of Creole and the controversy surrounding its definition, see Joseph Tregle, "Creoles and Americans" in *Creole New Orleans*, 131–85, and *Louisiana in the Age of Jackson*, 23–41.

13. Louis Caire, vol. 51, Act 816, August 24, 1834, and Louis Caire, vol. 53A, Act 846, September 23, 1836, NARC.

14. Tregle, *Louisiana in the Age of Jackson*, 112; Henry Herz, *My Travels in America* (Madison: State Historical Society of Wisconsin for the Department of History, University of Wisconsin, 1963), 89–93.

15. Succession of Rose Crocker No. 17513, April 4, 1861, City Archives, NOPL. A family meeting of friends was summoned to determine the guardianship of Rose Crocker's eleven-year-old son, Myrtille Raphaël Crocker. The meeting decided that Henry Louis Rey, Myrtille's brother-in-law, should act as his guardian. In attendance was the crème de la crème of the Afro-Creole community: Bazile Crocker, Drausin Macarty, Pierre Casanave, François Boisdoré, and François Lacroix.

16. 1850 Slave Schedule of the 1st Ward, 3rd Municipality in the Parish of Orleans. Accessed from ancestry.com.

17. Paul E. Laresche, vol. 2, Act 142; vol. 3, Act 100; vol. 5, Act 57; vol. 6, Act 57; vol. 8, Act 103; and vol. 10, Act 49, March 9, 1852, NARC.

18. Judith Kelleher Schafer, *Becoming Free, Remaining Free: Manumission and Enslavement, 1846–1862* (Baton Rouge: Louisiana State University Press, 2003), 80–81.

19. Ben Melvin Hobratsch, "Creole Angel: The Self-Identity of the Free People of Color of Antebellum New Orleans" (master's thesis, University of North Texas, 2006), 32–48. Creole historians such as Rodolphe Desdunes completely avoided any reference to slave ownership. See Rodolph Desdunes, *Our People and Our History*, trans. and ed. Sister Dorothea Olga McCants (Baton Rouge: Louisiana State University Press, 1973.) The Louisiana Civil Code of 1808 required the notary to label free persons of color in their legal documents, so it can be assumed that if there is no racial designation, the person was white.

20. Paul E. Laresche, vol. 10, Act 49, March 9, 1852, NARC.

21. Phillippe Pedesclaux, vol. 13, Act 655, NARC; John Adam Paxton, *New Orleans City Directory and Register of 1822* (New Orleans: Benjamin Levy, 1822); Chase, *Frenchmen, Desire, Good Children*, 96–99.

22. Roulhac B. Toledano, *A Pattern Book of New Orleans Architecture* (Gretna, LA: Pelican Publishing, 2010), 180–81.

23. Joseph Cuvillier, vol. 22, Act 127, May 20, 1839, NARC.

24. The Tremé Market was a masterpiece of nineteenth-century architecture. The WPA tore down the Tremé Market in 1932 to "beautify" the neighborhood. Today Armstrong Park occupies the area where Parish Prison and the Tremé Market once stood.

25. Gary A. Van Zante, *New Orleans 1867: Photographs by Theodore Lilienthal* (New York: Merrell Publishers, 2008), 109–10; Roulhac Toledano and Mary Louise Christovich, *New Orleans Architecture*, vol. 6 (Gretna, LA: Pelican Press, 1980), 63. The prison was demolished in 1895.

26. Jerah Johnson, *Congo Square in New Orleans* (New Orleans: Louisiana Landmarks Society, 1995), 2, 20, 34, 41.

27. Toledano and Christovich, *New Orleans Architecture*, 112–14.

28. Ibid., 142–43.

29. Bell, *Revolution, Romanticism*, 124.

30. Louis T. Caire, vol. 23A, Act 1048, November 12, 1832, *Testament de Veuve Bernard*, NARC.

31. Copy of a letter from Rodolphe Desdunes to René Grandjean, July 30, 1921, in Letterbook, 85-83, Grandjean Collection. Desdunes at this time was living with his son Daniel in Omaha.

32. Copy of a letter from René Grandjean to Rodolphe Desdunes, July 17, 1921, in Letterbook, 85-83, Grandjean Collection; Louis T. Caire, vol. 23A, Act 1048, November 12, 1832, *Testament de Veuve Bernard*, NARC.

33. Marie Anaise Rapp Collins was born on March 15, 1865, and died on January 1943. Ancestry.com.

34. Copy of a letter from René Grandjean to Rodolphe Desdunes, July 17, 1921, in Letterbook, 85-83, Grandjean Collection.

35. Donald E. DeVore and Joseph Logsdon, *Crescent City Schools: Public Education in New Orleans, 1841–1991* (Lafayette: University of Southwestern Louisiana, 1991), 42; Octave De Armas, vol. 40, Act 93, May 6, 1847, NARC.

36. Pierre-Aristide Desdunes, *Rappelez-vous Concitoyens! La poésie de Pierre-Aristide Desdunes*, ed. Caryn Cossé Bell (Shreveport, LA: Les Éditions Tintamarre, 2010), 20; Mary Niall (Molly) Mitchell, *Raising Freedom's Child: Black Children and Visions of the Future after Slavery* (New York: New York University Press, 2008), 16. According to Dr. Mitchell, the Catholic Institution was not just for orphans. In fact, most of the students were children from black Creole families who paid tuition, not penniless orphans. The inclusion of the word *orphan* in the school's name helped ensure partial funding from the state legislature and the city of New Orleans.

37. Octave De Armas, vol. 49, Act 110, February 1, 1851, NARC.

38. *Journal des Séances de la direction de l'institution Catholique pour l'instruction des Orphelins dans l'indigence*, vol. 1, April 26, 1851, 1 (hereafter cited as *Séance Book I*), AANO. The word *séance* in this context means a meeting, not a gathering to communicate with the dead.

39. Mitchell, *Raising Freedom's Child*, 17–18. In a poem titled "La Floraison—de 1848 à la guerre," Grandjean lists the following notables: Lacroix, Lanusse, Boguilles, Gérard, Crokère (Crocker), Cristophe, Lavigne, Lainez, Camps, Snaër, Trévigne, Chessé, Questy, Vigers, Rey, Thézan, Populus, and Adolphe Duhart. Letterbook, 85-83, Grandjean Collection.

40. *Séance Book I*, June 7, 1852, 89, AANO.

CHAPTER 2

1. Catherine L. Albanese, *A Republic of Mind and Spirit: A Cultural History of American Metaphysical Religion* (New Haven: Yale University Press, 2007), 180; Nancy Rubin Stuart, "The Raps Heard around the World," *American History* (August 2005), 42–48; Anne Braude, *Radical Spirits: Spiritualism and Women's Rights in Nineteenth-Century America* (Boston: Beacon Press, 1989), 11.

2. Albanese, *A Republic*, 181.

3. Ann Braude, *Radical Spirits*, 16.

4. Whitney R. Cross, *The Burned-over District: The Social and Intellectual History of Enthusiastic Religion in Western New York, 1800–1850* (New York: Harper & Row, 1950), 3. The Church of Jesus Christ of Latter-day Saints (Mormon Church), which had its genesis in the visions of Joseph Smith during the 1820s, is an exception to the ephemeral nature of religions and social reforms originating in the Burned-over District.

5. Cox, *Body and Soul*, 16–17.

6. Molly McGarry, *Ghosts of Futures Past: Spiritualism and the Cultural Politics of Nineteenth-Century America* (Berkeley: University of California Press, 2008), 177n1.

7. *New York Herald*, March 7, 1858.

8. Braude, *Radical Spirits*, 3, 56–57.

9. "The Night-Side of Nature," *Southern Literary Messenger* 17 (January 1851): 2–3; "Spiritual Manifestation," *Southern Literary Messenger* 19 (July 1853): 343–44.

10. "Credulity of the Times," *Southern Literary Messenger* 20 (June 1854): 344.

11. Clement Eaton, *The Freedom of Thought Struggle in the Old South* (New York: Harper & Row, 1964), 337.

12. Northwestern State University of Louisiana, Watson Memorial Library, Cammie G. Henry Research Center, Works Progress Administration, Federal Writers' Project (hereafter cited as NSU/WPA-FWP), Folder 91, 1 of 3, "The Ebony Enigma."

13. Hirsch and Logsdon, eds., *Creole New Orleans*, 92, 130.

14. Louisiana Rare Vertical File, Organizations, Société du Magnétisme de la Nouvelle-Orléans (1847), Louisiana Research Collection, Tulane University, New Orleans; Bell, *Revolution, Romanticism*, 189, 198.

15. Bell, *Revolution, Romanticism*, 189, 198; Emma Hardinge Britten, *Nineteenth Century Miracle or Spirits or Their Work in Every Country of the Earth* (1884; repr., New York: Arno Press, 1976), 11, 17; Cathy Gutierrez, *Plato's Ghost: Spiritualism in the American Renaissance* (New York: Oxford University Press, 2009), 7.

16. Bell, *Revolution, Romanticism*, 200–201; Tregle, "Creoles and Americans," 176.

17. *Daily Picayune*, July 31, 1852, Letter from Theodore Clapp. Dr. Clapp led his church from 1822 to 1856. For additional information about the church and Clapp, see Ripley, *Social Life in Old New Orleans*, 120–24.

18. "Spirit Rappers," *New Orleans Daily Crescent*, December 16, 1852.

19. Albanese, *A Republic*, 269; *Daily Picayune*, December 4, 1852, January 24, 1854, February 3, 1854, February 21, 1854.

20. *Daily Picayune*, October 2, 1853, May 9, 1854; Letter of Mrs. G. B. Bushnell Marks to Amy Post, January 16, 1854, Amy and Isaac Post Family Papers, University of Rochester Library, Department of Rare Books and Special Collections.

21. "Les Tables Tournantes," *Le Propagateur Catholique*, January 28, 1854.

22. Ibid.; John Monroe, "Making the Séance 'Serious': '*Tables Tournantes*' and Second Empire Bourgeois Culture, 1853–1861," *History of Religions* 38, no. 3 (February 1999): 220.

23. Monroe, "Making the Séance 'Serious,'" 223–25.

24. Albanese, *A Republic*, 207–8, 214; Bell, *Revolution, Romanticism*, 193–94.

25. Cox, *Body and Soul*, 12–13; Bell, *Revolution, Romanticism*, 193.

26. Cox, *Body and Soul*, 12; Bell, *Revolution, Romanticism*, 192, 194–97.

27. Gutierrez, *Plato's Ghost*, 175.

28. Emma Hardinge, *Modern American Spiritualism: A Twenty Years' Record of the Communion between Earth and the World of Spirits* (1869; repr., New Hyde Park, NY: University Books, 1970), 11.

29. James Martin Peebles, *What Is Spiritualism, Who Are These Spiritualists and What Has Spiritualism Done for the World?* (Battle Creek, MI: Peebles Institute Print, 1903), 7–12; Albanese, *A Republic*, 221–22.

30. Albanese, *A Republic*, 222–23.

31. Ibid., 236–38.

32. The periodical was later published in book form as Joseph Barthet, *Le Spiritualiste de la Nouvelle-Orléans*, vols. 1–2 (New Orleans: Joseph Barthet, 1857–1858).

33. Ibid.

34. For a more detailed account of the Barthet-Perché war of words, see Bell, *Revolution, Romanticism*, 206–15.

35. Death Certificate of Valmour, February 7, 1869, 252, City Archives, NOPL. Valmour's real name was John B. Averin. The death certificate is listed under John B. Averin with the name Valmour in parentheses.

36. Barthet, *Le Spiritualiste*, vol. 1, 245, vol. 2, 279.

37. Ibid., vol. 1, 136.

38. Bell, *Revolution, Romanticism*, 85–86; Mary Gehman, "The Mexico-Louisiana Creole Connection," *Louisiana Cultural Vistas* 11, no. 4 (Winter 2001–2002), 86. The noose around the embattled free people of color tightened during the turbulent 1850s. Manumissions—legal acts that freed slaves—were restricted in 1852 and then totally outlawed in 1857. In 1858, city ordinances were passed that limited the rights of speech, assembly, and religion. In 1859, the Louisiana legislature passed one last draconian measure: all free people of color were ordered to choose a master and voluntarily enslave themselves. For a more detailed analysis of self-enslavement, see Judith Kelleher Schafer, *Becoming Free, Remaining Free:*

Manumission and Enslavement, 1846–1862 (Baton Rouge: Louisiana State University Press, 2003), 145–162.

39. Mary Gehman, e-mail to author, July 16, 2008.

40. Barthet, *Le Spiritualiste*, vol. 2, 11, 15; Uriah Clark, *Plain Guide to Spiritualism: A Handbook* (Boston: William White, 1863), 72.

41. Barthet, *Le Spiritualiste*, vol. 2, 11, 15.

42. Braude, *Radical Spirits*, 30; *Banner of Light*, April 11, 1857, and other issues around that time. The name of the sales agent was listed as A. Dappemont, or sometimes A. D'Appemont. I have found no additional information about the agent. A yearly subscription sold for $2.50, and individual copies sold for 5 cents.

43. As quoted in Hardinge, *Modern American Spiritualism*, 420–25.

44. Clark, *Plain Guide to Spiritualism*, n.p.

45. *Banner of Light*, July 23, 1857, August 13, 1857, October 17, 1857, November 14, 1857, and January 6, 1858.

46. *New York Times*, January 2, 1885. Squire left the *Banner of Light* in 1861. Years later, Rollin Squire moved to New York City and became involved in turbulent city politics. Mayor Edson, a childhood friend, appointed him commissioner of public works in 1885, and Squire quickly became embroiled in scandals that were heavily publicized in the daily newspapers. Barthet, *Le Spiritualiste*, vol. 2, 11–13.

47. Barthet, *Le Spiritualiste*, vol. 2, 15–16.

48. Passport Application (1873) from ancestry.com. Thomas G. Forster was originally from South Carolina and fought in the Texas army in 1836 (*Banner of Light*, July 21, 1860). *New Orleans Daily True Delta*, February 14 and March 7, 1858. Squire as well as other lecture mediums complained about the high costs of renting a hall in New Orleans. Letter of January 29, 1858 in the February 20, 1858 issue of *Banner of Light*.

49. Letter of January 29, 1858, in the February 20, 1858, issue of *Banner of Light*.

50. "The Levee at New Orleans," *The Illustrated London News*, June 5, 1858, 552.

51. Letter of January 29, 1858, in the February 20, 1858, issue of *Banner of Light*.

52. Letter of February 25, 1858, in the March 13, 1858, issue of *Banner of Light*. The letter was signed "A.M."

53. Letter of March 12, 1858, in the April 3, 1858, issue of *Banner of Light*.

54. Letter of April 9, 1858, in the May 29, 1858, issue of *Banner of Light*.

55. Hardinge, *Modern American Spiritualism*, 419.

56. Barthet, *Le Spiritualiste*, vol. 2, 228.

57. Cox, *Body and Soul*, 166.

58. Grandjean Register 85-30, June 19, 1858, 1, Grandjean Collection. Both Thomas Gales Forster and J. Rollin M. Squire left the *Banner of Light* in 1861. Forster worked in the offices of the War Department in Baltimore. *Banner of Light*, January 31, 1863.

CHAPTER 3

1. US Census of 1850, ancestry.com; Grandjean Register 85-30, June 19, 1858, 1, Grandjean Collection.

2. Alexander Castaing, April 25, 1861, *Plan Book 41*, Folio 8, NARC.

3. Under duress from jealous white women, the Spanish governor Miró decreed in 1786 that free women of color had to wear tignons.

4. Grandjean Notes, 85–92, Grandjean Collection. This collection of notes is separate from the séance registers.

5. John W. Blassingame, *Black New Orleans 1860–1880* (Chicago: University of Chicago Press, 1973), 88.

6. Robert C. Reinders, "The Free Negro in the New Orleans Economy, 1850–1860," *Louisiana History* 6, no. 3 (1965): 273.

7. Mary Gehman, "Visible Means of Support: Businesses, Professions, and Trades of Free People of Color," in *Creole: The History and Legacy of Louisiana's Free People of Color*, ed. Sybil Kein (Baton Rouge: Louisiana State University Press, 2000), 209.

8. Rodolphe Lucien Desdunes, *Our People*, trans. Sister Dorothea Olga McCants (Baton Rouge: Louisiana State University Press, 1973), 97–108. Originally published in French in 1911.

9. Edward Larocque Tinker, *Les Écrits de la langue française en Louisiane au XIXe siècle* (1923; repr., Geneva: Shatkine, 1975); Auguste Viatte, "Complément à la bibliographie louisianaise d'Edward Larocque Tinker," *Revue de Louisiane/Louisiana Review* 3, no. 3 (Winter 1974): 12–57.

10. US Census 1850, ancestry.com. Adèle's maternal grandparents were Joseph Gignac and Manon Montreuil, who was born around 1775. Toledano and Christovich, *New Orleans Architecture*, 102.

11. Certificate of Baptism, St. Louis Cathedral, vol. 7, 116, April 3, 1803, AANO. The spelling of Pierre's mother's name is unclear. Pierre Crocker's name was written as "Pedro Croker" in the Baptismal Register, but in most legal documents and in the Grandjean Séance Registers, he is known as Pierre Crocker. This brings up the challenge of identification in the nineteenth century. In the case of Pierre Crocker, there were two other Pierre Crockers in his immediate family. His eldest legitimate son was also Pierre Crocker and an illegitimate son, Victor Pierre Crocker, sometimes went by his middle name. To complicate things further, there were several different spellings of "Crocker": Croker, Crokère, Croquier, and Crokin. The older Pierre Crocker was sometimes referred as Pierre Crocker Sr. and sometimes referred as Pierre Crocker Jr. in the Grandjean Séance Registers. There is the additional problem of nicknames that people sometimes used in legal documents and in the US Census. According to François Dubuclet, everybody called Pierre Crocker "Periquite." The US Census of 1850 lists Pierre Crocker as Periquite Crocker. Frequently, black Creoles reversed their name order. In other words, the middle name became the first name, and the first name became the middle name. Henry Louis Rey was actually baptized Louis Henry Rey, but he consistently used Henry as his first name throughout his adult life. A final problem of identification was the propensity to change first names to different languages, such as Pedro to Pierre, and Pierre to Peter. This may have been related to changes in the government of Louisiana or to the individual's preference. Henry Rey often used "Henri" in his séance registers, as the spirit messengers usually spoke French. This has

led to confusion for some Spiritualist historians, who identify him as Henri Rey. In fact, on every legal document, including all military records, he used "Henry," never "Henri."

Sometimes, the priest officiating the baptismal would translate the first name into his maternal language. Père Antoine, who officiated at many baptismals, spoke Spanish as his maternal language, so he often changed the French name to a Spanish name.

12. Carolyn Morrow Long, *A New Orleans Voudou Priestess: The Legend and Reality of Marie Laveau* (Gainesville: University Press of Florida, 2006), 239-240n52. Long lists the legitimate children of Pierre Crocker as Celeste (b. April 3, 1828), Rose (b. 1830, d. 1831), Marie Elizabeth (b. 1831, d. 1836), Pierre Jr. (b. 1833, d. ca. 1858), Adèle (no middle name) (b. 1837, d. July 22, 1890), Joseph Ernest (b. 1843, d. 1845), Florentine (b. 1839, d. 1846), and Myrtille Raphaël (b. March 25, 1849, d. August 1885). Both Rose Gignac and Pierre Crocker were natives of the city. (Toledano and Christovich, *New Orleans Architecture*, 99). Fatima Shaik, "The Economy Society and Community Support for Jazz," *Jazz Archivist* 18 (2004): 2; Rodolphe Desdunes, *Our People*, 77–78.

13. Martha Ward, *Voodoo Queen: The Spirited Lives of Marie Laveau* (Jackson: University Press of Mississippi, 2004), xv. Other biographers like Carolyn Morrow Long believe that the younger Marie Laveau was not involved in Voodoo. However, there are some notes in the Grandjean Collection which indicate that she assumed her mother's role as a Voodoo priestess.

14. Theodore Seghers, vol. 42, Act 70, February 25, 1842, NARC.

15. Long, *A New Orleans Voudou Priestess*, 66, 167.

16. *L'Abeille*, July 10, 1857. The wake took place at Crocker's home on "rue St. Philippe, entre Villere et Robertson," and the funeral was celebrated at St. Augustine Church at 5:00 p.m. Ludger Boguille was also a teacher at the Couvent School. Bell, *Revolution, Romanticism*, 124; Shaik, "The Economy Society and Community Support for Jazz," 2; Grandjean Register 85-34, November 30, 1871, 104, September 28, 1871, 52, Grandjean Collection.

17. *Séance Book*, vol. 1, April 26, 1851, 1, and other dates throughout 1851, 1852, and 1853, AANO.

18. Certificate of Marriage, Marriage PC, vol. 2, 1843–1869, 76, AANO.

19. Information about Lucia Rey accessed from ancestry.com. New Orleans Sale of Property, Jacques Monière and Catherine Thiebaud to Adèle Crocker, March 4, 1859, New Orleans Board of Conveyances, Book 77, Act 559.

20. Succession Papers of Rose Adèle Gignac, No. 17513, April 4, 1861, City Archives, NOPL.

21. The Rey residence is listed as being on Craps in the New Orleans City Directory of 1852. *Cohen's New Orleans City Directory of 1852* (New Orleans: Daily Delta, 1852). The name of the street was officially changed to Burgundy in 1850, but residents continued to call it Craps. See Chase, *Frenchmen, Desire, Good Children*, 96–99.

22. Grandjean Register 85-30, October 26, 1858, 3, Grandjean Collection.

23. Father J. M. Morisot to Father Stephen Rousselon, September 2, 1843; Father J. M. Morisot to Father Stephen Rousselon, November 5, 1843; Elizabeth Waggaman to Father Stephen Rousselon, May 5, 1853. All at University of Notre Dame, "Catholic Church.

Archdiocese of New Orleans," http://www.archives.nd.edu/calendar.htm (accessed September 20, 2015).

24. Father J. M. Morisot to Archbishop Anthony Blanc, March 3, 1859; Father Julian Benoit to Archbishop Anthony Blanc, July 21, 1859; Father J. M. Morisot to unknown recipient in New Orleans, September 1, 1862. All at ibid. (accessed September 20, 2015); Grandjean Register 85-43, July 25, 1872, 221, Grandjean Collection.

25. Grandjean Register 85-43, July 25, 1872, 221, Grandjean Collection.

26. Bell, *Revolution, Romanticism*, 216; Grandjean Register 85-30, October 26, 1858, 101, 104, November 20, 1858, 34, Grandjean Collection; Will of Jean Chatry Document, MSS 66, Louisiana and Lower Mississippi Valley Collections, Louisiana State University Libraries, Baton Rouge, Louisiana (hereafter cited as LSU Libraries). Neither Rey nor Dubuclet revealed the last name of Soeur Louise. She was described as a woman with black skin and a soul like a diamond. See Grandjean Notes, 85-92, Grandjean Collection. She appears as a spirit on July 11, 1870, indicating that she died sometime prior to that date.

27. Grandjean Register 85-30, October 26, 1858, 101, 104, Grandjean Collection.

28. Ibid., 104; Bell, *Revolution, Romanticism*, 125, 215–16; Pierre-Aristide Desdunes, *Rappelez-vous Concitoyens!*, ed. Caryn Cossé Bell, 14. In *Our People and Our History*, Rodolphe Desdunes described Samuel Snaër as a "musical genius" (84). Nelson Desbrosses was also a writer, and he contributed poems to *Les Cenelles* (1845), a seminal anthology of poems written by the black Creoles.

29. Grandjean Register 85-30, October 26, 1859, 107, Grandjean Collection.

30. Ibid., 102–4.

31. Emily Clark and Virginia Meacham Gould, "The Feminine Face of Afro-Catholicism in New Orleans, 1727–1852," *William and Mary Quarterly* 59 (2002), 436, 445; Bell, *Revolution, Romanticism*, 127–31.

32. Caryn Cossé Bell, "French Religious Culture in Afro-Creole New Orleans, 1718–1877," *U.S. Catholic Historian* 17, no. 2 (Spring 1999), 11–12; Rodolphe Desdunes, *Our People*, 99.

33. Hardinge, *Modern American Spiritualism*, 419, 427–28.

34. Letter of October 14, 1860, *Banner of Light*, November 24, 1860. "*Chercheur*" is French for seeker. Correspondents often used initials or pseudonyms.

35. Odd Fellow's Hall was a massive, four-storied building on Camp Street, between Lafayette and Poydras in the American business sector. J. Curtis Waldo, *Illustrated Visitors' Guide to New Orleans* (New Orleans, 1879). Images from this guide can be seen on the NOPL website, nutrias.org. at Images of the Month Gallery, March 2004.

36. Hardinge, *Modern American Spiritualism*, 428–29.

37. Ibid.; "Spiritualism in the South," *Banner of Light*, January 28, 1860.

38. Hardinge, *Modern American Spiritualism*, 429–39, 425; Grandjean Séance Margin Notes in Register 85-64, 16. Hardinge's quote is in English in Grandjean's Margin Notes. Grandjean's notes corroborate with what Hardinge described in *Modern American Spiritualism*. See "Spiritualism in the South," *Banner of Light*, January 28, 1860. Emma Hardinge Britten, *Nineteenth Century Miracle or Spirits or Their Work in Every Country of the Earth* (1884; repr. New York: Arno Press, 1976), 38.

39. *Banner of Light*, June 18, 1857; Hardinge, *Modern American Spiritualism*, 201, 457.

40. James V. Mansfield Papers, William L. Clements Library, University of Michigan (hereafter cited as WLCL); Mrs. J. H. Conant, "The Messenger," *Banner of Light*, December 12, 1857.

41. Finding aid for James V. Mansfield Papers, Manuscripts Division, WLCL, Bethany Anderson, 2008; *Daily Picayune*, December 30, 1860.

42. James V. Mansfield Papers, WLCL. See chapter 6 and the Epilogue for more information about J. W. Allen.

43. Ibid.; *New Orleans Daily Crescent*, November 16, 1860.

44. "The Great Rebellion," *Banner of Light*, April 27, 1861.

45. Ochs, *A Black Patriot*, 68.

46. Grandjean Register 85-30, pullout sheet, Grandjean Collection.

47. James G. Hollandsworth Jr., *The Louisiana Native Guards* (Baton Rouge: Louisiana State University Press, 1995), 3–4; *New York Times*, November 5, 1862. The *New York Times* article is a reprint of an article from *L'Union* published on October 15, 1862, which reported the Christmas toast.

48. *New York Times*, November 5, 1862.

49. Chester G. Hearn, *When the Devil Came Down to Dixie: Ben Butler in New Orleans* (Baton Rouge: Louisiana State University Press, 1997), 59–61, 71.

50. Rodolphe Desdunes, *Our People*, 118–20; Hollandsworth, *Louisiana Native Guards*, 15–16; G. William Quatman, *A Young General and the Fall of Richmond: The Life and Career of Godfrey Weitzel* (Athens: Ohio University Press, 2015), 71.

51. Rodolphe Desdunes, *Our People*, 114.

52. *New York Times*, November 5, 1862; US Pension Record No. 1127637, Department of the Interior, Bureau of Pensions, Washington, DC. A devastating fire destroyed Rey's house in 1875, which may be the reason why no photographs exist.

53. Hollandsworth, *Louisiana Native Guards*, 18.

54. General Orders No. 28, May 15, 1862, *Official Records of the Union and Confederate Armies, War of the Rebellion*, 128 vols. (Washington, DC, 1880–1901), vol. 15, 426. Hereafter cited as ORA.

55. François Dubuclet was a séance circle participant who later related to his son-in-law, René Grandjean, what transpired at the séances and gave him insights into the social, political, and historical backgrounds of the black Creoles. See Introduction of this volume for more information.

56. *New York Times*, November 5, 1862.

57. Grandjean Notes, 85-92, Grandjean Collection. These notes are separate from the Grandjean Séance Registers.

58. W. C. Corsan, *Two Months in the Confederate States: An Englishman's Travels through the South*, ed. Benjamin H. Trask (Baton Rouge: Louisiana State University Press, 1996), 19.

59. Ochs, *A Black Patriot*, 75, 77; Hollandsworth, *Louisiana Native Guards*, 17–18.

60. *L'Union*, September 27, 1862. This was the premier issue of *L'Union*. Some of the mediums and participants of Rey's séance circles were contributors to the newspaper. Among these writers were Joanni Questy, Charles Testat, and Louis Fouché.

61. Ibid., October 18, 1862.

62. Corsan, *Two Months*, 21; Letter from General Weitzel to General Butler, October 24, 1862, *ORA*, series 1, vol. 15, 159; Quatman, *A Young General*, 114; Hollandsworth, *Louisiana Native Guards*, 33, 38–40; *L'Union*, November 8, 1862. Confederate General Richard Taylor was the son of US president Zachary Taylor.

63. US Pension Record No. 1127637, Department of the Interior, Bureau of Pensions, Washington, DC; Hollandsworth, *Louisiana Native Guards*, 38–40.

64. Ibid., 33–35. Benjamin F. Butler, *Private and Official Correspondence of General Benjamin Butler during the Period of the Civil War*, ed. Jessie Ames Marshall, vol. 2 (Norwood, MA: Plimton Press, 1917), 490, 426–28.

65. Hollandsworth, *Louisiana Native Guards*, 43–46.

66. Pierre-Aristide Desdunes, *Rappelez-vous Concitoyens!*, ed. Caryn Cossé Bell, 36, 52, 141.

67. US Army Discharge Papers, April 4, 1863, National Archives and Records Administration, Washington, DC.

68. Grandjean Séance Margin Notes in Register 85-30, 34, 125, Grandjean Collection.

69. Henry Joseph Rey was born on April 14, 1860. See ancestry.com.

CHAPTER 4

1. Nathan W. Daniels, *Thank God My Regiment an African One: The Civil War Diary of Colonel Nathan W. Daniels*, ed. C. P. Weaver (Baton Rouge: Louisiana State University Press, 1998), 107–8.

2. Hearns, *When the Devil Came*, 212, 215, 218; Theresa Arnold-Scriber and Terry G. Scriber, *Ship Island, Mississippi: Rosters and History of the Civil War Prison* (Jefferson, NC: McFarland, 2008), 426–31.

3. Van Zante, *New Orleans 1867*, 100–103.

4. The description of occupied New Orleans is adapted from Charles W. Boothby's letter of August 18, 1862, Charles W. Boothby Papers, MSS. 4847, Louisiana and Lower Mississippi Valley Collections, LSU Libraries, Baton Rouge, Louisiana (hereafter cited as Boothby Papers, LSU Library), and Laura De Force Gordon's letter of July 30, 1864, which appeared in the August 20, 1864 issue of *Banner of Light*. Gordon was a celebrated Spiritualist lecturer who accompanied her husband, a Union army doctor, to New Orleans in 1864.

5. Jay Dearborn Edwards, *A Closer Look: The Antebellum Photographs of Jay Dearborn Edwards 1858-1861*, ed. Jessica Dorman and Erin Greenwald (New Orleans: The Historic New Orleans Collection, 2008), 45–46; Corsan, *Two Months*, 18.

6. Noah André Trudeau, *Like Men of War: Black Troops in the Civil War 1862–1865* (Boston: Little, Brown, 1998), 26, 41–43, 45.

7. Ochs, *A Black Patriot*, 1–4.

8. Henry S. Laver, "Refuge of Manhood: Masculinity and the Militia Experience in Kentucky," in *Southern Masculinity: Perspectives on Masculinity in the Old South*, ed. Craig Thompson Friend and Lorri Glover (Athens: University of Georgia Press, 2004), 15.

9. Grandjean Register 85-30, July 17, 1863, 156–58, Grandjean Collection.

10. Grandjean Register 85-38, February 9, 1872, 420, Grandjean Collection; Grandjean Register 85-32, June 2, 1871, 33, Grandjean Collection.

11. Grandjean Register 85-57, June 2, 1871, 33½ (in English), Grandjean Collection; Hollandsworth, *Louisiana Native Guards*, 28.

12. Michaelides, ed., *Paroles d'honneur*, 48.

13. Justin A. Nystrom, *New Orleans after the Civil War: Race, Politics, and a New Birth of Freedom* (Baltimore: The John Hopkins University Press, 2010), 43; Ochs, *A Black Patriot*, 5.

14. US Pension Record No. 1018808, Department of the Interior, Bureau of Pensions, Washington, DC. Thanks to Alaina Wallace, a descendent of Hippolyte Rey, for the pension records.

15. US Pension Record No. 1118825, Department of the Interior, Bureau of Pensions, Washington, DC; Trudeau, *Like Men of War*, 28.

16. US Pension Record No. 1018808, Department of the Interior, Bureau of Pensions, Washington, DC; Grandjean Margin Notes in 85-65, 330, Grandjean Collection, and information obtained from http://www.nutrias.org/~nopl/exhibits/lacroix/hacker.htm, a NOPL website; Grandjean Séance Margin Notes in Register 85-30, 34, 125, Grandjean Collection.

17. Daniels, *Thank God My Regiment an African One*, 108–9, 115, 151, 153.

18. Julia LeGrand, *The Journal of Julia LeGrand, New Orleans 1862–1863*, ed. Kate Mason Rowland and Mrs. Morris L. Croxall (Richmond, VA: Everett Waddy, 1911), 162, 131, 98.

19. Robert J. Chandler, "In the Van: Spiritualists as Catalysts for the California Women's Suffrage Movement," *California History* 73 (Fall 1994): 194; Letter of July 30, 1864, in the *Banner of Light*, August 20, 1864. Laura Gordon is most noted as an activist for women's suffrage in her adopted state of California after she abandoned her life as a Spiritualist speaker. She became the second woman lawyer in California. Spiritualism, women's rights, and radical abolitionism were closely intertwined in the antebellum years. After the Civil War, some popular women mediums and lecturers abandoned Spiritualism as women's rights were catapulted into the forefront of the women activists' political agenda.

20. *New Orleans Times*, November 6, 1863. Shaik, "The Economy Society," 2–4. The third building, known as Economy Hall, was demolished in 1965 after sustaining major damage from Hurricane Betsy.

21. *New Orleans Times*, November 6, 1863.

22. Ibid. Grandjean described Pinchback as "very, very capable" and a man with great oratorical skills, earning him the epithet of "silver tongue." See Grandjean Notes, 85-92, Grandjean Collection. Interestingly, on the following day (November 7, 1863), the *New Orleans Times* apologized for misidentifying another speaker, C. C. Morgan, as colored. The reporter explained, "It would have required a connossieur [sic] and daylight to distinguish between free color and white." See the *New Orleans Times*, November 7, 1863. Bell, *Revolution, Romanticism*, 248.

23. David C. Rankin, "The Origins of Black Leadership in New Orleans during Reconstruction," *Journal of Southern History* 40, no. 3 (August 1974), 422.

24. Logsdon and Bell, "Americanization of Black New Orleans," 206, Table 1.

25. Pension records describe Rey as a "bright mulatto." US Pension Record No. 1127637, Department of the Interior, Bureau of Pensions, Washington, DC.

26. *New Orleans Tribune*, September 14, 1865. The *New Orleans Tribune/La Tribune de la Nouvelle-Orléans* was the successor to *L'Union*.

27. Grandjean Séance Margin Notes in Register 85-41, 422, Grandjean Collection.

28. Zante, *New Orleans 1867*, 106–9; Johnson, *Congo Square*, 20. The Carondelet Canal was eventually filled in during the twentieth century, becoming Lafitte Street with railroad tracks along the road. An Interstate (I-10) Interchange is located where the turning basin once existed. Today a linear park, the Lafitte Greenway, stretches from near City Park to Basin Street in Tremé, adjacent to the nineteenth-century venues of the Cercle Harmonique's séances.

29. Grandjean Notes, 85-92, and Grandjean Séance Margin Notes in Register 85-31, 20, Grandjean Collection. François Dubuclet informed Grandjean that Valmour's real name was John B. Averin. Valmour's death certificate is filed under "Averin," but in parentheses it is noted as "Also Valmour." Dubuclet signed the death certificate as a witness, indicating that the two were close friends. Death Certificate of Valmour, February 7, 1869, 252, City Archives, NOPL.

30. Grandjean Séance Margin Notes in Register 85-31, 37, Grandjean Collection. See chapter 6 for additional information about the French Creole registers.

31. Grandjean Notes, 85-91, Grandjean Collection. Original French: "*Oh! trop tard, je suis perdue, moi.*" These notes are separate from the séance registers and include 85-91 and 85-92.

32. Barthet, *Le Spiritualiste*, vol. 2, 138.

33. Grandjean Register 85-43, November 28, 1872, 172. It is not clear who Abner was. Grandjean Notes, 85-91, Grandjean Collection.

34. Caryn Cossé Bell, "Pierre-Aristide Desdunes (1844–1918), Creole Poet, Civil Rights Activist: *The Common Wind*'s Legacy," *Louisiana History* 55, no. 3 (Summer 2014), 204n55.

35. Ibid., 287; Rodolphe Desdunes, *Our People*, 53.

36. Ward, *Voodoo Queen*, 176. See Epilogue for more information about Voodoo and Spiritual and Spiritualist churches.

37. Grandjean Register 85-31, December 1, 1865, 15, Grandjean Collection.

38. John Hope Franklin, *Reconstruction after the Civil War* (Chicago: University of Chicago Press, 1994), 34–36. The official name of the Freedmen's Bureau was the Bureau of Refugees, Freedmen, and Abandoned Lands.

39. Ibid., 63–64; Eric Foner, *Reconstruction: America's Unfinished Revolution, 1864–1877* (New York: HarperCollins, 1989), 261–62.

40. James Hogue, *Uncivil War: Five New Orleans Street Battles and the Rise and Fall of Radical Reconstruction* (Baton Rouge: Louisiana State University Press, 2006), 34, 40; *House Report No. 16: Report of the Select Committee on New Orleans Riots*, 39th Cong., 2d Sess. (Washington, DC: US Government Printing Office, 1867), 2 (hereafter cited as *House Report No. 16*).

41. James Hollandsworth Jr., *An Absolute Massacre: The New Orleans Race Riot of July 30, 1866* (Baton Rouge: Louisiana State University Press, 2001), 99–113; *House Report No. 16*, 54.

42. Daniels, Nathan W., 1836–1867, Nathan W. Daniels diary and scrapbook, 1861–1867, New Orleans Correspondence of June 16, 1867 to the *National Anti-Slavery Standard*, https://lccn.loc.gov/mm2002084934; Hollandsworth, *An Absolute Massacre*, 116; *House Report No. 16*, 15.

43. Hollandsworth, *An Absolute Massacre*, 42–44; *House Report No. 16*, 160, 199, 354, 54–55.

44. *House Report No. 16*, 2, 12; Foner, *Reconstruction*, 263.

45. Hollandsworth, *An Absolute Massacre*, 50–51; Reed, *Life of A. P. Dostie*, 338; *House Report No. 16*, 384.

46. Grandjean Register 85-31, February 21, 1869, 101–3, Grandjean Collection. Some nouns have been capitalized in the spirit messages that would have normally not been capitalized. I have retained the original capitalization.

47. Grandjean Register 85-36, November 18, 1871, 153, Grandjean Collection. The entry was written in English.

CHAPTER 5

1. Daniels, *Thank God My Regiment an African One*, 175; "The River," *Daily Picayune*, May 30, 1867. The chapter title is borrowed from the subtitle of Henry Clay Warmoth's memoir, *War, Politics, and Reconstruction: Stormy Days in Louisiana* (Columbus: University of South Carolina Press, 1930).

2. Cora Daniels's maiden name was Scott, but she was most recognized by her first husband's last name, Hatch. After the death of Colonel Daniels, she remarried twice and is also known by the last names of Tappan and Richmond. Cora always included her two middle initials, L.V., when she signed her name.

3. Harrison Barrett, *Life Work of Cora L. V. Richmond* (Chicago: Hack & Anderson, 1895), 4; Braude, *Radical Spirits*, 86; McGarry, *Ghosts of Futures Past*, 30; Benjamin F. Hatch, *Spiritualists' Iniquities Unmasked and the Hatch Divorce Case* (New York: B. F. Hatch, 1859), 35n1.

4. Daniels, *Thank God My Regiment an African One*, 173.

5. Ibid., 151, 153, 147–48, 172; Daniels, Nathan W., 1836–1867, Nathan W. Daniels diary and scrapbook, 1861–1867, transcription by C. P. Weaver of March 1865 diary entry of Nathan Daniels, https://lccn.loc.gov/mm2002084934.

6. Ibid., 173; *Daily True Delta* (Louisiana), December 21, 1865. The Reverend John Pierpont was the maternal grandfather of J. Pierpont Morgan, the famous banker and entrepreneur.

7. Letter to Amy Post from Cora L. V. Daniels, February 18, 1867, Amy and Isaac Post Family Papers, University of Rochester Library, Department of Rare Books and Special Collections, Rochester, NY. Cora wrote, "Our lovely little 'Etta' unfolds every day in beauty and intelligence like the rose." Daniels's child and his first wife shared the same name, Henrietta.

8. Daniels, *Thank God My Regiment an African One*, 175. Cora Daniels had discontinued her Spiritualist work because, as she wrote to Amy Post, "I am so much of a mother that I am almost wholly absorbed in my babe, and so much of a wife that husband and Rosebud are ever paramount in my thoughts." Letter to Amy Post from Cora L. V. Daniels, February 18, 1867, Amy and Isaac Post Family Papers, University of Rochester Library, Department of Rare Books and Special Collections, Rochester, NY.

9. Daniels, *Thank God My Regiment an African One*, 175.

10. *New Orleans Tribune*, July 30, July 31, 1867.

11. Death Certificate of Nathan W. Daniels, October 2, 1867, and Death Certificate of Henrietta Daniels, October 17, 1867, City Archives, NOPL; Daniels, *Thank God My Regiment an African One*, 176. Thanks to Clare Weaver for copies of the death certificates. Charles Boothby in his letter of March 24, 1864, reported that "since the Federals have been here, New Orleans has been as healthy as any city in the United States, and every precaution will be taken to make the same state of health the summer to come." Coincidently, Boothby contacted yellow fever the same month as Daniels in 1867 but was able to recover. See Boothby Papers, LSU Libraries. Jefferson City is today part of New Orleans. The Daniels lived on Magazine Street, near the cross street of Lyons.

12. *New Orleans Tribune*, October 3, 1867, obituary as quoted in Daniels, *Thank God My Regiment an African One*, 176; *Cincinnati Daily Gazette*, December 24, 1867.

13. Bell, *Revolution, Romanticism*, 265, 291; Minutes of the Fraternité #20 Masonic Society, Box 40, in the George Longe Collection, Amistad Research Center, Tulane University, New Orleans.

14. Logsdon and Bell, "Americanization of Black New Orleans," 235.

15. Ibid., 245.

16. Letter of July 16, 1863, Boothby Papers, LSU Library.

17. Grandjean Notes, 85-92, Grandjean Collection; Kimberly S. Hanger, *Bounded Lives, Bounded Places: Free Black Society in Colonial New Orleans, 1769–1803* (Durham, NC: Duke University Press, 1997), 15–16.

18. The capital of Louisiana remained in New Orleans throughout Reconstruction. The location later moved from the Mechanics' Institute to the St. Louis Hotel in the French Quarter (Toledano and Christovich, *New Orleans Architecture*, vol. 6, 107).

19. Grandjean Notes, 85-92 and Grandjean Séance Margin Notes in Register 85-31, 57, Grandjean Collection. Valmour had moved from his house/blacksmith shop seven blocks further north on St. Louis Street (in the direction of Lake Pontchartrain) between Miro and Galvez Streets. His new residence still fronted the Carondelet Canal. Rey's new residence was on St. Louis Street between Derbigny and Claiborne Streets.

20. Brett Carroll, *Spiritualism in Antebellum America* (Bloomington: Indiana University Press, 1997), 131.

21. Grandjean Séance Margin Notes in Register 85-31, 62, 67 and January 8, 1869, 62, Grandjean Collection; Bell, *Revolution, Romanticism*, 215–16. The banking district moved a few years later to the emerging financial district around Carondelet and Gravier Streets, today known as the Central Business District in New Orleans (Campanella, *Bourbon Street*, 74).

22. Grandjean Séance Margin Notes in Register 85-31 and February 6, 1869, 91, Grandjean Collection; Drew Gilpin Faust, *This Republic of Suffering: Death and the American Civil War* (New York: Vintage Books, 2008), 10; NSU/WPA-FWP, Folder 73, "A Custom."

23. Death Certificate of John B. Averin (Valmour), February 7, 1869, 252, City Archives, NOPL; *New Orleans Times*, October 4, 1868; Grandjean Notes, 85-92, Grandjean Collection.

24. *New Orleans Tribune*, February 7, 1869.

25. Mourning customs are described in Ward, *Voodoo Queen*, 94–95.

26. *Official Journal of the Proceedings of the Convention for Framing a Constitution for the State of Louisiana* (New Orleans: J. B. Roudanez, 1868), 17, 242.

27. Ibid., 149.

28. Ibid., 122, 199.

29. *New Orleans Tribune*, January 12, 1869.

30. Donald E. DeVore and Joseph Logsdon, *Crescent City Schools: Public Education in New Orleans* (Lafayette: University of Southwestern Louisiana, 1991), 70.

31. *Séance Book II*, December 30, 1869 and April 14, 1870, 157–158, 163, AANO.

32. Letter from Rodolphe Desdunes to René Grandjean, August 12, 1921, Letterbook 85-83, Grandjean Collection.

33. *Séance Book II*, Attendance Rolls for 1871–1873, AANO.

34. Grandjean Register 85-64, June 10, 1871, 29, Grandjean Collection.

35. Logsdon and Bell, "Americanization of Black New Orleans," 234.

36. Bambra Pitman, "Culture, Caste, and Conflict in New Orleans Catholicism: Archbishop Francis Jassens and the Color Line," *Louisiana History* 49, no. 4 (Fall 2008): 436.

37. Grandjean Register 85-31, February 13, 1869, 123, Grandjean Collection.

38. Grandjean Register 85-34, October 30, 1871, 83, Grandjean Collection. The French word for black, *noir*, was capitalized in the communication.

39. Grandjean Register 85-31, March 11, 1869, 176, Grandjean Collection.

40. Bell, "French Religious Culture in Afro-Creole New Orleans," 13.

41. Bell, *Revolution, Romanticism*, 68–73; Latrobe, *Impressions*, 166.

42. Bell, *Revolution, Romanticism*, 214–15; Barthet, *Le Spiritualist de la Nouvelle-Orléans*.

43. Toledano and Christovich, *New Orleans Architecture*, 100; Tinker, *Les Écrits*, 448.

44. Grandjean Register 85-31, May 22, 1870, 271, Grandjean Collection.

45. *New Orleans Tribune*, September 15, 1865. Dunn was born free in New Orleans in 1826. Some historical sources have erroneously reported that he was a slave who bought his freedom.

46. As quoted in Joe Gray Taylor, *Louisiana Reconstructed 1863–1877* (Baton Rouge: Louisiana State University, 1974), 218.

47. Warmoth, *War, Politics, and Reconstruction*, 120.

48. Grandjean Notes, 85-93, Grandjean Collection; Warmoth, *War, Politics, and Reconstruction*, 120; Marcus B. Christian, "The Theory of the Poisoning of Oscar J. Dunn," *Phylon* 6, no. 3 (3rd qtr. 1945): 254–66; *The Louisianian*, January 11, 1872, November 26, 1871. Lieutenant Governor Dunn was interred in St. Louis Cemetery No. 2.

49. Grandjean Register 85-34, November 30, 1871, 160, Grandjean Collection. Dubuclet observed that at this séance Rey's daughter, Lucia, and her classmates were present.

50. Ibid., December 8, 1871, 194.

51. Grandjean Register 85-35, December 26, 1871, 225, Grandjean Collection.

52. Grandjean Register 85-37, November 22, 1872, 329, Grandjean Collection. Capitals proliferate in the communications.

53. *Edward's Annual Directory in the City of New Orleans 1873* (New Orleans: Southern Publishing Co., 1873), 874. Warmoth was able to appoint a mayor because of his expanded

role during Radical Reconstruction. Ordinarily, the mayor of New Orleans would have been elected. The address 18 Royal Street represents the old numbering; today it is the 100 block of Royal, one block from Canal Street. B. M. Norman, *Norman's New Orleans and Environs: Containing a Brief Historical Sketch* (New Orleans: B. M. Norman, 1845), 86, 100. The building was destroyed by fire on December 3, 1960 (*Times-Picayune*, December 4, 1960).

54. The dates for Rey's tenure as Third District assessor are taken from a plaque that used to be on display at the Third District assessor's office in New Orleans's City Hall. The New Orleans assessor's office has been reorganized, and the plaque is no longer displayed. Grandjean frequently mentioned Rey's role as assessor in his margin notes, emphasizing the increased wealth from that position.

55. *William George v. Board of State Assessors, Jack Wharton and others*, Historical Archives of the Supreme Court of Louisiana, New Orleans, 24 La. Ann. 410 (1872), Special Collections, Earl K. Long Library, University of New Orleans. Henry Rey and two other tax assessors alleged that they were entitled to their offices and that they should not have to return the $1,000 advanced to them for their public services. The Louisiana Supreme Court affirmed the lower court's decision, which said that Rey had been legally appointed but that the appointment expired on March 5, 1872, leaving that office vacant. The court also ruled that Rey had to repay the $1,000 advanced to him. House Miscellaneous Document No. 211, *Testimony Taken by the Select Committee to Investigate the Condition of Affairs in the State of Louisiana* (Washington, DC: Government Printing Office, 1872), 411.

56. Grandjean Register 85-39, March 14, 1872, 300, Grandjean Collection. B. P. Blanchard replaced Rey, and Blanchard's tenure ended on January 18, 1873. Ovide C. Blandin succeeded Blanchard and remained assessor until April 22, 1886. The dates for Blanchard's and Blandin's tenure as Third District assessor are taken from a plaque that used to be on display at the Third District assessor's office in the New Orleans City Hall. The New Orleans assessor's office has been reorganized, and the plaque is no longer displayed.

CHAPTER 6

1. Faust, *This Republic*, 6–10; Braude, *Radical Spirits*, 24–25.

2. *Banner of Light*, October 1, 1864; Faust, *This Republic*, 183–85. Drew Faust states that according to the database of the National Park Service, the soldiers who were supposedly channeled by Conant were fictional creations, and in fact the "*Banner of Light* did not present the story of any reader's actual kin" (184).

3. "Spiritualism. Its Rise and Progress—Something of Its History in New Orleans. A Times Reporter Caught in the Toils of the Rappers—What He Saw and Heard," *New Orleans Times*, July 5, 1874.

4. Ibid.

5. Information obtained from ancestry.com. The daughter's name was misspelled in the article as "Maybell." There is no explanation why Kendall consented to work with a rival newspaper. New *Orleans Times*, July 5, 1874.

6. Ibid.

7. "Ticket of Leave Spirits. Remarkable Demonstrations," *Daily Picayune*, July 12, 1874.
8. Ibid.
9. "Spiritualism. A Times Reporter Enters the Field as an Investigator," *New Orleans Times*, February 22, 1875.
10. *Daily Picayune*, December 17, 1871.
11. Joseph O. Barrett, *The Spiritual Pilgrim: A Biography of James M. Peebles* (Boston: William White, 1872), 301; *New Orleans Times*, February 13, 1876; Cox, *Body and Soul*, 198, 206; Claude F. Jacobs and Andrew J. Kaslow, *Spiritual Churches of New Orleans: Origins, Beliefs and Rituals of an African-American Religion* (Knoxville: University of Tennessee Press, 1991), 35–36.
12. "Letting in Light. How Spiritualism is Said to do that by Opening the Windows of the Soul. The Trance Lecture of the Rev. J.W. Allen on Sunday Morning," *New Orleans Times*, March 13, 1876.
13. *Daily Picayune*, May 27, 1877.

CHAPTER 7

1. Grandjean Séance Margin Notes in Register 85-63, 65, 311, Grandjean Collection.
2. Ibid.; Coroner's Office Record of Inquest, vol. 21, May 1871, City Archives, NOPL.
3. Grandjean Register 85-35, December 12, 1871, 16. Hacker's store did not have a special name other than "hardware store."
4. Freedman's Bank Records accessed on ancestry.com, May 20, 1873.
5. John Magill, "The History of Banking in New Orleans," *Louisiana Cultural Vistas* 18, no. 1 (Spring 2007): 44.
6. Cox, *Body and Soul*, 185.
7. Grandjean Register 85-44, Grandjean Séance Margin Notes, 180, Grandjean Collection. The *Banner of Light* ceased publication in 1907.
8. Grandjean Register 85-31, April 24, 1867, 55, Grandjean Collection.
9. Grandjean Register 85-34, December 10, 1871, 210, Grandjean Collection. Moni was Father Aloysius Leopold Moni, the pastor of St. Louis Cathedral. Father Moni passed away in August 1842.
10. Grandjean Register 85-33, June 16, 1871, 68, Grandjean Collection.
11. Grandjean Register 85-40, pullout sheet, Grandjean Collection. See pages 126–127 for the artwork.
12. Grandjean Register 85-59, February 28, 1875, 136, Grandjean Collection; Bliss Broyard, *One Drop: My Father's Hidden Life—A Story of Race and Family Secrets* (New York: Little, Brown, 2007), xiv. *One Drop* is based on Bliss Broyard's black Creole ancestry. Her great-great-grandfather was Henry Broyard, who was white but passed for black in order to marry a black Creole woman in New Orleans. From this communication it can be inferred that Broyard was integrated into the black Creole community.
13. Grandjean Register 85-38, February 10, 1872, 452, Grandjean Collection. The identity of Myrtile is unclear other than that she was a young child.
14. Grandjean Register 85-42, June 13, 1872, 149, Grandjean Collection.

15. Rodolphe Desdunes, *Our People*, 60–70. Rodolphe Desdunes and René Grandjean were friends and correspondents during Desdunes's later years. The two men shared a common interest in the history and legacy of nineteenth-century black Creoles. Desdunes's book first appeared in French in 1911. The spirits often addressed Henry Rey as Henri.

16. Grandjean Register 85-31, March 9, 1869, 159–163, Grandjean Collection. Desbrosses was also a medium, author, and teacher at the Couvent School.

17. Grandjean Register 85-31, March 12, 1869, 178–81, Grandjean Collection.

18. Toledano and Christovich, *New Orleans Architecture*, 15. In 1798, real estate tycoon Claude Tremé laid out rue St. Claude perpendicular to present-day Esplanade Avenue. He named it after his patron saint, St. Claude, and the original name for Esplanade Avenue was rue Ste. Julie in honor of his wife. La Société d'Economie et d'Assistance Mutuelle Minute Book (MSS 267), Society d'Economie et d'Assistance Mutuelle Collection, Special Collections, Earl K. Long Library, University of New Orleans.

19. Ochs, *A Black Patriot*, 27; Blassingame, *Black New Orleans*, 229, Table 6; Letter of November 5, 1866, Boothby Papers, LSU Libraries.

20. Nathaniel Cortlandt Curtis, *New Orleans: Its Old Houses, Shops and Public Buildings* (Philadelphia: J. B. Lippincott, 1933), 87. The building still exists.

21. Grandjean Margin Notes in Register 85-36, 409, Grandjean Collection; Magill, "History of Banking in New Orleans," 37, 41. The Société des Arts et Métiers was another venue for séances.

22. Grandjean Register 85-36, August 19, 1872, 409, and Grandjean Séance Margin Notes, 406, Grandjean Collection; Albanese, *A Republic*, 225.

23. Grandjean Register 85-36, Grandjean Séance Margin Notes, 176, Grandjean Collection.

24. Grandjean Register 85-33, June 17, 1871, 74 and 85-31, March 12, 1869, 178–81, Grandjean Collection.

25. Grandjean Register 85-64, May 7, 1872, 15, Grandjean Collection. This register contains séance transcriptions from 1890 as well as earlier ones from 1871 and 1872. Emanuel Swedenborg is discussed in more detail in chapter 2.

26. Grandjean Register 85-32, August 5, 1870, 54–55, Grandjean Collection.

27. Grandjean Séance Margin Notes in Register 85-36, 177, Grandjean Collection; Bell, *Revolution, Romanticism*, 217.

28. US 1850 Census, ancestry.com. Similar to Rey's father and mother, Duhart's father was born in Cuba, and his mother was born in Saint-Domingue. Bell, *Revolution, Romanticism*, 124–25; Michaelides, ed., *Paroles d'honneur*, 38–39, Grandjean Séance Margin Notes in Register 85-42, 302, Grandjean Collection.

29. Ancestry.com; Bruce Chessé, "The Chessés in Louisiana," *La Créole: A Journal of Creole History and Genealogy* 3, no. 1 (October 2010), 39–41. The younger Herriman later moved his family to Los Angeles as a result of increasingly harsh Jim Crow laws during the 1890s. His son, George J. Herriman, created the famous *Krazy Kat* cartoon strip, which was published daily from 1913 until his death in 1944. The cartoonist hid his black Creole ancestry from the public.

30. Uriah Clark, *Plain Guide to Spiritualism: A Handbook* (Boston: William White, 1863), 72.

31. Grandjean Séance Margin Notes in Register 85-42, 302, and Grandjean Register 85-34, November 28, 1871, 250, Grandjean Collection; Cox, *Body and Soul*, 13.

32. Grandjean Collection. Determining the sex of some spirit messengers was problematic, so the percentages are an approximation. Often the first name was omitted in the index.

33. Grandjean Register 85-32, March 18, 1870, 6, Grandjean Collection.

34. Grandjean Notes, 85-91; Grandjean Séance Margin Notes in Register 85-64, 13, and Grandjean Register 85-38, January 8, 1872, 102, Grandjean Collection. I have not found any additional information about Mrs. Rice, although she was mentioned several times in the séance registers.

35. Grandjean Register 85-34, November 7, 1871, 95, and Grandjean Register 85-30, November 21, 1858, 19, Grandjean Collection.

36. Grandjean Register 85-31, March 25, 1869, 205, Grandjean Collection. Marquise de Sévigné (1626–1696) was a French aristocrat, remembered for her letter writing.

37. Grandjean Register 85-53, January 7, 1874, 83, Grandjean Collection.

38. René Grandjean frequently penciled in *et soeurs* (and sisters) behind the word "*frères*" (brothers) as if to breathe some gender equality into the séance registers.

39. Paul F. Lachance, "The Foreign French," *Creole New Orleans*, 119–20; Shaik, "The Economy Society and Community Support for Jazz," 3.

40. Pitman, "Culture, Caste, and Conflict," 426.

41. Bell, "Pierre-Aristide Desdunes," 291–95.

42. Grandjean Register 85-32, August 5, 1870, 54–55, Grandjean Collection.

CHAPTER 8

1. Michael A. Ross, *The Great New Orleans Kidnapping Case: Race, Law, and Justice in the Reconstruction Era* (New York: Oxford University Press, 2015), 214; Orleans Parish School Board Minutes, January 9, 1875-February 7, 1877, Orleans Parish School Board Collection, Special Collections, Earl K. Long Library, University of New Orleans; DeVore and Logsdon, *Crescent City Schools*, 354–55.

2. Ross, *The Great New Orleans Kidnapping Case*, 11–12.

3. Ibid.; DeVore and Logsdon, *Crescent City Schools*, 73, 354–55; Hogue, *Uncivil War*, 69, 72–73.

4. Orleans Parish School Board Minutes, January 9, 1875-February 7, 1877, Orleans Parish School Board Collection, Special Collections, Earl K. Long Library, University of New Orleans.

5. Information obtained from the Biographical/Historical Note in Charles W. Boothby Papers, LSU Libraries; Letter of March 16, 1867, Orleans Parish School Board Minutes, January 9, 1875-February 7, 1877, Orleans Parish School Board Collection, Special Collections, Earl K. Long Library, University of New Orleans; Devore and Logsdon, *Crescent City Schools*, 73. Monthly meetings were held on the first Wednesday of the month at 7:30 p.m.

6. Curtis, *New Orleans*, 205.

7. Letter of September 25, 1874, Boothby Papers, LSU Libraries. Boothby was able to return to his office the next day. Henry C. Castellanos, *New Orleans As It Was: Episodes of Louisiana Life* (Baton Rouge: Louisiana State University Press, 2006), 203–4.

8. Letter of September 25, 1874, Boothby Papers, LSU Libraries.

9. White Leaguers executed at least seventy black leaders in a confrontation over a courthouse in Colfax, Louisiana, on Easter Sunday, April 13, 1873.

10. *L'Abeille de la Nouvelle-Orléans* (*The Bee of New Orleans*), September 13, 1874; *New Orleans Times*, September 13, 1874.

11. Stuart Omar Landry, *The Battle of Liberty Place: The Overthrow of Carpet-bag Rule in New Orleans* (New Orleans: Pelican Press, 1955), 122; Ross, *The Great New Orleans Kidnapping Case*, 214.

12. Nystrom, *New Orleans After the Civil War*, 170–73; Judith K. Schafer, "The Battle of Liberty Place: A Matter of Historical Perception," *Louisiana Cultural Vistas* 5, no. 1 (Spring 1994), 9–17.

13. The once magnificent St. Louis Hotel was demolished in 1916 because of damage sustained by the hurricane of the year before. The Omni Royal Orleans Hotel now occupies most of the block.

14. Letter of September 25, 1874, Boothby Papers, LSU Libraries.

15. Cox, *Body and Soul*, 185.

16. Grandjean Register 85-57, September 14, 1874, 8, 37, Grandjean Collection.

17. Ibid., September 15, 1874, 39½, 44.

18. Ibid., October 2, 1874, 86½. Monatte did not appear in the casualty lists, so it is unclear what his role was in the Battle of Liberty Place. The Battle of Liberty Place Monument was erected in 1891, near the location of the 1874 insurgency. In the wake of antiracism protests in 1993, the controversial obelisk monument was moved to a more obscure location between the Aquarium of the Americas and Canal Place.

19. DeVore and Logsdon, *Crescent City Schools*, 76.

20. Grandjean Register 85-58, December 28, 1874, n.p., pullout sheet, Grandjean Collection.

21. Ibid., 178.

22. Grandjean Séance Margin Notes in Register 85-61, 38, Grandjean Collection. Dubuclet mentioned numerous times that Rey's house on Villere burned on December 3. I have done extensive research to verify the fire and have not found any newspaper articles reporting it. At this time, there was no standardized method of reporting and documenting fires in the city. A Rey descendent confirmed the fire in an email. Elisha Robinson and Roger H. Pidgeon, *Robinson's Atlas of the City of New Orleans* (New York: E. Robinson, 1883), plate 21, square 627.

23. Orleans Parish School Board Minutes, February 7, 1877, April 4, 1877; Orleans Parish School Board Collection, Special Collections, Earl K. Long Library, University of New Orleans; *New Orleans Times*, March 5, 1877.

24. Hough, *Uncivil Wars*, 6.

25. The term *Bourbons* refers to the French royalists who were restored to power after the fall of Napoleon Bonaparte in France. Here it is used to describe the Redeemers.

26. James Gill, *Lords of Misrule: Mardi Gras and the Politics of Race in New Orleans* (Jackson: University of Mississippi Press, 1997), 123.

27. Foner, *Reconstruction*, 589.

28. Orleans Parish School Board Minutes, June 4, July 3, 1877. Orleans Parish School Board Collection, Special Collections, Earl K. Long Library, University of New Orleans.

29. Logsdon and Devore, *Crescent City Schools*, 87.

30. Ibid., 88–89; Paul Trévigne lived at 155 Columbus Street, and Rey lived at 95 Columbus Street. See ancestry.com.

31. Ibid.

32. Grandjean Register 85-32, July 11, 1870, 6, Grandjean Collection.

33. *New York Times*, February 8, 1875.

34. Information obtained from the New Orleans Public Library website, http://www.nutrias.org/~nopl/exhibits/lacroix/intro.htm; Shirley Elizabeth Thompson, *Exiles at Home: The Struggle to Become American in Creole New Orleans* (Cambridge, MA: Harvard University Press, 2009), 145.

35. Shaik, "The Economy Society and Community Support for Jazz," 4–5.

36. Constitution et Statues Organiques de la Société d'Economie et d'Assistance Mutuelle, 1, Louisiana Rare Vertical Files, Jones Library, Tulane University, New Orleans; Shaik, "The Economy Society and Community Support for Jazz," 2, 5–6; *Daily Picayune*, April 25, 1874.

37. *Daily Picayune*, April 25, 1874.

38. Société d'Economie et d'Assistance Mutuelle Minute Book (MSS 267), March 1, 1877, 1, June 12, 1877, 76–77, Société d'Economie et d'Assistance Mutuelle Collection, Special Collections, Earl K. Long Library, University of New Orleans; Keith Weldon Medley, *We as Freemen*: Plessy v. Ferguson (Gretna, LA: Pelican Publishing, 2003), 120, 127.

39. Société d'Economie et d'Assistance Mutuelle Minute Book (MSS 267), June 13, 1877, 78, Société d'Economie et d'Assistance Mutuelle Collection, Special Collections, Earl K. Long Library, University of New Orleans.

40. Ibid.

41. Grandjean Séance Margin Notes in Grandjean Register 85-37, 48, 558, Grandjean Collection; Grandjean Séance Margin Notes in Grandjean Register 85-65, 311, Grandjean Collection.

42. Grandjean Register 85-63, November 22, 1877, 553, May 29, 1877, 124, July 30, 1877, 221 (in English), November 24, 1877 (pullout paper), Grandjean Collection.

43. As quoted in Logsdon and Bell, "Americanization of Black New Orleans," 251–52.

44. Nystrom, *New Orleans After the Civil War*, 188.

CHAPTER 9

1. Neutral ground is the distinctively New Orleanian term for the traffic medium. In his family research, Derrick Pitard discovered several employees of his great-great-grandfather had worked for decades in the hardware store. Some employees were relatives of the owner.

2. Thanks to Derrick Pitard for information about his great-great-grandfather's store. The store was torn down in the 1930s to make way for F. W. Woolworth, a five-and-dime store. On September 9, 1960, civil rights activists with the Congress on Racial Equality (CORE) staged a sit-in at the whites-only lunch counter. Henry Rey, no doubt, would have been proud of their civil rights activism (*New Orleans Times-Picayune*, September 10, 1960). Woolworth was demolished in 2015. The modern numbering for the store is 1031 Canal. Melissa Lee Smith, *Remembering New Orleans* (Nashville, TN: Turner Publishing, 2010), 26.

3. Hollandsworth, *An Absolute Massacre*, 154. The Mechanics' Institute was later demolished, and today the Roosevelt Hotel occupies the space.

4. St. Charles Avenue changes its name to Royal Street at the Canal Street intersection. It was near this intersection that Rey worked in the Third District assessor's office on Royal Street. The old City Hall is now Gallier Hall, named after the architect.

5. Smith, *Remembering New Orleans*, 23.

6. *New Orleans Tribune*, October 25, 1864.

7. Medley, *We as Freemen*, 33.

8. The huge live oak trees and traffic circle no longer exist. They were victims of the controversial construction of the elevated portion of Interstate 10 on Claiborne Avenue during the late 1960s. The construction hastened the decline of Tremé by dividing its two major portions and denying its inhabitants a green space on Claiborne Avenue to gather. In 1854, a city-owned market opened in the space occupied today by the Circle Food Store (*New Orleans Times-Picayune*, August 3, 2012).

9. Charles Vincent, "Aspects of the Family and Public Life on Antoine Dubuclet: Louisiana's Black State Treasure, 1868–1878," *Journal of Negro History* 66, no. 1 (Spring 1981): 31–33.

10. Medley, *We as Freemen*, 95–96, 104.

11. Certificate of Death of Adèle Crocker Rey, July 23, 1890, City Archives, NOPL.

12. Grandjean Register 85-64, Grandjean Collection. Within the same register are transcriptions of séances from 1871 and 1872. The register may have been used in those years, or the communications may have been copies from earlier spiritual messages.

13. Ibid., April 8, 1890, 3, April 22, 1890, 4.

14. Medley, *We as Freedmen*, 118, 127.

15. Ibid., 158–60. At this time the Louisiana Supreme Court was located in the Cabildo, next to St. Louis Cathedral and across from Jackson Square.

16. As quoted in Logsdon and Bell, "Americanization of Black New Orleans," 261.

17. US Pension Record No. 1127637, Department of the Interior, Bureau of Pensions, Washington, DC.

18. Ibid.

19. Ibid.

20. US Pension Record No. 1018808, Department of the Interior, Bureau of Pensions, Washington, DC.

21. US Pension Record No. 1118825, Department of the Interior, Bureau of Pensions, Washington, DC.

22. Information obtained from ancestry.com.

23. Death Certificate of Henry Louis Rey, April 20, 1894, City Archives, NOPL. The reasons for Henry Rey's death by anthrax remain a mystery. Typically, in the nineteenth century anthrax was contracted by direct contact with animals in a rural setting. I have no evidence that would indicate Henry Rey spent time in rural Louisiana during the 1890s. However, New Orleans at this time had livestock living on many open lots within the city limits.

24. Grandjean Séance Margin Notes in Register 85-63, 511, Grandjean Collection. Henry Louis Rey's body is interred in the crypt of Pierre Crocker, which is located in St. Louis Cemetery No. 1, near Marie Laveau's crypt. The crypt is marked La Famille de P. Crocker, and Rey's name does not appear on the crypt's plate. Thanks to the Office of Archives, Archdiocese of New Orleans, for its help in locating the burial site.

25. *Plessy v. Ferguson*, 163 US 537 (1896). Majority decision by Justice Henry Brown and dissent by Justice John Harlan.

26. Medley, *We as Freemen*, 209–214.

27. US Censuses of 1900 and 1930. Accessed on ancestry.com.

28. Bruce Chessé, "The Chessés in Louisiana," *La Créole* 3, no. 1 (October 15, 2010): 41–42; Biographical information obtained from the Grandjean Finding Aid, Grandjean Collection.

29. Grandjean Séance Margin Notes in Register 85-34, 41, Grandjean Collection. Thanks to Michael Tisserand for biographical information about George Herriman Jr. and his son.

30. Bliss Broyard, *One Drop*; Grandjean Register 85-59, February 28, 1875, 136, Grandjean Collection.

31. Laussat, *Memoirs of My Life*, 105.

EPILOGUE

1. Carroll, *Spiritualism in Antebellum America*, 179. For a detailed discussion of New Thought, Christian Science, and Theosophy, see Albanese, *A Republic*, 270–339.

2. *Daily Picayune*, March 27, 1881.

3. Joseph O. Barrett, *Spiritual Pilgrim*, 301; *Daily Picayune*, March 30, 1891; "For Forty-four Years: The Anniversary of Modern Spiritualism," *New Orleans Item*, April 1, 1892.

4. *New Orleans Times-Picayune*, March 30, 1891; "For Forty-four Years. The Anniversary of Modern Spiritualism," *New Orleans Item*, April 1, 1892.

5. "Spiritualists in Convention. Meeting of the National Spiritualists Association in Washington. The Association Represents 125,000 Professed Spiritualists," *Daily Picayune*, October 20, 1895; "Church of the Soul. First Society of Spiritualists Adopts Another Name. Mrs. Cora L.V. Richmond Takes Charge of the Congregation," *Daily International Ocean* (Chicago), June 8, 1896.

6. *New York Herald*, March 5, 1893.

7. "Could See Spirit Seated at Table, Is Claimed of Psychics," *Seattle Daily Times*, January 5, 1923; *Watertown* (NY) *Daily Times*, February 16, 1922. Peebles's wife, Mary M. Corkey, was from around Watertown, New York. According to newspaper articles from across the nation, Dr. Peebles actually attended his one hundredth birthday party. The centennial birthday celebration was held as planned, and a chair was reserved at the head of the table

for the spirit of Dr. Peebles. Dr. Guy Bogart read a message from him: "I sit here this glorious day for just a short time listening to such songs as no earth birds can sing." *San Diego Evening Tribune*, March 24, 1922.

8. Letter of March 7, 1917, Grandjean Collection 85-78. All of the letters from this era were written in English.

9. R. Waite Joslyn, *Criminal Law and Statutory Penalities of Illinois* (Chicago: T. H. Flood, 1920), 64; Letter of August 11, 1917, Grandjean Collection 85-78.

10. Letter of December 18, 1919, Grandjean Collection 85-78.

11. Letter of May 8, 1924, Grandjean Collection 85-78.

12. Federal Writers' Project of the WPA, *New Orleans City Guide* (Cambridge, MA: The Riverside Press, 1938), xxxi. The three churches listed were the First Church of Divine Fellowship, 823 Spain Street; the First Church of Spiritual and Psychic Research, 720 Girod Street; and the Sacred Heart Spiritual Church, 1734 Amelia Street.

13. Biographical information about Oscar L. Clark was accessed from ancestry.com. I used the following sources from the online service: Massachusetts Town and Vital Records, town of Plymouth; World War I Draft Registration Cards 1917–1919; 1910 US Federal Census; and New Orleans Passenger Lists, arrival date of September 17, 1928, from Honduras. *New Orleans Times-Picayune*, January 25, 1937; Folder 85-123, Schedule of services, First Church of Divine Fellowship of Spiritualism, n.d., Grandjean Collection; *New Orleans Times-Picayune*, March 30, 1929; Folder 85-123, Schedule of services, First Church of Divine Fellowship of Spiritualism, n.d., Grandjean Collection; *New Orleans Times-Picayune*, March 30, 1929.

14. *New Orleans Times-Picayune*, September 12, 1929, October 24, 1931.

15. Hans Baer, *The Black Spiritual Movement: A Religious Response to Racism* (Knoxville: University of Tennessee Press, 2001), 38–44.

16. *New Orleans Times-Picayune*, April 16, 1921; Albanese, *A Republic*, 474. The congregation of the Pleasant Grove Baptist Church purchased the church after Leafy Anderson's death (*New Orleans Times-Picayune*, May 2, 1931).

17. Jacobs and Kaslow, *Spiritual Churches*, 137.

18. Cox, *Body and Soul*, 206.

19. Albanese, *A Republic*, 474; Robert Tallant Collection, ca. 1937, NOPL.

20. Hans A. Baer, "The Limited Empowerment of Women in Black Spiritual Churches: An Alternative Vehicle to Religious Leadership," *Sociology of Religion* 54, no. 1 (Spring 1993), 66.

21. Federal Writers' Project, *New Orleans City Guide*, 199–211.

22. "Fanatic Cults, Mother Catherine," NSU/WPA-FWP, Folder 91, 2 of 3; Marcus B. Christian, "A Black History of Louisiana," chapter 12, 51, typescript in Marcus B. Christian Collection, Special Collections, Earl K. Long Library, University of New Orleans.

23. Albanese, *A Republic*, 474–75.

24. Jacobs and Kaslow, *Spiritual Churches*, 17.

25. Ibid., 86.

26. "Fanatic Cults"; Ward, *Voodoo Queen*, 113–14.

27. Helene d'Aquin Allain memoir, Manuscripts Collection M-781, Louisiana Research Collection, Howard-Tilton Memorial Library, Tulane University, New Orleans; Jacobs and Kaslow, *Spiritual Churches*, 129, 132.

Bibliography

PRIMARY SOURCES

Archival Materials

Amistad Research Center, Tulane University, New Orleans
  George Longe Collection

Archives of the Archdiocese of New Orleans
  Baptismal Records, St. Louis Cathedral
  Burial Records, St. Louis Cemetery No. 1
  "Journal des Séances de la direction de l'Institution Catholique pour l'instruction des orphelins dans l'indigence," vols. 1 and 2
  Marriage Records, Saint Augustine Church

Earl K. Long Library, Special Collections, University of New Orleans
  Marcus B. Christian Collection
  Historical Archives of the Supreme Court of Louisiana, New Orleans
  Orleans Parish School Board Collection
  René Grandjean Collection
  Société d'Économie et d'Assistance Mutuelle Collection

Historic New Orleans Collection
  Vieux Carré Survey

Howard-Tilton Memorial Library, Jones Hall, Louisiana Research Collection, Tulane University, New Orleans

Helene d'Aquin Allain Memoir
Louisiana Rare Vertical Files

Louisiana and Lower Mississippi Valley Collections, Louisiana State University Libraries, Baton Rouge
    Charles W. Boothby Collection
    Jean Chatry Collection

National Archives and Records Administration, Washington, DC
    Record Group 15: Records of the Veterans Administration
        Pension Records
    US Army Discharge Papers

New Orleans, Recorder of Conveyances, Orleans Parish, Louisiana
    Conveyance Office Index to Purchasers and Vendors and Conveyance

New Orleans Public Library, New Orleans
    City Archives
        Coroner's Office Record of Inquest
        Death Certificates
        Robert Tallant Collection
        Succession and Probate Records

Notarial Archives Research Center, New Orleans
    Original Acts of Orleans Parish, Notaries
        Louis Caire
        Joseph Cuvillier
        Octave DeArmas
        Paul E. Laresche
        Phillippe Pedesclaux
        Carlile Pollock
        Theodore Seghers
    Plan Books
        Alexander Castaing
        Tourné F. Nicholas
        James Strehler

University of Rochester Library, Rochester, New York
    Amy and Isaac Post Family Papers Collection

Watson Memorial Library, Cammie G. Henry Research Center, Northwestern State University, Natchitoches, Louisiana

Louisiana Writers' Project. Unpublished Interviews and Research Materials, 1935–1943, Federal Writers' Collection

William L. Clements Library, University of Michigan
James V. Mansfield Pwapers

Public Documents

House Miscellaneous Document No. 211: *Testimony Taken by the Select Committee to Investigate the Condition of Affairs in the State of Louisiana*, Washington, DC: US Government Printing Office, 1872.
House Report No. 16: *Report of the Select Committee on New Orleans Riots*, 39th Cong., 2d Sess. Washington, DC: US Government Printing Office, 1867.
Official Journal of the Proceedings of the Convention for Framing a Constitution for the State of Louisiana. New Orleans: J. B. Roudanez, 1868.
The War of the Rebellion: A Compilation of the Official Records of the Union and Confederate Armies. 128 vols. Washington, DC: US Government Printing Office, 1880–1901.

Online Sources

Ancestry.com
Library of Congress website: https://lccn.loc.gov/mm2002084934. Daniels, Nathan W., 1836–1867. Nathan W. Daniels diary and scrapbook, 1861–1867.
New Orleans Public Library website: http://www.nutrias.org/~nopl/exhibits/lacroix
University of Notre Dame website: http://www.archives.nd.edu/calendar.htm

Published Memoirs, Letters, Articles, Documents, Literary Works, and Historical Narratives

Barrett, Harrison. *Life Work of Cora L. V. Richmond*. Chicago: Hack & Anderson, 1895.
Barrett, Joseph O. *The Spiritual Pilgrim: A Biography of James M. Peebles*. Boston: William White, 1872.
Barthet, Joseph. *Le Spiritualiste de la Nouvelle-Orléans*, vols. 1, 2. New Orleans: Joseph Barthet, 1857, 1858.
Britten, Emma Hardinge. *Nineteenth Century Miracle or Spirits or Their Work in Every Country of the Earth*. 1884. Reprint, New York: Arno Press, 1976.
Butler, Benjamin F. *Butler's Book: A Review of his Legal, Political and Military Career*. Boston: A. M. Thayer, 1892.
———. *Private and Official Correspondence of General Benjamin Butler During the Period of the Civil War*. Vol. 2. Edited by Jessie Ames Marshall. Norwood, MA: Plimton Press, 1917.
Castellanos, Henry C. *New Orleans As It Was: Episodes of Louisiana Life*. 1895. Reprint, Baton Rouge: Louisiana State University Press, 2006.
Claiborne, William C. C. *Official Letter Books of W. C. C. Claiborne 1801–1816*. Vol. 5. Edited by Dunbar Rowland. Jackson: Mississippi Historical Association, 1917.

Clark, Uriah. *Plain Guide to Spiritualism: A Handbook*. Boston: William White, 1863.
Cohen's New Orleans City Directory of 1852. New Orleans: Daily Delta, 1852.
Corsan, W. C. *Two Months in the Confederate States: An Englishman's Travels Through the South*. Edited by Benjamin H. Trask. Baton Rouge: Louisiana State University Press, 1996.
Daniels, Nathan W. *Thank God My Regiment an African One: The Civil War Diary of Colonel Nathan W. Daniels*. Edited by C. P. Weaver. Baton Rouge: Louisiana State University Press, 1998.
Desdunes, Rodolphe Lucien. *Our People and Our History*. Translated and edited by Sister Dorothea Olga McCants. Baton Rouge: Louisiana State University Press, 1973.
Edward's Annual Directory in the City of New Orleans 1873. New Orleans: Southern Publishing, 1873.
Hardinge (Britten), Emma. *Modern American Spiritualism: A Twenty Years' Record of the Communion Between Earth and the World of Spirits*. 1869. Reprint, New Hyde Park, NY: University Books, 1970.
Hatch, Benjamin F. *Spiritualists' Iniquities Unmasked, and the Hatch Divorce Case*. New York: B. F. Hatch, 1859.
Herz, Henry. *My Travels in America*. Madison: State Historical Society of Wisconsin for the Department of History, University of Wisconsin, 1963.
Latrobe, Benjamin Henry Boneval. *Impressions Respecting New Orleans, Diary and Sketches 1818–1820*. Edited by Samuel Wilson Jr. New York: Columbia University Press, 1951.
Laussat, Pierre Clément de. *Memoirs of My Life*. Edited by Robert D. Bush. Translated by Sister Agnes-Josephine Pastwa. Baton Rouge: Louisiana State University Press, 1978.
Parton, James. *General Butler in New Orleans*. New York: Mason Brothers, 1864.
Paxton, John Adam. *New Orleans City Directory and Register of 1822*. New Orleans: Benjamin Levy, 1822.
Peebles, James Martin. *What is Spiritualism, Who are These Spiritualists and What has Spiritualism Done for the World?* Battle Creek, MI: Peebles Institute Print, 1903.
Percy, Stephen E., and Edward Augusta Michel. *New Orleans City Directory and Register of 1832*. New Orleans: Stephen E. Percy, 1832.
Robinson, Elisha, and Roger H. Pidgeon. *Robinson's Atlas of the City of New Orleans, Louisiana*. New York: E. Robinson, 1883.
Warmoth, Henry Clay. *War, Politics and Reconstruction: Stormy Days in Louisiana*. 1930. Reprint, Columbia: University of South Carolina Press, 2006.

Newspapers and Periodicals

Banner of Light, Boston
Boston Post
Cincinnati Daily Gazette
Daily International Ocean, Chicago
Daily Picayune, New Orleans
Frank Leslie's Illustrated Newspaper

Harper's Weekly
The Illustrated London News
New Orleans Bee (*L'Abeille de la Nouvelle-Orléans*)
New Orleans Daily Crescent
New Orleans Item
New Orleans Le Courier
New Orleans Times
New York Daily Reformer
New York Herald
New York Times
The Progressive Thinker, Chicago
Le Propagateur Catholique, New Orleans
San Diego Evening Tribune
Seattle Daily Times
Southern Literary Messenger
Sunday Delta, New Orleans
Tribune/La Tribune de la Nouvelle-Orléans
L'Union, New Orleans
Watertown Daily Times, Watertown, New York
Weekly Louisianian, New Orleans

SECONDARY SOURCES

Books

Albanese, Catherine L. *A Republic of Mind and Spirit: A Cultural History of American Metaphysical Religion*. New Haven, CT: Yale University Press, 2007.

Arnold-Scriber, Theresa, and Terry G. Scriber. *Ship Island, Mississippi: Rosters and History of the Civil War Prison*. Jefferson, NC: McFarland, 2008.

Baer, Hans. *The Black Spiritual Movement: A Religious Response to Racism*. Knoxville: University of Tennessee Press, 2001.

Bell, Caryn Cossé. *Revolution, Romanticism, and the Afro-Creole Protest Tradition in Louisiana, 1718–1868*. Baton Rouge: Louisiana State University Press, 1997.

Blassingame, John W. *Black New Orleans, 1860–1880*. Chicago: University of Chicago Press, 1973.

Braude, Ann. *Radical Spirits: Spiritualism and Women's Rights in Nineteenth-Century America*. Boston: Beacon Press, 1989.

Broyard, Bliss. *One Drop: My Father's Hidden Life—A Story of Race and Family Secrets*. New York: Little, Brown, 2007.

Campanella, Richard. *Bienville's Dilemma: A Historical Geography of New Orleans*. Lafayette: University of Louisiana at Lafayette Press, 2008.

———. *Bourbon Street*. Baton Rouge: Louisiana State University Press, 2014.

———. *Lincoln in New Orleans: The 1828–1831 Flatboat Voyages and Their Place in History.* Lafayette: University of Louisiana at Lafayette Press, 2010.

Carroll, Bret E. *Spiritualism in Antebellum America.* Bloomington: Indiana University Press, 1997.

Chase, John. *Frenchmen, Desire, Good Children, and Other Streets of New Orleans.* Gretna, LA: Pelican Press, 2004.

Cox, Robert S. *Body and Soul: A Sympathetic History of American Spiritualism.* Charlottesville: University of Virginia Press, 2003.

Cross, Whitney R. *The Burned-over District: The Social and Intellectual History of Enthusiastic Religion in Western New York, 1800–1850.* Ithaca, NY: Cornell University Press, 1950.

Curtis, Nathaniel Cortlandt. *New Orleans: Its Old Houses, Shops and Public Buildings.* Philadelphia: J. B. Lippincott Company, 1933.

Desdunes, Pierre-Aristide. *Rappelez-vous concitoyens! La poésie de Pierre-Aristide Desdunes.* Edited by Caryn Cossé Bell. Shreveport, LA: Les Éditions Tintamarre, 2010.

DeVore, Donald E., and Joseph Logsdon. *Crescent City Schools: Public Education in New Orleans, 1841–1991.* Lafayette: Center for Louisiana Studies, University of Southwestern Louisiana, 1991.

Dubois, Laurent. *Avengers of the New World.* Cambridge, MA: Harvard University Press, 2004.

Eaton, Clement. *The Freedom of Thought Struggle in the Old South.* New York: Harper & Row, 1964.

Edwards, Jay Dearborn. *A Closer Look: The Antebellum Photographs of Jay Dearborn Edwards 1858–1861.* Edited by Jessica Dorman and Erin Greenwald. New Orleans: The Historic New Orleans Collection, 2008.

Faust, Drew Gilpin. *This Republic of Suffering: Death and the American Civil War.* New York: Vintage, 2008.

Federal Writers' Project of the Works Progress Administration (WPA). *New Orleans City Guide.* Cambridge, MA: The Riverside Press, 1938.

Foner, Eric. *Reconstruction: America's Unfinished Revolution 1863–1877.* New York: Harper Collins, 2002.

Franklin, John Hope. *Reconstruction after the Civil War.* Chicago: University of Chicago Press, 1994.

Friend, Craig Thompson, and Lorri Glover, eds. *Southern Masculinity: Perspectives on Masculinity in the Old South.* Athens: University of Georgia Press, 2004.

Gutierrez, Cathy. *Plato's Ghost: Spiritualism in the American Renaissance.* New York: Oxford University Press, 2009.

Hanger, Kimberly S. *Bounded Lives, Bounded Places: Free Black Society in Colonial New Orleans, 1769–1803.* Durham, NC: Duke University Press, 1997.

Hearn, Chester G. *When the Devil Came Down to Dixie: Ben Butler in New Orleans.* Baton Rouge: Louisiana State University Press, 1997.

Hirsch, Arnold R., and Joseph Logsdon, eds. *Creole New Orleans: Race and Americanization.* Baton Rouge: Louisiana State University Press, 1992.

Hogue, James. *Uncivil War: Five New Orleans Street Battles and the Rise and Fall of Radical Reconstruction.* Baton Rouge: Louisiana State University Press, 2006.

Hollandsworth, James G., Jr. *An Absolute Massacre: The New Orleans Race Riot of July 30, 1866.* Baton Rouge: Louisiana State University Press, 2001.

———. *The Louisiana Native Guards: The Black Military Experience During the Civil War.* Baton Rouge: Louisiana State University Press, 1995.

Jacobs, Claude F., and Andrew J. Kaslow. *Spiritual Churches of New Orleans: Origins, Beliefs, and Rituals of an African-American Religion.* Knoxville: University of Tennessee Press, 1991.

Kein, Sybil, ed. *Creole: The History and Legacy of Louisiana's Free People of Color.* Baton Rouge: Louisiana State University Press, 2000.

Landry, Stuart Omar. *The Battle of Liberty Place: The Overthrow of Carpet-bag Rule in New Orleans.* New Orleans: Pelican Press, 1955.

Long, Carolyn Morrow. *A New Orleans Voudou Priestess: The Legend and Reality of Marie Laveau.* Tallahassee: University Press of Florida, 2006.

McGarry, Molly. *Ghosts of Futures Past: Spiritualism and the Cultural Politics of Nineteenth-Century America.* Berkeley: University of California Press, 2008.

Medley, Keith Weldon. *We as Freemen:* Plessy v. Ferguson. Gretna, LA: Pelican, 2003.

Michaelides, Chris, ed. *Paroles d'honneur: Écrits de Créoles de couleur néo-orléanais.* Shreveport, LA: Éditions Tintamarre, 2004.

Mitchell, Mary Niall. *Raising Freedom's Child: Black Children and Visions of the Future after Slavery.* New York: New York University Press, 2008.

Nystrom, Justin A. *New Orleans after the Civil War: Race, Politics, and a New Birth of Freedom.* Baltimore: The Johns Hopkins University Press, 2010.

Ochs, Stephen J. *A Black Patriot and a White Priest: André Cailloux and Claude Paschal Maistre in Civil War New Orleans.* Baton Rouge: Louisiana State University Press, 2000.

Quatman, G. William. *A Young General and the Fall of Richmond: The Life and Career of Godfrey Weitzel.* Athens: Ohio University Press, 2015.

Ross, Michael A. *The Great New Orleans Kidnapping Case: Race, Law, and Justice in the Reconstruction Era.* New York: Oxford University Press, 2015.

Schafer, Judith Kelleher. *Becoming Free, Remaining Free: Manumission and Enslavement in New Orleans, 1846–1862.* Baton Rouge: Louisiana State University Press, 2003.

Scott Rebecca J., and Jean M. Hébrard. *Freedom Papers: An Atlantic Odyssey in the Age of Emancipation.* Cambridge, MA: Harvard University Press, 2012.

Smith, Melissa Lee. *Remembering New Orleans.* Nashville, TN: Turner, 2010.

Sublette, Ned. *The World That Made New Orleans: From Spanish Silver to Congo Square.* Chicago: Lawrence Hill Books, 2008.

Taylor, Joe Gray. *Louisiana Reconstructed, 1863–1877.* Baton Rouge: Louisiana State University Press, 1974.

Thomas, Shirley Elizabeth. *Exiles at Home: The Struggle to Become American in Creole New Orleans.* Cambridge, MA: Harvard University Press, 2009.

Tinker, Edward Larocque. *Les Écrits de langue française en Louisiane au XIXe siècle.* Geneva: Slatkine, 1975.

Toledano, Roulhac. *A Pattern Book of New Orleans Architecture.* Gretna, LA: Pelican Press, 2010.

Toledano, Roulhac, and Mary Louise Christovich. *New Orleans Architecture: Faubourg Tremé and the Bayou Road.* Vol. 6. Gretna, LA: Pelican Press, 1980.

Tregle, Joseph G., Jr. *Louisiana in the Age of Jackson: A Clash of Cultures and Personalities.* Baton Rouge: Louisiana State University Press, 1999.

Trudeau, Noah André. *Like Men of War: Black Troops in the Civil War, 1862–1865.* Boston: Little, Brown, 1998.

Tunnel, Ted. *Crucible of Reconstruction: War, Radicalism, and Race in Louisiana, 1862–1877.* Baton Rouge: Louisiana State University Press, 1984.

Vella, Christina. *Intimate Enemies: The Two Worlds of the Baroness de Pontalba.* Baton Rouge: Louisiana State University Press, 1997.

Ward, Martha. *Voodoo Queen: The Spirited Lives of Marie Laveau.* Jackson: University Press of Mississippi, 2004.

Whitten, David O. *Andrew Durnford: A Black Sugarplanter in the Antebellum South.* New Brunswick, NJ: Transaction, 1995.

Zante, Gary A. *New Orleans 1867: Photographs by Theodore Lilienthal.* New York: Merrell Publishers, 2008.

Articles, Pamphlets, and Theses

Baer, Hans A. "The Limited Empowerment of Women in Black Spiritual Churches: An Alternative Vehicle to Religious Leadership." *Sociology of Religion* 54, no. 1 (Spring 1993): 65–68

Bell, Caryn Cossé. "French Religious Culture in Afro-Creole New Orleans, 1718–1877." *U.S. Catholic Historian* 17, no. 2 (Spring 1999): 1–16.

———. "Pierre-Aristide Desdunes (1844–1918), Creole Poet, Civil Rights Activist: The Common Wind's Legacy." *Louisiana History* 55 (Summer 2014): 282–312.

Berry, Mary F. "Negro Troops in Blue and Gray: The Louisiana Native Guards, 1861–1863." *Louisiana History* 8 (Spring 1967): 165–90.

Chandler, Robert J. "In the Van: Spiritualists as Catalysts for the California Women's Suffrage Movement." *California History* 73 (Fall 1994): 188–201.

Chesse, Bruce. "The Chessés in Louisiana." *La Créole: A Journal of Creole History and Genealogy* 3, no. 1 (October 2010): 39–41.

Christian, Marcus B. "The Theory of the Poisoning of Oscar J. Dunn." *Phylon* 6, no. 3 (3rd qtr., 1945): 254–66.

Clark, Emily, and Virginia Meacham Gould. "The Feminine Face of Afro-Catholicism in New Orleans, 1727–1852." *William and Mary Quarterly* 59, no. 2 (April 2002): 409–48.

Gehman, Mary, "The Mexico-Louisiana Creole Connection." *Louisiana Cultural Vistas* 11, no. 4 (Winter 2001–2002): 68–76.

Hobratsch, Ben Melvin. "Creole Angel: The Self-Identity of the Free People of Color of Antebellum New Orleans." Master's thesis, University of North Texas, 2006.

Johnson, Jerah. *Congo Square in New Orleans*. New Orleans: Louisiana Landmarks Society, 1995.

Joshi, Manoj K., and Joseph P. Reidy. "'To Come Forward and Aid in Putting Down This Unholy Rebellion': The Officers of Louisiana's Free Black Native Guard During the Civil War Era." *Southern Studies* 21 (Fall 1982): 326–42.

Lachance, Paul F. "The 1809 Immigration of Saint-Domingue Refugees to New Orleans: Reception, Integration and Impact." *Louisiana History* 29 (Spring 1988): 109–41.

Lepore, Jill. "Historians Who Love Too Much: Reflections on Microhistory and Biography." *Journal of American History* 88, no. 1 (June 2001): 129–44.

Magill, John. "The History of Banking in New Orleans." *Louisiana Cultural Vistas* 18, no. 1 (Spring 2007): 42–48.

Monroe, John. "Making the Séance 'Serious'; *'Tables Tournantes'* and Second Empire Bourgeois Culture, 1853–1861," *History of Religions* 38, no. 3 (February 1999): 219–46.

Pitman, Bambra. "Culture, Caste, and Conflict in New Orleans Catholicism: Archbishop Francis Janssens and the Color Line," *Louisiana History* 49 (Fall 2008): 423–62.

Rankin, David C. "The Origins of Black Leadership in New Orleans During Reconstruction." *Journal of Southern History* 40, no. 3 (August 1974): 417–40.

Reinders, Robert C. "The Decline of the New Orleans Free Negro in the Decade before the Civil War." *Journal of Mississippi History* 24 (January–October 1962): 88–98.

———. "The Free Negro in the New Orleans Economy, 1850–1860." *Louisiana History* 6 (1965): 260–88.

Schafer, Judith K. "The Battle of Liberty Place: A Matter of Historical Perception." *Cultural Vistas* 5, no. 1 (Spring 1994): 9–17.

Shaik, Fatima. "The Economy Society and Community Support for Jazz." *Jazz Archivist* 17 (2004): 1–9.

Tregle, Joseph G., Jr. "Thomas J. Durant, Utopian Socialism, and the Failure of Presidential Reconstruction in Louisiana." *Journal of Southern History* 45 (November 1979): 485–512.

Viatte, Auguste. "Complément à la bibliographie louisianaise d'Edward Larocque Tinker." *Revue de Louisiane/Louisiana Review* 3, no. 3 (Winter 1974): 12–57.

Vincent, Charles. "Aspects of the Family and Public Life of Antoine Dubuclet: Louisiana's Black State Treasurer, 1868–1878." *Journal of Negro History* 66 (Spring 1981): 26–36.

Index

Page numbers in **bold** indicate illustrations.

Abner, 71
abolitionism, 20, 22–23, 30
Academy of Music, 100
Adams, Thomas E., 74–75
Adolphe, Canon J., 87
Afro-Creoles. *See* black Creoles
Albanese, Catherine, 20, 25, 30
Alexi, Joseph, 109
Allen, J. W., 52, 100, 150
Ambroise, Père, 31, 90, 124
American Spiritualist, 100
Anderson, Leafy, 154, 184n16
Anderson, W. P., 79
Annunciation Church, 17, 45
Antoine, C. C., 105, 125, 141
Antoine, Père (Antonio de Sedella), 41, 71, 89–90, 109, 112, 124, 167n11
Article 135, 85–86, 130
Averin, John B. *See* Valmour

Badger, Algernon Sydney, 119–20
Banks, Nathaniel, 61
Banner of Light, 33–37, **33**; Civil War, 53, 67; "The Messenger," 96; "Movements of Mediums," 34; Spiritual Postmaster, 50–52, 150
Barthet, Joseph: Catholic Church, 26, 31–33; circle, 32, 90; *Le Spiritualiste de la Nouvelle-Orléans*, 30–37; mesmerism, 23–24, 37
Basin Street, 69
Battle of New Orleans, 53

Bee of New Orleans. *See L'Abeille de la Nouvelle-Orléans*
Beecher, Thomas K., 51
Bell, Caryn Cossé, 24, 81, 108
Benjamin, Judah P., 54
Bertonneau, Arnold, 60, 81, 127, 130
black Creoles, xix, 68, 112–23, 136, 141–48
Black Hawk, 99–100, 154–55
"Black History of Louisiana, A" (Christian), 155
Black Independence Day, 76, 138
black suffrage, 67–68, 80–82, 102, 130, 134
Blanc, Anthony, 45
Blassingame, John, 40
Body and Soul: A Sympathetic History of American Spiritualism (Cox), xix, 154
Boguille, Ludger, 43, 167n16
Boisdoré, François, 11, 44, 68
Bonée, Marie, 148
Booth, Edwin, 51
Booth, John Wilkes, 51
Booth, Junius Brutus, 51
Booth, Mary Devlin, 51
Boothby, Charles W., 82, 117–21, 174n11
Bouligny, Louis, 10
Bourbon Street, 10
Bourbons. *See* Redeemers
Britten, Emma. *See* Hardinge, Emma
Britten, Samuel Byron, 21, 27
Brodie, William, 151
Brown, William, 122
Broyard, Anatole Paul, 148

Broyard, Henry, 104–5, 148
Burke, Edward Austin, 140
Burned-over District, 21, 149
Butler, Andrew, 61
Butler, Benjamin F., 54–62, 74, 80

Cailloux, André, 62–64, **64**, 80
Camasac, Celeste, 41
Campanella, Richard, 10
Canal Street, 61–62, 137–39
Carondelet Canal, 14, 69–70, 84–85, 139, 172n28
carpetbaggers, 73–74, 81, 93, 102, 117, 119–22, 124–27
Carroll, Brett, 83
Casey, James, 118
Catholic Church: Afro-Catholicism, 48–49; Americanization, 89–90; corruption, 88; French language, 113–14; racism, 88
Catholic Institution. *See* Couvent School
Cercle Harmonique: aphorisms, 103; attendance, 109; composition, 108–9; demise, 135, 149; forgiveness, 90–91; French writers, 31, 113–14; gender, 109–13, 155; heyday, 96–97; importance to Rey, 144–45; martyrs, 76; mediums, 114; messengers, 109–11; participants, 108; protocol, 106–7; replacement, 149; role of medium, 107–8; symbolism, 103–4; topics, 104–5; venues, 83
Chalon, Père Gabriel, 88
Chartres Street, 9–10, 120
Chassaigne, Eugène, 81
Chatry, Jean François, 45–46
Chessé, Alexander Laurent, 108
Chessé, Leda Marie, 147
Chicago, 146–47, 151–52
Church of the Innocent Blood (New Orleans), 154
Church of the Soul (Chicago), 151
Citizens' Committee (Comité des Citoyens), 134, 141–43, 145
Claiborne, William C. C., 6
Claiborne streetcar, 139–40
Clapp, Theodore, 25, 164n17

Clark, Oscar Lewis, 152–53, 184n13
Clay, Henry, statue of, 119, 138–39
Colby, Luther, 34
Collins, Marie, 16, 162n33
Columbus Street, 43, **133**, 139, 140, 144
Compromise of 1877, 122–23
Conant, Jeannie "Fanny" H., 34, 51, 96
Condé Street, 9–10
Congo Square, 14–15
Constitutional Convention (1868), 81–82
Conway, Thomas, 86
cosmos cartography, 28, 109
Couvent, Marie Justine Cirnaire, 16, 41, 110, 139
Couvent School, 15–17, 106, 108, 139, 141, 162n36
Cox, Robert S., 21, 28, 102
Creoles (political division), 13
Creoles of color. *See* black Creoles
Crescent City Schools: Public Education in New Orleans, 1841–1991 (DeVore and Logsdon), 116
Crocker (Rey), Adèle, 11, 40–41, 43, 46–48, 140, 166n10
Crocker, Bazile, 42
Crocker, Pierre: birth, 41; children of, 43, 167n12; Couvent School, 41, 43; death, 43, 167n16; Economy Society, 42–43; and Marie Laveau, 42–43; other names, 166n11; parents, 41; and Barthélemy Rey, 41–43
Crocker, Pierre, Jr., 43, **52**
Croker, Rafael, 41
Crowder, John, 63–64, **128**

Daily Picayune, xvii, 26, 87, 90, 141
Daniels, Cora L. V. Hatch, xvi–xvii, 34, 78–81, 173n2, 173n8. *See also* Richmond, Cora L. V.
Daniels, Henrietta, 79, 173n7, 173n8
Daniels, Nathan W., 66, 75, 78–81
Dankin, James H., 93
D'Appemont, A., 165n42
Dastugue, Jeanne, 111
Davis, Andrew Jackson, 27–29

Davis, Edgar, 54
De Laussat, Pierre Clémont, 148
De Paule, Vincent, 71, 88–89, 103, 107, 112, 121
Delille, Henriette, 48
Democrats (Louisiana). *See* Redeemers
Dent, Julia, 117
Déruisé, Donatien, 109
Desbrosses, Nelson, 46, 71–72, 84, 105, 107, 109, 114, 168n28, 178n16
Desdunes, Aristide, 59
Desdunes, Daniel, 141
Desdunes, Rodolphe, xv, 16–17, 55, 72, 87, 98, 141–42
Dessalines, Jean-Jacques, 5
Dotsie, Anthony, 75–76
Dubuclet, Antoine, 72–73, 83, 106, 140
Dubuclet, Assitha, 111. *See also* Grandjean, Assitha
Dubuclet, August, 72–73, 83
Dubuclet, François, xiv, **xix**, 2, 72, 83–86; oral history, xv, 103, 106–7, 109–10, 145, 151–52
Dubuclet, Laurent, 146–47
Dubuclet, Sidney, 152
Duhart, Adeline, 108
Duhart, Adolphe, 46, 108, 160n2
Duhart, Pierre, 67
Dunn, Oscar James, 82, 91–92, 94, 135, 175n45, 175n48
Durant, Thomas Jefferson, 68–69
Durel, Paulin (Paul), 70, 152

Economy Hall, 43, 67–68, 134, 171n20
Economy Society (La Societé d'Économie et d'Assistance Mutuelle), 42, 53, 106, 113, 132–35, 141
education, 87. *See also* public education
Eternal Life Christian Church (New Orleans), 154
Eternal Life Spiritualist Church (Chicago), 154
Eureka, Mexico, 32
Exchange Alley, 9

Farragut, David, 54
Faubourg Marigny, xiv, 13–15, 42, 139
Faubourg St. Mary (Ste. Marie), 13
Faubourg Tremé, xiv, 13–15, **47**, 139
Federal Writers' Project (WPA), 72, 152, 154
Ferguson, John Howard, 141–42
First Church of Divine Fellowship of Spiritualism (New Orleans), 152–53, **153**
First Society of Spiritualists, 151
First Spiritual Church of Chicago, 151
Fish, Leah, 19–20
Flanders, Benjamin Franklin, 92–93
Fletcher, Henry, 16
foreign French, 23
Forster, Thomas Gales, xvi, 33–38, 165n48, 165n58
Fort Pike, 65
Forts Jackson and St. Philip, 54
Fortune Telling Law, 152
Foster, Murphy J., 146
Fouché, Louis Nelson, 10, 32, 81, 169n60
Fourteenth Amendment, 73, 115
Fox, Kate, 19–22, 151
Fox, Maggie, 19–22, 151
Franklin, John Hope, 73
Fraternité #20, 81
free people of color, xiii, 5–6, 8, 89–90; occupations, 10, 40, 106; percentage of population (New Orleans), 6, 68–69; slave ownership, 11–13, 161n19
Freedman's Bank, 102
Freedmen's Bureau, 73, 172n38
Freemasonry, 81, 132
French language, 113–14
French Quarter, 139
Frère, Rositte, 8
Friends of Universal Suffrage, 69, 86

G. Pitard's Hardware Store, 101, 135, 137–39, 144, **147**, 181n1, 182n2
Gallier Hall (New Orleans City Hall), 118, 182n4
Garden District, 139
Gauthier, Odette Dubuclet, 152
Gehman, Mary, 40

General Order No. 28, 56
Gignac, Joseph, 166n10
Gignac (Crocker), Rose Adèle, 41, 43–44, 92
Girodeau, Virginie, 41, 110
Glapion, Christophe, 42
Glapion, Marie Heloïse Euchariste, 42–43. *See also* Laveau, Marie
Godin, Marie Antoinette, 10
Good Death, 84, 96
grandfather clause, 145–46
Grandjean, Assitha, xv, 147, 151
Grandjean, René, xv, **xviii**, 141, 151, 153–54, 163n39. *See also* René Grandjean Séance Registers
Grant, Ulysses S., 117, 120
Great Harmonia, The (Davis), 66
Greeley, Horace, 20–21, 23
griffe, 82
Grimes, J. Stanley, 27
Grunewald Hall, 150
Gutierrez, Cathy, 24

Hacker, Agathe, 101
Hacker, Eugène, 39–40, 65, 101, 144
Hahn, Michael, 75
Haitian (Saint-Domingue) Revolution, 4
Hamlin, Cyrus, 75
Hardinge (Britten), Emma, xvi, 29–30, 37–38, 49–50, 110, 114
Harmonial philosophy, 27–29, 83, 104, 109, 111
Harmonialists and the Brothers of the Swedenborgian, 99
Harris, Thomas Lake, xvi, 25–27, 45, 49, 114
Harrison, Benjamin, 142
Hatch, Benjamin, 78–79
Hatch, Cora L. V. *See* Daniels, Cora L. V. Hatch
Hayes, Rutherford, 122
Henderson, John, 75–76, **128**
Herriman, George, Jr., 108, 147–48, 178n29
Hewlett's Exchange, 9, 160n5
Hobratsch, Ben, 12
Honto, 152
Hurston, Zora Neale, 72
Hydesville, New York, 19–20

Illinois legislature, 152
Illustrated London News, 35
immortelle, 84
Ingraham, James, 58, 60
Invalid Pension claims (Civil War), 142–43

Jacob, Claude, 156
Jamaica, 151
Jim Crow legislation, 141–42, 145–46, 148
Johnson, Andrew, 73, 76, 117
Joubert, L. J., 141

Kaslow, Andrew, 156
Kellogg, William Pitt, 117, 119–20, 141
Kendall, George, 98
Kendall, Mabel, 98

La Balize, 3, 148
La Société du Magnétisme de la Nouvelle-Orléans, 23–24
L'Abeille de la Nouvelle-Orléans (*The Bee*), 65, 143
L'Album littéraire, 114
Lachance, Paul, 113
Lacroix, François, 11, 16–17, **44**, 130–32
Lacroix, Victor, 76, 130–31
Ladder of Progress (Echelle de Progression), 126–27, **126**, **127**
Lafayette Square, 118
Lafourche Crossing, 58, 142–43
Lalaurie, Madame Delphine, 37
Lamotte, Louisa, 41
Lanusse, Armand, 17, 46, 86, 114
Laresche, Paul, 11
Lavigne, Joseph Vignaud, 105–6, 109, **131**, 134–35
Lavigne, Lucien, 107, 109
Laveau, Marie, 42–43, 70–71, 156, 167n13. *See also* Glapion, Marie
Le Propagateur Catholique, 26, 31
Le Spiritualiste de la Nouvelle-Orléans, 30–37
Leclerc, Charles, 5
LeGrand, Julia, 66–67
Lepore, Jill, xx

Les Cenelles (Lanusse, ed.), 41, 114
Les Écrits de langue française en Louisiane au XIXe siècle (Tinker), 41
les gens de couleur libre. See free people of color
Liberty Place (Battle), 119–21, 180n18
Lincoln, Mary Todd, 49, 79
Lincoln, Willie, 49, 79
Logsdon, Joseph, xv–xvi, 81
Longstreet, James, 116–17, 119–20
Los Angeles, 147–48
Lost Cause, 73, 117
Louisiana Bureau of the Treasury, 106
Louisiana State Bank, 106
Louisiana State Militia, 117
Louise (schooner), 4, 159n2
Louverture, Toussaint, 4–5
Lovell, Mansfield, 54
L'Union, xvi, xx, 57, 113, 130, 169n60
Luscy, Emile, 109
Lusher, Robert M., 122

Maistre, Claude, 63, 80
Mallet, Jules, 109, 135
Manehault, Constantine, 16
Mansfield, James, xvi, 22, 50–52, 150
manumissions, 11–12, 164n38
Marigny, Bernard, 13
Marks, G. B. Bushell, 26
Martin, Victor Dorsin, 144
Martinet, Louis A., 129
Mary, Aristide, 127–29
Massel's, 39
Mechanics' Institute (building), 25, 74–75, 83, 138, 182n3
Mechanics' Institute Massacre, 74–78, 80
mediums, 21–22, 32, 29, 150–51, 155, 171n19
Memphis riot, 73–74
Merchants' Exchange, 93, 139, 175n53
Mesmer, Franz Anton, 24
mesmerism, 23–24, 26–27
Michaelides, Chris, xix–xx
Mickline, Elizabeth, 6, 8
microhistory, xx
Minerva Hall, 99, 150

Mitchell, Archibald, 127–28
Mitchell, Mary (Molly), 17
Modern American Spiritualism, xvii, 50, 67, 149–51; beginnings, 19–21; black Creoles' interest, 57–58; Catholic Church opposition, 26; France, 26; New Orleans, 26; secular philosophy, 29–30; South, 23; theoretical framework, 28–29; women as leaders, 22. *See also* Spiritualism
Modern American Spiritualism (Hardinge), 29–30, 88, 112–14
Moni, Aloysius Leopold, 71, 90, 103–5, 107, 177n9
Monière, Jacques, 43
Monroe, John, 27
Monroe, Mayor John T., 53, 74
Montesquieu, 103
Montreuil, Manon, 42, 166n10
Moore, Thomas Overton, 53
Moreau (Moró), Julia, 13
Moreau, Manuel, 67
Morisot, Joseph, 17, 45
Mothers, 154
Mountain Cove (Virginia), 25
mulatto, 12
My Travels in America (Herz), 11

National Spiritualists Association, 151, 153
Native Americans, 154
Native Guards (Confederate), 53–57, 106
Native Guards (Union), 57–60, 62–66, 68–69, 74, 106, 142–43
New Jerusalem Church, 41
New Orleans: banking district, 83–84; center for Spiritualism, 37; fall to Union, 54–56; literary scene, 41; occupation, 61–62, 68
New Orleans City Guide (Federal Writers' Project of the WPA), 152, 154
New Orleans Daily Crescent, 25
New Orleans Race Riot. *See* Mechanics' Institute Massacre
New Orleans Spiritualist Association, 52, 150

New Orleans Times, xvii, 96–97, 99
New Orleans Tribune/La Tribune, 20–21, 108, 113, 123
New York Times, 55–56, 132
New York Tribune, 20–21
Nicholls, Francis T., 125–26, 140

Odd Fellow's Hall, 35, 49–50
Ogden, Frederick Nash, 119
Old Basin Canal. *See* Carondelet Canal
Old Canal Steam Brewery, 70
old numbering, 160n9
One Drop (Broyard), 148
Orleans Parish Schools, 116–19, 121–23, 127–30, 179n5
Our People and Our History: Fifty Creole Portraits (Rodolphe Desdunes), xv, 41

Packard, Stephen, 125
Panic of 1837, 15
Parish Prison (Orleans), 14, 39, 162n24, 162n25
Paroles d'honneur: Écrits de Créoles de couleur néo-orléanais 1837–1872 (Michaelides), xix–xx
passe à blanc (passing), 146
Peebles, James Martin, xvi, 22, 29–30, 99–100, 150–51, 154, 183n7
Perché, Abbé Napoléon Joseph, 31–32, 37–38, 87
Pierpoint, John, 79, 173n6
Pinchback, P. B. S., 60, 68, 91–92, 135–36, 171n22
Pitard, Gustave, 101. *See also* G. Pitard's Hardware Store
Planchard, Emilien, 109, 135
planchette, 95
Plessy, Homer, 139–42
Plessy v. Ferguson, 129–30, 141–42, 145
Pollard, Claire, 73, 111
Pollock, Carlile, 8–9, 160n4
Port Hudson (battle), 59, 63–66
Post, Amy, 20–21, 23
Post, Isaac, 20–21, 23
Poydras Market, 14

Prion, Maitre, 107–9
Prion, Myrthil J., 134
Protestantism, 87
public education, 85–86, 126–27

quadroon, 41
Quaker beliefs, 20
Questy, Joanni, 46, 108

Rabelais, 88
Rabutin-Chantal, Marie de (Marquise de Sévigné), 111
Radical Republicans, 76, 82, 124–25
Radical Spirits: Spiritualism and Women's Rights in Nineteenth-Century America (Braude), 22
Rapp, Eugène, 16, 54
Red Fox (schooner), 32
Redeemers, 125–27, 130, 136, 140, 144, 181n25
Reinders, Robert, 40
René Grandjean Séance Registers, xiv–xvi; anti-clericalism, 88–89; artwork, 104; documentation, 96–97; education, 87; final message, 135; Index, 123–24, **124, 125**; as a primary document, xviii–xix, 70; Séances Harmoniques (1890), 141
Republican Party, 60, 69, 77, 80, 82, 92, 120, 122–25, 139
Revolution, Romanticism, and the Afro-Creole Protest Tradition in Louisiana 1718–1868 (Bell), xviii–xix
Rey, Alfred Louis, 144, 146, 170n69
Rey, Barthélemy: children of, 161n11; role in Couvent School, 15–17; and Pierre Crocker, 41–42; death, 17–18, 44–45; and François Lacroix, 131–32; marriage, 8–9; parents, 6; real estate, 10–11, 13; residence, 10, 13; as slave owner, 11–13
Rey, Elizabeth, 10
Rey, Henriette, 16
Rey, Henry Joseph, 144, 146, 170n69
Rey, Henry Louis, xiii, xiv; appearance, 55; baptism, 10; bookbinder, 39; Couvent School, 86–87, 144; and Nathan Daniels, 65–66, 81; death, 145, 183n23, 183n24; early years of Spiritualism, 45–46;

Economy Society, 134–35; education, 15; fire on Villere Street, 122, 135; first séance register (85-30), 38, 44; marriage, 43; as medium, 65–66; name change, 166n11; Native Guards, 54, 56–60; as Orleans Parish School Board Director, 116–17, 122–23, 144; political activism, 69; public education, 85–86, 130; resignation from US Army, 59–60; as Third District assessor, 92–93

Rey, Hippolyte, 57, 65, 81, 108, 143

Rey, Joseph, 6, 10, 13

Rey, Lucia Rose, 43, 92, 144, 146, 175n49

Rey, Marie Josephine, 45–46

Rey, Octave, 32, 46, 54–55, 57, 65, 81, 120, 143

Reynès, Constant, 71

Rice, Mrs., 110

Richmond, Cora L. V., 151. *See also* Daniels, Cora L. V. Hatch

Rochester, New York, 20

Roudanez, Louis Charles, 57

Rousselon, Etienne, 45

Royal Street, 93

Ruth (steamboat), 78

Sacriste (Rey), Rose Agnès, 8–9

Sacriste, Jean Marie, 8

Saint-Domingue, 4

Santiago de Cuba, 4, 6, 9

Sauvenet, Charles, 54–55

scalawags, 64, 73–74, 102

Schafer, Judith, 11

Scott, David W., 78

Scott, James, 25

Seals, Catherine, 154–56

séance circles, 97

Second Wave of Emigration (1809–1810), xiii–xiv, 6, 13

Select Committee on the New Orleans Riots, 75

Separate Car Act of 1890, 129, 140–41

Shaik, Fatima, 67

Shepley, George, 68

Ship Island, 56, 61, 65–66

Sisters of the Holy Family, 48

slave trade, 4

Snaër, Samuel, 46, 80, 168n28

Soeur (Sister) Louise, 46, 110–11, 140–41

Soul Circle Church (Chicago), 152

Soulé, Pierre, 11, 90–91

Southern Literary Messenger, 22–23

Southern University, 136

Spiritual churches, 72, 99–100, 150, 152–56, 184n12

Spiritual Pilgrim, 99–100. *See also* Peebles, James M.

spiritual protocols, 30

spiritual telegraph, 21

Spiritualism: African Americans, 38; comparison to Spiritual churches, 155–56; comparison to Voodoo, 72, 155–56; lectures, 99; mediums, 110; musical instruments, 98–99; slate writing, 98–100, 150; unpopularity, 97, 100. *See also* Modern American Spiritualism

Spiritualist churches, 152–53

Spiritualist newspapers, 21, 29–30, 33–34

Squire, J. Rollin M., 33–38, 165n46, 165n58

St. Augustine Church, 15

St. Bernard Circle, 140

St. Charles streetcar, 139, 182n4

St. John's Eve (La Fête de St. Jean), 72

St. Louis Cathedral, 15, 89

St. Louis Cemetery No. 2, 139

St. Louis Hotel, 180n13

St. Philip Street, 42

Stafford, Spencer H., 58

Stowe, Harriet Beecher, 51

Sue, Eugène, 87

Swedenborg, Emanuel, 27–28, 107

tables tournantes, 26–27

Tallant, Robert, 154

Tampico, Mexico, 32

Taylor, Richard, 58, 170n62

Testut, Charles, xx, 24–25

"Theory of the Poisoning of Oscar J. Dunn, The" (Christian), 91–92

Thiebaud, Catherine, 43

Thomas, Chazal, 10

three-tiered racial system (tripartite), xiii, 13, 87, 90, 101, 112
tignon, 39–40
transatlantic linkages, xviii, 112–14
Tregle, Joseph, 10
Tremé, Claude, 13
Tremé Market, 14–15, 39–40, **48**, 162n24
Trévigne, Paul, 17, 46, 81, 127–30, 143, 181n30
Tyson, Dora, 154

US Custom House, 55, 61–62, 139

Valmour: Cercle Harmonique, xiv, 83; and Nathan Daniels, 66; death, 83–85; and Emma Hardinge, 50; name (John B. Averin), 164n35, 172n29; and Abbé Perché, 31; register, 70; residence, 69–70, 174n19; Séances Harmoniques, 140–41; as spirit messenger, 121, **129**; Voodoo, 70–72
Valmour, Dianah, 70, 85

Valmour, Johnny, 70
Veque, Charles, 45
Vicksburg, 64
Villere Street, 14, 70, 122, 180n22
Voodoo (Voudou), 37, 43, 70–72, 155–56
Voodoo Queen: The Spirited Lives of Marie Laveau (Ward), 42, 167n13

Waples, Rufus, 80
Warbourg, Eugène, 105
Ward, Martha, 42, 72
Warmoth, Henry Clay, 68, 76, 82, 85–86, 91–94, 117, 175n53
Washington, Booker T., 136
Weekly Louisianian, 91–92
Weitzel, Godfrey, 58
Wells, J. Madison, 74
White League, 118–22, 180n9
Wiltz, Louis Alfred, 125

yellow fever, 62, 80

www.ingramcontent.com/pod-product-compliance
Lightning Source LLC
Chambersburg PA
CBHW031812220426
43662CB00007B/619